Mary Stewart

Mary Stewart
Queen in Three Kingdoms

Edited by Michael Lynch

Basil Blackwell

Copyright © Basil Blackwell Ltd 1988

First published 1988

Basil Blackwell Ltd
108 Cowley Road, Oxford, OX4 1JF, UK

Basil Blackwell Inc.
432 Park Avenue South, Suite 1503
New York, NY 10016, USA

Published in association with *The Innes Review*, the journal of the Scottish Catholic
Historical Association

British Library Cataloguing in Publication Data

Mary Stewart: queen in three kingdoms.
1. Mary, *Queen of Scots* 2. Scotland −
Kings and rulers − Biography
I. Lynch, Michael, *1946 June 15−*
941.105′092′4   DA787.A1

ISBN 0−631−15263−6

Library of Congress Cataloging in Publication Data

Mary Stewart, queen in three kingdoms/edited by Michael Lynch.
p.   cm.
Bibliography: p.
Includes index.
ISBN 0−631−15263−6
1. Mary, Queen of Scots. 1542−1587. 2. Scotland − History − Mary
Stuart. 1542−1567. 3. France − History − Francis II. 1559−1560.
4. Great Britain − History − Elizabeth. 1558−1603. 5. Scotland − Kings
and rulers − Biography. 6. France − Queens − Biography. I. Lynch,
Michael. 1946−   .
DA787.A1M28   1988
941.105′092′4 − dc19
[B]   87−35488
CIP

Typeset in Bembo on 10/12 pt by Setrite Typesetters Limited
Printed in Great Britain

For Anthony Ross OP

Contents

Preface

This volume has been a long time in the making. It was born of two beliefs: that there was still much to discover or reassess about the career of Mary, queen of Scots, and that no one historian could deal with it satisfactorily in all its aspects, French and English as well as Scottish, literary as well as religious or political.

A collection such as this is an opportunity for making new friendships as well as cementing (and trying) old ones. So it has proved. It is unlikely that all the contributors agree with everything which each has written, or with what the editor has gleaned from them, but there has been clear agreement, both on the gaps in current knowledge of the subject and on the direction the volume should take.

I owe many personal debts of thanks. Menna Prestwich, Geoffrey Parker and J. J. Scarisbrick gave constructive help and encouragement in its planning. The editorial board of the Scottish Catholic Historical Association gave backing to the project throughout. My greatest debts are to Leslie Macfarlane, whose idea it first was, and to John Durkan, who unstintingly gave me the benefit of his scholarship and friendship throughout.

A final and very real debt is owed to my wife and family. If any bear a greater burden than wives of authors, it must be wives of editors.

M. L.

List of Contributors

Simon Adams is Lecturer in the Department of History, University of Strathclyde

Ian B. Cowan is Professor in the Department of Scottish History, University of Glasgow

John Durkan is Senior Research Fellow in the Department of Scottish History, University of Glasgow

Julian Goodare is a Research Student in the Department of Scottish History, University of Edinburgh

M. Greengrass is Lecturer in the Department of Modern History, University of Sheffield

P. J. Holmes is a Teacher at Hills Road Sixth Form College, Cambridge

Michael Lynch is Lecturer in the Department of Scottish History, University of Edinburgh

M. H. Merriman is Lecturer in the Department of History, University of Lancaster

Allan White OP is Honorary Catholic Chaplain to the University of Edinburgh

Abbreviations and Conventions

All sums of money in £ are given, unless otherwise stated, in £ Scots, which was rated at *4:1* against £ sterling in 1560, *5.5:1* in 1567, and *7.33:1* by 1587; a merk was two-thirds of £ Scots. With dates the year is deemed to have begun on 1 January. All printed state paper references are to pages. The abbreviations used for sources are generally those recommended in *List of Abbreviated Titles of the Printed Sources of Scottish History to 1560* (*Scottish Historical Review* supplement, 1963). The following are the abbreviations most commonly used:

Add. MSS	Additional MSS, British Library
Adv. MSS	Advocates MSS, National Library of Scotland
AGS	Archivo General de Simancas
AN	Archives Nationales, Paris
APS	*The Acts of the Parliament of Scotland,* ed. T. Thomson and C. Innes (Edin., 1814–75)
AUL	Aberdeen University Library
BHR	*Bibliothèque d'Humanisme et de la Renaissance*
BL	British Library, London
BN	Bibliothèque Nationale, Paris
BUK	*The Booke of the Universall Kirk of Scotland: Acts and Proceedings of the General Assemblies of the Kirk of Scotland from the year 1560,* ed. T. Thomson (Bannatyne and Maitland Clubs, 1839–45)

BUPG   Bibliothèque Universitaire et Pub-
                             lique de Genève

Calderwood, *History* ,   *History of the Church of Scotland by*
                             Mr. David Calderwood (Wodrow Soc.,
                             1842—9)

Codoin   *Collección de Documents inéditos para la*
                             Historia de España

CSPF   *Calendar of State Papers Foreign,*
                             Elizabeth, ed. J. Stevenson et al.
                             (1863—1950)

CSP Rome   *Calendar of State Papers, Rome*, ed. J.
                             M. Rigg (1916—26)

CSP Scot   *Calendar of State Papers relating to*
                             Scotland and Mary, Queen of Scots,
                             1547—1603, ed. J. Bain et al. (1898—
                             1969)

CSP Spain   *Calender of State Papers, Spanish,*
                             Elizabeth, ed. M. A. S. Hume (1892—9)

CSP Ven.   *Calendar of State Papers, Venetian*, ed.
                             R. Brown and C. G. Bentinck (1864—
                             98)

Diurnal   *Diurnal of Remarkable Occurents that*
                             have passed within the country of Scot-
                             land . . . (Bannatyne and Maitland
                             Clubs, 1833)

DNB   *Dictionary of National Biography*

Donaldson, *First Trial*   G. Donaldson, *The First Trial of*
                             Mary, Queen of Scots (1969)

Donaldson, *Mary*   G. Donaldson, *Mary, Queen of Scots*
                             (1974)

Donaldson, *Queen's Men*   G. Donaldson, *All the Queen's Men:*
                             Power and Politics in Mary Stewart's
                             Scotland (1983)

Donaldson, *Scotland*   G. Donaldson, *Scotland: James V to*
                             James VII (1965)

Ellis, *Original Letters*   H. Ellis (ed.), *Original Letters illustra-*
                             tive of English History (1824—46)

ER   *Exchequer Rolls of Scotland*, ed. J.
                             Stewart et al. (1878—1908)

ESL   *Early Scottish Libraries*, ed. J. Durkan
                             and A. Ross (1961)

EUL   Edinburgh University Library.

Forbes Leith, *Narratives*	W. Forbes Leith, *Narratives of Scottish Catholics under Mary Stuart and James VI* (1885)
Foreign Corresp.	*Foreign Correspondence with Marie de Lorraine, Queen of Scotland, from the originals in the Balcarres Papers* (SHS, 1923–5)
Fraser, *Mary*	A. Fraser, *Mary, Queen of Scots* (1969)
GD	Gifts and Deposits series, Scottish Record Office
Gilbert, 'Usual money of Scotland'	J. Gilbert, 'The usual money of Scotland and exchange rates against foreign coin', in *Coinage in Medieval Scotland*, ed. D. M. Metcalf (British Arch. Reports, xlv, 1977)
GUL	Glasgow University Library
Hay Fleming, *Mary*	D. Hay Fleming, *Mary, Queen of Scots* (1897)
Herries, *Memoirs*	Lord Herries, *Historical Memoirs of the Reign of Mary, Queen of Scots* (1836)
HMC	Historical Manuscripts Commission
HMC Bath	*Calendar of MSS of Marquess of Bath at Longleat* (1907)
HMC Pepys	*Calendar of Pepys MSS preserved at Magdalene College, Cambridge* (1911)
HMC Salisbury	*Calendar of MSS of the Marquess of Salisbury* (1883–5)
IR	*The Innes Review*
Keith, *History*	R. Keith, *The History of the Affairs of the Church and State in Scotland* (1844–50)
Knox, *History*	*John Knox's History of the Reformation in Scotland*, ed. W. C. Dickinson (1949)
Knox, *Works*	*The Works of John Knox*, ed. D. Laing (Wodrow Soc., 1846–64)
Labanoff	Prince Labanoff, *Lettres, instructions et mémoires de Marie Stuart* (1844)
Leslie, *History* (Bann.)	J. Leslie, *The History of Scotland from the Death of King James I in the Year 1436 to the Year 1561* (Bannatyne Club, 1830)
Lynch, *Edinburgh*	M. Lynch, *Edinburgh and the Reformation* (1981)

Mary of Lorraine Corresp.	*The Scottish Correspondence of Mary of Lorraine, 1542–1560,* ed. A. I. Cameron (SHS, 1927)
McRoberts, *Scottish Reformation*	D. McRoberts (ed.), *Essays on the Scottish Reformation, 1513–1625* (1962)
Melville, *Memoirs*	Sir James Melville of Halhill, *Memoirs of his own Life, 1549–93* (Bannatyne and Maitland Clubs, 1827)
Michel, *Français*	F.-X. Michel, *Les Français en Ecosse. Les Ecossais en France* (1862)
NLS	National Library of Scotland, Edinburgh
Papal Negs.	*Papal Negotiations with Mary Queen of Scots during her Reign in Scotland, 1561–1567,* ed. J. H. Pollen (SHS, 1901)
Phillips, *Images*	J. E. Phillips, *Images of a Queen* (1964)
Pitcairn, *Trials*	R. Pitcairn, *Criminal Trials in Scotland from 1488 to 1624* (1833)
PRO	Public Record Office, London
PSAS	*Proceedings of Society of Antiquaries of Scotland*
RMS	*Registrum Magni Sigilli Regum Scotorum,* ed. J. M. Thomson et al. (1882–1914)
RPC	*The Register of the Privy Council of Scotland,* ed. J. H. Burton et al. (1877–98)
RSS	*Registrum Secreti Sigilli Regum Scotorum,* ed. M. Livingstone et al. (1908–)
SHR	*Scottish Historical Review*
SHS	Scottish History Society
SP	*Scots Peerage,* ed. Sir J. Balfour Paul (1904–14)
SP	State Papers series, Public Record Office, London
SRO	Scottish Record Office, Edinburgh
SRS	Scottish Record Society
STS	Scottish Text Society
TA	*Accounts of the Lord High Treasurer of Scotland,* ed. T. Dickson and Sir J. Balfour Paul et al. (1877–)
Teulet, *Papiers*	A. Teulet (ed.), *Papiers d'état... relatifs à l'histoire de l'Ecosse au XVIᵉ siècle* (1852–60)

Teulet, *Relations*   A. Teulet (ed.), *Relations politiques de la France et de l'Espagne avec l'Ecosse au XVIe siècle* (1862)

Thirds of Benefices   *Accounts of the Collectors of Thirds of Benefices, 1561−1572,* ed G. Donaldson (SHS, 1949)

Warrender Papers   *Warrender Papers,* ed. A. I. Cameron (SHS, 1931−2)

Wright, *Elizabeth*   T. Wright, *Queen Elizabeth and her Times* (1838)

1

Introduction

MICHAEL LYNCH

Mary, queen of Scots, was a legend, even before her own lifetime. There were excited rumours in the north of England, at the time of the Pilgrimage of Grace in 1536, of a child queen's imminent arrival, which would liberate this Catholic heartland from the oppression and heresy of Henry VIII.[1] The quick-witted child, transported to France at the age of six, dazzled even the glittering and sophisticated Valois court. Her marriage to the Dauphin, François, in 1558 was, as Marcus Merriman shows, the climax of a series of triumphal entries, fêtes and court rituals, overlaid with imperial imagery and mythology, which promised the arrival of an 'age of gold' for both France and Scotland. Her own court in Scotland, set up after her return in 1561, was an acknowledged centre of learning, with the queen, 'a miracle of nature', as its fulcrum;[2] this was a world inhabited by painters, musicians, poets, both Latin and vernacular, many of whom had been in France in the 1550s, as well as by what many historians still insist on seeing as the unsophisticated Scots nobility, despite their many contacts with France. It seemed to promise a return, as one of those poets put it, to 'the golden age of Saturn'.[3]

Over the course of her nineteen years of captivity in England, two different sets of images developed, each preparing the ground for the martyrology debate which followed her execution on 8 February 1587. In an age where court portraiture, not least of Elizabeth I, was part of a cult of political symbolism, it is hardly surprising that Mary became a virtual Catholic icon to the exiled Catholic communities abroad, both Scottish and English.[4] To the English Catholic community, with whom she had surprisingly little contact, she was, for most, the legitimate heir to the throne but also, as Peter Holmes argues, a potential source of political embarrassment. In France, where Mary had been cast off as a Catholic *cause célèbre* by the crown for some fifteen years and even by the Guises after 1585, she was able effortlessly to make the transition to Catholic martyr within days of her death, on the basis both of the well-established literature of her captivity, which had increased in volume as the 1580s progressed, and the genuine outrage felt by popular Catholic opinion, especially in Paris. Yet the mythology of Mary, like that of Geneva,[5] depended as much on the hysteria of her enemies as on the religious fervour, real or forced, of her friends. Andrew Melville, the doyen of the second generation of Calvinist ministers in the Scottish reformed church, could in 1584 use the apocalyptic context of the Book of Daniel to prophesy her return as a latter-day Nebuchadnezzar, 'fed', for her sins, 'these two seven years with hay' as retribution for the sins of the Scottish people.[6] Much of the English anti-Marian literature originated, however, in an earlier, and rather different period, and had climaxed in the aftermath of the Ridolfi plot of 1571,[7] which was the last Marian escapade that posed any serious threat to Elizabeth. The English secret service won what was a cynically contrived game largely of its own making in the Babington plot of 1586; but it lost the end game — the war of words, which took even veteran manipulators of opinion like Walsingham by surprise with the speed and vehemence of the reaction to Mary's death, both in France and Scotland. As James VI predicted, his mother's execution gave to Catholic politics 'a new head, more formidable than a sickly woman' — the head of a Catholic martyr.[8]

Some of this picture of Mary is familiar, but other parts are not. Yet it genuinely reflects contemporary opinion, as it unfolded over the course of Mary's life. There was a Marian mythology, but it needs to be distinguished from the genre of Marian martyrology, which came later and was largely confessional in motivation. Admiration for Mary's charm, wit and learning was shared by Protestant and Catholic observers alike during her personal reign; in this respect at least, John Knox, whose immensely quotable *History* has done more to diminish the personal accomplishments of the queen than any other source, was the odd man out. Both of the hymns of praise cited earlier were made by convinced Protestants: one was Patrick Adamson, a minister and author of a waspish tract on the papist superstitions of Aberdeen's university establishment, but also a poet and disciple of Buchanan, Latin court poet in all but name at Holyrood.[9] The other was Pietro Bizzari, Italian Protestant, client of that most precise Protestant, the earl of Bedford, but also a humanist and historian. He visited Mary's court in 1564, but published his opinion as late as 1568, eighteen months after the murder of Darnley.[10] Adamson penned his extravagant verses to mark the birth of Mary's son, three months after the Protestant demonstration which took the form of the collective murder of the queen's servant, David Riccio.[11] Taken together, these views reflect a widely felt contemporary admiration for Queen Mary, a view shared by some of her early English captors,[12] and may indicate that judgement was merely suspended for a time rather than finalized after the succession of calamitous events of 1567.

By the end of six years of a bitterly fought civil war in Scotland between supporters of the queen and her infant son, opinions had hardened, on all sides, both in Scotland and outside it. The cause in Scotland of the change of mood was not so much the fabricated evidence produced at her first trial, at York in 1568—9, as the course of the war itself; elsewhere the Ridolfi plot and the Massacre of St Bartholomew had confirmed the division of most of Europe into confessional stances, which had been presaged by the final session at Trent. One of the casualties of the new atmosphere was the personal reputation of the queen of Scots. When Bizzari published a second edition of his work, in 1573, the section praising Mary was excised.[13] By then the two confessional moulds of Mary — Catholic martyr and papist plotter — had been cast.

It is in part the very black and white nature of historiographical opinion about her that has fuelled the Mary, queen of Scots, industry. But the perennial fascination with the most famous of all Scotland's monarchs is also explained by the fact that here history shares — and can seemingly be explained by — the essential ingredients of popular fiction: sex, murder and intrigue, with a dash of religiosity. Equally, the material is endlessly recyclable because, like a good murder mystery, the evidence can point in different directions — as indeed it was designed to do, for much of it was the product of competing intelligence networks, which operated in a half-real world, at once international and closeted, conditioned to think in terms of plotting and counter-espionage. Although the volume of contemporary evidence is huge, it needs to be understood that it was in the nature of such a world that other evidence was deliberately destroyed, such as the copies of the personal correspondence from the 1580s between Mary and David Chalmers, her former privy councillor, which were held at one stage by Elizabeth's minister, Burghley. There is also a serious imbalance in the evidence as to the personal reign: the most sustained and compelling accounts of it came from the pens of Protestant apologists, such as Knox, Buchanan and Thomas Randolph, English ambassador in Edinburgh; Catholic accounts, by contrast, such as the *Narrative* of John Leseli, bishop of Ross,[14] largely disappoint, in both their scope and the amount of detail they provide. Much of the impression of an aimless drift in Mary's policy between 1561 and 1566 stems from the absence of a specifically contemporary apologia; the accounts of the Marian courtiers, Sir James Melville and Lord Herries, both written much later, have the whiff of rationalized memoirs about them. By contrast, the role and reputation of other leading figures in Scottish politics of the 1560s stem directly from their contemporary apologists: Randolph, who had helped rescue the young earl of Arran from France in 1559, was until 1566 a spokesman for the Hamiltons as well as English ambassador;[15] Buchanan was a brilliant advocate for his patron, James Stewart, earl of Moray, who was in greater need of a good defence lawyer than most in the 1560s; and Knox, with equal verve, conducted his own defence. Yet missing from this list is the Lennox Stewart interest, which had no such apologist; its central role in the events of 1564−6 has, as a result, formed a curious *lacuna* in analyses of the period, as both Simon Adams and Julian Goodare recognize.[16]

There are, therefore, particular difficulties in arriving at a balanced treatment, either of Mary's reign or her political career as a whole, spanning as it did three decades and three countries. Too many historians have, it must be said, consulted their own prejudices first and the sources second. Yet others have, less deliberately, fallen into the traps laid by sixteenth-century apologists, who have done their work well. The escape route taken by popular historians or biographers out of these difficulties posed by the evidence is usually to indulge in some form of personal determinism, often recognizable by stock phrases like 'the ill-fated queen'. There is material in this collection for them, but it is not always what it may seem at first sight. It would be possible, for example, to draw contrasts between Mary's various Catholic *personae*: the *ingénue* who looked for a time on her half-brother, James, who had held the commendatorship of the priory of St Andrews since childhood, as a churchman and who expected her nobles to accept her invitation, made early in 1566, to return to the mass; the Catholic queen who laid low her greatest Catholic magnate in 1562, and distributed his exquisite collection of Catholic relics and treasures around her court; the *politique* who, it was rumoured in 1562, wore her religion lightly enough to contemplate, on Guise orders, a conversion to Anglicanism to consolidate her claim to the English throne; or the deepening but still rather conventional faith of the Catholic pietist in exile. Yet the cult or exploration of Mary's personality will not in itself explain these seemingly different or conflicting facets of her character. They are better explained as reactions to the series of shifts in the personalities around her, which marked her career, both in Scotland and England. Marianism was itself a shifting commodity; the queen's conduct was as much a reflection of this basic fact of both Scottish and international politics as the cause of it.

There are three extra dimensions to the career of Queen Mary which are highlighted in this volume. It is surprising that more is known of Mary's household when in captivity than in her personal reign. The composition of the queen's friends at the Scottish court has recently been analysed,[17] but not the 250-strong household itself.[18] Here the most important contribution came, not from the famous four Marys, but from the talented corps of confessors, tutors and advisers, most of whom she had also brought with her from France. Their role in Mary's policy has been deeply obscure. A second aspect is the size of her jointure as a dowager queen of France, which supported her household and gave her a unique opportunity amongst Scottish monarchs, both to extend the size and impressiveness of the royal court without indulging in punitive taxation and to act as a patron, whether of poets, scholars or distressed clergy. As Mark Greengrass demonstrates, the fact that the revenues from her jointure continued to reach her administrative council in Paris, even if in reduced sums, allowed her patronage to continue on a remarkable scale, even after she fled to England.[19] The jointure was, even after Thomas Morgan laid his unscrupulous hands on it around 1574, more than a campaign fund for Marian conspirators; it sustained the fairly harmless exile of some of the English rebels of 1569 well into the 1580s; it funded Scots scholars in France as well as pensioners, such as John Gordon and David Chalmers, who produced defences of the queen.[20] Mary, it might be said, was more faithful to her pensioners than many of them were to her.

The third dimension which has not received the attention it should lies in dynastic politics. Mary's actions and policy in the 1560s became enmeshed with the aims and fate of not just one noble house but three: that of the Hamiltons and the Lennox Stewarts as well as that of Guise-Lorraine. There was in Scotland, as in England, a debate on the succession that lasted throughout the 1560s, even if it took a more muted form. Each of these houses had its own distinctive dynastic mentality and family strategy, which had its own rationality and continuity but which produced seemingly bewildering shifts in court politics. Each considered the fortunes of its house in an international perspective.

After 1561 and the collapse of prospect of a match between Arran and Elizabeth I, the Hamiltons were as concerned with the loss of the French duchy of Châtelherault, which had returned to the family of Diane de Poitiers, as with their position in Scottish domestic politics; the result was, first, a reconsideration of their attitude towards the English amity, which temporarily allied them with the Catholic magnate, the earl of Huntly, and eventually, in what was virtually a war of the Scottish succession after 1568, a determined pro-Marian stance.[21] The house of Lennox Stewart, which has misleadingly been seen as 'anglicized',[22] was able to pick up with remarkable ease the threads of contacts with the pro–English faction of the mid-1540s, despite twenty years' absence from Scotland. It was also able to exploit the odd situation after Mary's return to Scotland, in which she, although a Stewart monarch, had virtually no close, legitimate kin around her.[23] A Lennox Stewart dynasty could thus be portrayed as the consolidator of a dangerously narrowly based royal Stewart dynasty.[24] In England, in the early 1560s, the Lennox interest had fluctuated in its tactics, as Simon Adams shows, threatening the Catholic card in 1562 in order to persuade Elizabeth to allow a restoration of their position and estates in Scotland. The flexible religious habits of the Lennoxes in the past should stifle any surprise that Lennox returned as a Protestant, but by late 1565 both he and his son Darnley, now husband of Mary, were attending the mass. What is interesting is not their change of mind but why they chose the Catholic ground to further their family interest at this point, for this was arguably the essential prelude to Mary's attempt to persuade her nobility back to the mass early in 1566.

With the house of Lorraine Mary belonged to a dynasty which was not only an important power at the French court, especially after the death of Henri II in 1559, but also a sovereign family, with its own court at Nancy, closely tied to developments in the Empire, and even its own printing press, at Rheims. With the marriage in May 1566 of Anne d'Este, the Ferrarese dowager duchess of Guise, to the duke of Nemours, a cadet of the house of Savoy[25] (which explains the prominent position given to the Savoyard delegation at the baptism of Mary's son in 1566)[26] there was an important extra dimension, in the northern half of Italy, given to Guise interests. It may be that too much attention has conventionally been paid to the Guise factor in Mary's policy and not enough to the way she, like Anne d'Este, that other Guise dowager, fitted into Guise policy. The projected match between Mary and the Archduke Charles in 1563 was only one of a chain of prospective marriages in a 'matrimonial campaign' of the house of Lorraine;[27] some were realistic, others more important as bargaining counters, such as the proposal to marry Charles IX to Elizabeth I, eighteen years his senior. In the heady atmosphere of the French court, which saw 'a non-stop cultivation of protectors and suitors',[28] Mary, like other Guise assets, was not necessarily consulted until after negotiations had actually begun. This may help explain the rumours, which often originated in English dispatches from the French court, as to her intentions, religious as well as matrimonial. From 1563 the two greatest Guise assets were the two dowagers, who were likened by Brantôme, recalling seeing them dance together in happier days, to 'two suns that had appeared to bewilder the world'.[29] Yet Guise policy, with so much to consider and to lose, fluctuated considerably, even in the 1560s. It was Thomas Randolph's inability to decipher the complexities and ambiguities in Mary's relations with the Guises that lay at the root of the confusions in English foreign policy and led to its miscalculations over a marriage in 1564—5. In both the personal reign and after, Guise influence on Mary was probably more important for the fears it provoked in English policy-makers than for the tangible influence it had on Mary's own policy and actions. The prospect of the captive Mary becoming the fulcrum of a French invasion of England was a tempting one for Guise policy, but not as tempting as English agents thought. Guise contacts need to be considered as carefully as policy. By the late 1570s Guise influence was greater on the Marian exiles in France than on Mary herself. Yet even here distinctions have to be made, for, with the significant exception of John Leslie, there was more Guise contact with English seminary activists than with Scots.[30] And there was another basic irony: the France Mary had left in 1561, on the very eve of the Colloquy of Poissy, had been hypnotized by the prospect of religious conciliation on Gallican lines. By 1562 it no longer existed. Mary's consistent attachment throughout her years in Scotland to a certain liberty of conscience would, in France, have resulted in her being branded 'more politique than dévot' — by her own family.[31]

The core of any judgement of Mary must, however, rest on the personal reign. Yet there are immediate difficulties of context, for it is flanked by two of the most obscure regencies of the sixteenth century, those of Mary's mother (1554—60) and her half-brother, Lord James, earl of Moray (1567—70). For some, the case against Queen Mary is buttressed by assumptions about the governments of these two regencies. Despite some success in recent attempts to rehabilitate the reputation of Mary of Guise,[32] it is becoming clear that her government was hit by recurrent crises *before* the Reformation crisis of 1559—60, on issues other than the Protestant one.[33] The result was that any government which followed would be likely to treat the most contentious issues — finance, patronage and the authority of the crown as well as the religious question — with a cautious conservatism. And Mary was followed by a regent who, although he did supervise the institutions of government more closely and experiment with them, was arguably a good deal less fitted to rule than his half-sister; he was wittily compared by one courtier to a bad tennis player, unable to anticipate or control the flow of the game, so 'runnyng ever efter the ball'.[34] Those who stress the unpopularity and ineptitude of the queen need to explain why the Regent Moray was confronted between 1568 and 1570 by the opposition of more than two-thirds of the greater nobility.[35]

The Reformation crisis of 1559−60 had seen a parliament of uncertain status adopt a Protestant confession, proscribe the mass and abolish papal jurisdiction, but this hardly amounted to a religious revolution: not a single major office in the executive or judicial functions of government changed hands and nothing was done to phase out the structure of the old church and little to phase in that of the new.[36] It is often said, rather loosely, that the Treaty of Edinburgh (July 1560) which preceded the parliament marked both the end of French influence and the birth of the amity with England. Yet great issues are seldom settled so quickly. As Allan White shows, the two great territorial magnates, Huntly and Châtelherault, could think of putting their religious differences aside because of common reservations about the pro-English drift implied in the pursuit of the English succession, which had united Mary and the Protestant leaders of her privy council, Lord James Stewart and William Maitland, after had return in 1561. In many ways, the real political litmus test in the first year of Mary's personal reign was not the religious question, which was for the moment safely contained, but the auld alliance and the new, with England; and, for the moment, divisions threatened between factions that were not so much Catholic and Protestant as pro- and anti-English.[37] The point was not lost on Mary, for the marriage with Darnley offered an escape route from a policy which had demonstrably failed, despite prolonged negotiations with England, to produce tangible benefits. The 1565 match offered not so much, as is often said, a union of the best two Catholic claims to the English throne as the enticing prospect of an independent monarchy. Darnley could help turn Mary into a patriot queen.[38]

The English issue thus remained near the centre of Scottish politics throughout the personal reign. It would have been surprising if this had not been the case. The breach with both France and Rome in 1560 had not taken place as the climax of a longer-term process, distancing Scotland from either the papacy or the auld alliance. Both relationships were, as Ian Cowan and Marcus Merriman point out, actually becoming closer in the 1550s. Scotland had never been directly represented in Rome and there had been only occasional visits made by a papal nuncio to Scotland, as in 1514 and 1543. Yet the grant to Cardinal Beaton of the status of *legatus a latere* in 1544 had strengthened rather than weakened the links between Scotland and the Holy See, as was its purpose. And the second half of the 1550s saw a stream of queries from Rome, such as that of the cardinal protector, Sermoneta, or of papal visitors, like the bishop of Amiens, in the unusual guise of a French legate with papal faculties.[39] Viewed without benefit of hindsight, Mary's personal reign saw a continuance, despite obvious difficulties, of the new and closer interest taken by popes since the 1540s in the affairs of Scotland. There had also been a sustained effort made by the French crown from 1551 onwards to put more flesh on the bones of the alliance: there had been not one 'brain-washing expedition', such as that of 1550, but several and exposure to the majesty and ritual of the royal court was calculated to do just that. In addition, Scots, such as Lord James, who had already held the Augustinian priory of St Andrews since childhood, were offered the commendatorship of abbeys the length and breath of France as well as pensions.[40] As the 1550s went on, and the spread of heresy among some of the various Scots colonies in France became more obvious, these efforts redoubled. A good deal of energy was expended, not least by Mary herself, on finding a suitable and Catholic bride for the central figure of the troubled young earl of Arran, whose Protestant views had survived a term in a French prison.[41] The background to John Knox's consistent fear after 1560 of a Counter-Reformation lay not only in the numerical weakness of Protestantism in Scotland, but also in the very real links which still existed with both France and Rome.

There is, on the personal reign itself, still a basic and sharp difference of opinion — between 'failure as [a] Catholic ruler'[42] and a somewhat older but still widely held view of a deliberately equivocal policy which was 'a conspicuous success'.[43] Yet the terms of this debate have been oddly constrained. The reign of Mary has recently been used to examine the attitudes of her *subjects,* which often turned on views of sovereignty and the bonds of kinship rather than religion.[44] Yet the new thinking about the nature of Stewart kingship which has marked so much of the recent study of the reigns of all six Jameses has been conspicuously absent in discussion of Queen Mary. There has been a certain amount of special treatment accorded to Mary as queen, both by her detractors and her defenders. There have also been some double standards. Mary was inept, it is sometimes claimed, because she neglected the ordinary business of government, preferring to stay away from meetings of her privy council to enjoy the pleasures of her court.[45] This is a judgement largely based on the practice of James VI, thirty years later. It passes, without comment, over the fact that Elizabeth I also did not regularly attend her council, except on special occasions, such as on the eve of the expedition to France in 1562.[46] It also forgets that hunting, dancing and even playing cards were all kingly pursuits, which had been specifically recommended to James V as essential tools of the art of government.[47]

Mary's council was in 1561 dominated by the same largely Protestant combination of nobles as had masterminded the rebellion of 1559—60 and staffed the provisional government until her return. Her household, in contrast, was firmly and unambiguously Catholic; it acted not only as a centre for the mass but also, to a greater degree than has been appreciated, as a Catholic publishing centre, supporting both Ninian Winzet and René Benoist, her confessor, in the first year after her return. Yet did this not make sense, as a Scottish solution to a distinctive, Scottish problem? The operation of the queen's two spheres — council and household — was quite appropriate to a country where Protestant reform had been adopted by parliament but not fully established and where the bulk of the ordinary population, both rural and urban, was still not converted to the new faith.[48] Her mother had, after all, been criticized for *failing* to maintain a division between her French household and her administration. Mary's court was, in a real sense, a place where minds could meet, for in the still Erasmian atmosphere of the early 1560s this remained possible; it could, as Randolph sourly complained, 'draw men to her by gentle letters and fair words.'[49]

There are four sets of questions which are normally asked in measuring the success and failure of Stewart kingship: its relationship with the church, its finances, its relationship with the great nobles and the points of contact it maintained, in what was still a highly decentralized realm, between centre and localities. The first two of these criteria are easiest to answer briefly. Queen Mary had, in her attitude towards the church, the same distinctive Stewart combination of personal piety and venality as James IV and V. She may or may not have personally devised the plea to Rome in 1555 for the continuance of taxation of the church under the indults granted to her father by Clement VII and Paul III, but she did little after 1560 to reverse the curious situation whereby a Catholic queen was, in terms of the disposal of major benefices, the chief beneficiary of the break with Rome made by the Reformation parliament.[50]

The key to the stability of any Stewart reign lay in finance. As Ian Cowan argues, it is only to be expected that Mary's first interest lay, not in promoting the old church or giving some tacit recognition to the new, but in restoring the revenues of the crown. For this reason, Mary's pursuit of a papal subsidy and her acceptance of the various windfall profits accruing from the Reformation, including the settlement on both the crown and the new ministers of the thirds of benefices, were of a piece with the actions of her mother in the 1550s.[51] Yet in other respects Mary's fiscal policy stands at odds with that of her immediate predecessors, for it was marked by an extreme financial prudence, which, more than any other aspect of her policy, demonstrates the queen's natural conservatism. The 1560s were the first decade since the 1530s to call a halt to the spiralling burden of ordinary taxation. By the early 1550s more than twenty burghs were in arrears in their tax payments and at least one major town was threatened with bankruptcy. There was widespread criticism of Mary of Guise's package of taxes between 1555 and 1557, which stemmed as much from her breach of the tacit promise to the parliament of 1552, which had indicated some relief from the weight of taxation during the eight-year war with England, as from its size or partly novel basis.[52] There was no repetition by Mary of her mother's fiscal demands; the only taxation came at the baptism of her son in 1566. The precise amounts of Mary's revenue and expenditure, like those of her father, remain something of a mystery. The revenues from customs averaged only £2,155, only forty per cent of the level of 1542. The thirds yielded a good deal more: sums varying between £12,700 in 1562 and £32,033 in 1565 went to the crown.[53] There were profits, too, from the active market in land, as well as from royal justice. This was, however, still a modest income. Yet there were two vital differences between the 1530s and the 1560s. The great period of impressive − and prohibitively expensive − royal building was over. And the expense of the royal household was met by the regular income from Mary's jointure; its 60,000 *livres* (some £30,000 Scots) was modest by French standards but exercised a disproportionately large impact on the royal finances. Although there were already difficulties in its collection by 1566, the falling value of the Scots pound more than made up for the shortfall.[54] Scotland not only had a royal court, the first for two decades, but also one which cost little.

How diligent a ruler was Mary? It is difficult to measure this by the volume of her correspondence, although it is unlikely that she ever approached the phenomenal 216 letters a year written by Catherine de Médicis. Many of Mary's letters have been lost or destroyed and it was not her usual practice, at least before 1564, to make copies.[55] Yet, in another respect, there is a striking analogy between them − in royal progresses. In January 1564 Catherine and the young king, Charles IX, embarked on a spectacular tour of the kingdom, which lasted twenty-seven months.[56] Mary spent two-thirds of the thirteen months between August 1562 and September 1563 on progress, covering over 1,200 miles. Her entourage was, of course, much smaller than that of the French court, but the rate of progress was correspondingly greater: in fifty-four days in July−September 1564 it covered 460 miles, visiting the north-east and Inverness for a second time. And in the first nine months of the year of her marriage to Darnley, the queen again spent two-thirds of her time on progress. Like Charles IX, Mary took her court to the frontiers of her kingdom − in the north-east, west and south-west.[57] Her administration for the most part went with her. Given the importance placed by so many recent historians on the delicate balances involved in governing a still highly decentralized feudal realm, it is surprising that the queen's conventional absence from her privy council is stressed rather than the conspicuous degree of access she gave to her subjects, both at Holyrood and in her peripatetic court.

Like the tour of Charles IX, progresses were a political education for herself as well as a ritual demonstration of royal power and accessibility, all made the more necessary by the political crisis her realm had gone through in recent years. Here Mary was acting within the best traditions of both Scottish and French practice. Few Stewarts had taken so literally the recommendation of the Scots parliament to James IV that the king 'ryd in proper person, anis in the yeir, throch all partis of the realme'.[58] And Mary must have been aware of the stress put by her husband, François, on the need that the prince 'recoipt et donne accès sans ecception de personne à tous ceux qui sont affligez, et preste l'oreille aux plus pauvres qui ont recours à la justice que Dieu a mis en sa main pour la leur distribuer'[59] − even to the point of granting access to that turbulent subject, John Knox. By the end of 1565, when Randolph complained (in a letter which also repeated the familiar gossip that the queen had spent the night playing cards) that 'every man does what he likes if he has either credit or friend at court',[60] the mutual expectations of the queen and her subjects had been transformed.

There were real risks and serious casualties, however, in this process of restoring the patronage and authority of the crown. The queen's first progress had claimed the first and greatest victim, the earl of Huntly, the queen's most powerful Catholic magnate. Here the stakes, as described by Allan White, were high and had little to do with religion, other than in the invitation made by the 'pope of the north-east' for the queen to attend a flagrantly illegal private mass. Mary risked a provincial destabilization (of, as it happened, her most Catholic province) to avoid the risk of a national war of religion, as had already begun to engulf France. What was at stake was the credibility of both the pursuit of the English succession and the policy, established in the first days after her return, of a religious standstill.

Yet if the issues seemed clear-cut in 1562, it can nevertheless be argued that it was then that Mary sowed the first seeds of doubt in the minds of her nobility. The almost ritual humiliation of a great magnate was both in the long tradition of Stewart royal brutality and a particularly extreme example of it, perhaps unmatched since the hounding of the Black Douglases in the 1450s. The treatment of the head of the house of

Hamilton in 1565 had certain analogies, even if his religion was different. Within four years Mary had forced her two greatest magnates, one Catholic and one Protestant, into rebellion and defeated them. The elevation of 'men of base degree', like Riccio, or the queen's habit of fraternizing with lesser lords and gentry at court,[61] would not have had the effect they did unless there was already, as Julian Goodare argues, a feeling of insecurity amongst those who liked to term themselves the 'ancient nobility'; they were, in fact, mostly *arrivistes* of the 1450s and thus all the more conscious of the fact that their position rested on the whim of the Stewart monarchy. In her relationship with her nobility Queen Mary was every inch a Stewart monarch. Yet it may be there, as with James III and potentially with James V, that her fatal flaw lay. Arguably her most serious error was not so much the attempt in itself to re-establish Catholicism, but her decision to seek her first converts amongst her nobility, for a number of them were already convinced that the real issue at stake in 1566 was their traditional power and status.[62]

The accumulated evidence so far discussed suggests a revised balance sheet for the personal reign and a certain recasting of the issues at stake. It also points to a different chronological perception of the reign. Mary's apologists tend to stress the years of success, 1561—4, and to gloss over the seemingly inexplicable turmoil of 1565—7; her detractors, even if they do not dwell on the period started by the unsuccessful putsch of August 1565, tend to be conditioned by it. There are two sets of issues that both miss. One was the need by 1564—5 for an alternative policy to the dead-end that seemed increasingly to be the prospect offered by the 'amity' with England; this change implied a reduction in the volume of the accompanying 'Puritan choir' which had been led by Moray and Leicester. The other was the purpose and contemporary perception of the marriage with Darnley. It is difficult to exaggerate either the significance of the Lennox Stewart restoration, which began with the return of the earl in September 1564, or the excitement at court and elsewhere triggered off by the prospect of a marriage between Mary and his son. 1560 had been a triumph for the Hamiltons in Scotland, and a disaster for the Lennox Stewart interest in England;[63] 1565 was nothing short of a dynastic counter-revolution. The Hamilton interest was threatened not only at court but in those localities in which it had been consolidating its influence since Lennox's flight in 1544. It was forced, with great reluctance, to return, for example, the office of baillie of the regality (and with it virtual control) of Glasgow in July 1565.[64] The twenty-year absence had done little to harm either the Stewart kinship network, which had been in search of a leader for most of that time, or the earl's old contacts with a group of pro-English lairds of the 1540s. The pro-English party as a result was coming apart, even before Moray strained their two sets of loyalties, to the amity and the crown, in his abortive coup of 1565.

The Lennox Stewart restoration offered not only a place at court but ennoblement on a large scale: it was Lennox himself who, as Julian Goodare points out, drew up the list knighted in May 1565. Earldoms were on offer, too, in a dramatic inflation of honours in the summer of 1565, which closely parallels the creation of forty *chevaliers de l'ordre* by Charles IX between August 1564 and February 1565. It may also have added to the instability felt by some of the old nobility. With ennoblment came a new, and very French humanist stress on the concept of honour, an interest also heavily reflected in Mary's library.[65] The foil to a patriot queen (and king) would be, it was intended, a patriot nobility — a seductive concept (later put to good use by Buchanan)[66] which might transcend their differences, personal as well as religious. This indeed was the theme of Mary's speech from what she thought was her death bed, in October 1566 — in a remarkably fluent appeal to the twin notions of gentility and order.[67] The natural climax to this process was the investiture of Darnley in the order of St Michael, which was still the ultimate mark of honour in French chivalry; Darnley had lobbied the French court for it since the marriage.[68] This was the point, early in 1566, when Mary tried to persuade her nobility to return to the mass. The two policies — the pursuit of honour and the encouragement of Catholicism by degrees — came together at Candlemas. Some nobles were enticed, most were not; but the now joint policy survived the murder of Riccio, which came just four weeks after the investiture. It found a new focus, not in the quixotic figure of Darnley, but in his infant son, born in June, and baptized Charles James (after Charles IX) by Catholic rites in December.[69]

The prospect offered by the birth of a prince, like that offered by the marriage, was at root that of an independent kingdom, able to restore itself to its rightful and equal status with its neighbour. As Randolph complained, towards the end of 1565, the Scots (for whom he had a thinly veiled contempt) by 'their bostes and braggynges' think 'our whole countrie as good as their owne'.[70] It could appeal with equal force to those whose actions in 1559 had been governed by fear of undue French influence and to those who, with the experience of the fruitless English negotiations of the early 1560s behind them, sought a more equitable relationship with Elizabeth. It went hand in hand with an emphasis on the restoration of royal authority, for that alone, it was argued, would guarantee peace and security. The emphasis in the contemporary literature on Mary and Henry as the bringers of peace is so striking that the wonder is that it has been so ignored. There were clear analogies, too, with the emblematic imagery of peace and war in the Valois court of the 1550s and 1560s. And for Scots apologists, they were also the restorers of 'eternal kingship', secured 'in the power of the Stewart family'.[71] This was traditional rhetoric, but all the more convincing for it. It could and did survive the bizarre conduct of Darnley over the course of most of 1566. But if Darnley did not destroy the credibility of Mary's polity in life, he certainly did in death, which came in that eternal murder mystery of 10 February 1567. Whether Bothwell was chosen as a replacement husband because he was 'twice the man' that Darnley was, or because he continued the policy of an anti-English stance, the gap between his standing and that of the Lennox Stewart with two royal blood lines was too blatant for the polity to convince. Mary fell victim to the very persuasiveness of the advertising campaign that had accompanied the restoration of the Lennox Stewarts. No wonder her enemies could use the image of the infant prince demanding revenge; their campaign was a natural sequel to that of 1565–6.

It is now possible to come to some judgement both of the role of the royal court during the personal reign and the sense of the queen's attitude towards the religious question. The importance and accomplishments of Mary's court have scarcely been recognized. It was the inspiration, it has recently been recognized, of the bulk of the Bannatyne Manuscript, the comprehensive anthology of late Scots medieval poetry; for when else would the love poetry, which makes up half of the collection, be compiled but in the distinctive milieu brought about by the Darnley courtship and marriage?[72] This was also the occasion of the first published work of Scots secular literature since the Reformation, in the form of Latin verses celebrating the marriage by the lawyer, Thomas Craig.[73] Mary's court deserves to be restored, as John Durkan makes clear, to its due and honoured place in the history of Scottish culture, both Latin and vernacular. It was as glittering a Renaissance court as that of her father or her son. And in its specific interests in French and Italian literature there are direct links, such as provided by Alexander Montgomerie, a kinsman of the Catholic Lord Eglinton and an imitator of Ronsard, and by John Stewart of Baldynneis, a relative of Mary Beaton and a translator of Ariosto, as well as by Mary's own library, with what is conventionally seen as a literary revival centred on the Castalian band of James VI.[74] With the weight of new evidence of Mary's personal accomplishments, as literary patron, book collector and student of the art of government, the notion of the empty-headed queen, intent only on the pleasures of her court, can safely be laid to rest.

The court, whether in its elaborate ritual and entertainments or in its patronage, was also an instrument of monarchical authority. One of the most significant groups of Mary's clients was a circle of lawyers, some with Catholic sympathies, like David Chalmers and James Balfour who were both promoted to the privy council in the changes of 1565–6.[75] It was they, who were also linked with Bothwell, who were almost certainly the moving forces in the commission set up in 1566 which resulted in the first printed edition of the acts of the Scottish parliament.[76] Both it and Chalmers's manuscript dictionary of Scots law, also the first of its kind, reflected a concern to codify a body of 'municipal' (or national) law, as the first step in giving greater administrative cohesion to a decentralized feudal kingdom. All this was of a piece with the more general policy of the restoration of the power and status of the Stewart monarchy.

There were also a series of connections between the court as a literary centre and as a Catholic devotional centre. Some were personal: Alexander Scott, poet and musician, had links with both the court and the chapel royal at Stirling; so had George Clapperton, provost of Edinburgh's Trinity College and perhaps also a minor poet. Others were overtly political. Mary's confessors, Benoist and Winzet, were pamphleteers as well as preachers to the royal household. There is a paradox here, for one of the curiosities of the Reformation of 1559–60 had been the near-silence of the Catholics in print. The real battle with Protestant spokesmen, both in print and in disputations, came after 1560 and the royal household had a greater role in it than has previously been thought. Although both Benoist and Winzet went abroad in 1562, their campaign in print continued. Its effects are hard to judge, but it is noticeable that the queen, with eight of Benoist's tracts in her library,[77] was interested in the strictly orthodox defence of both the mass and images which had emerged in France by 1562 with the Colloquy of Saint-Germain and which featured in his work; this, after all, was the priest who denied Henri III new kinds of devotion.[78] By 1565 it is striking that some influential Protestants, particularly Moray, were anxious enough about the effects of Italian influence on the court to have reissued in an Edinburgh edition two esoteric Italian works criticizing monasticism and the papacy. A client of Moray had financed the printing of the *Book of Common Order* in 1564 and one of the ex-canons of Moray's Augustinian priory at St Andrews collaborated in the production of a metrical psalter showing distinct traces of Huguenot influence in 1566.[79] By the mid-1560s there was a battle of the books in and around the court; a wave of Catholic or royalist literature, some produced in Edinburgh and some abroad, with the queen acting either as its inspiration or its direct mentor, was met by a determinedly Protestant counterblast, which had Moray as its patron and perhaps also Buchanan as a fellow worker in the vineyard. The question to be answered by historians who view the 1560s in Scotland in terms of the untrammelled growth and consolidation of Protestantism is why there was such widespread anxiety, felt by Knox as much as by Moray, by 1565.[80]

In one sense, Mary's attempts at encouraging Catholic reform were modest and unimaginative. There had been little effort made in the direction of diocesan-based reform, such as Mary Tudor and Cardinal Pole had inspired in England.[81] At least one of the three Catholic bishops Mary appointed never visited his diocese: the efforts of John Leslie (of Ross) and William Chisholm (of Dunblane) were needed elsewhere, both at court and in Rome or Paris. Yet Mary, it should be noted, had in Winzet and Leslie advisers who were sharply critical of the pre-Reformation hierarchy and unlikely to neglect the role of bishops in a Catholic revival. According to Leslie, the parliament scheduled to meet in March 1566 (which was overtaken by the crisis triggered by the Riccio murder) was to discuss 'allowing bishops and rectors the full exercise of their ancient religion'. This seems to reflect Trent's reaffirmation of the authority and jurisdiction of the episcopate.[82] Also in line with Tridentine decrees was her selection, as reported by her confessor, Roch Mamerot, in December 1565, of four 'Catholic men of learning' for public preaching; they were probably John Black, Andrew Abercrombie, both Dominicans, and John Roger, a Franciscan. All three were seasoned, gifted preachers and Knox, revealingly, reports that they were now 'using' another 'style' than in 1559. The fourth may perhaps have been Clapperton.[83]

The queen's chapel at Holyrood, described as 'a college'[84] later in 1566, was one instrument of Mary's emerging Catholic *risorgimento*; the other, as yet less developed, was the episcopate. The target was the nobility at court and the inducement, for those who could not bring themselves to return to the mass, was liberty of conscience — for all, it is likely, except Calvinists.[85] The stick would be provided, as Ian Cowan makes clear, by means of a papal subsidy, which Mary had been pursuing since September 1565. These demands made of the papacy were of a quite different dimension from the modest £15,000 Scots (30,000 *livres*) of a pension which had been sought in 1555.[86] The scale of the queen's intentions in 1565−6 can be judged by the size of the sums involved: 300,000 ducats (approximately £530,000 Scots or

£97,000 sterling) represented forty per cent of the amount spent by Philip II in defence of the Mediterranean against the Turks in 1565–6.[87] Yet this was not a preposterous demand if viewed in the light of the £400,000 (800,000 *livres*) which the French had budgeted to spend in Scotland in 1549,[88] or the large but unquantifiable total the papacy had been willing to grant to James V in the 1530s, in the form of taxation of the church and virtual capitulation to the crown of the *ius nominandi* to religious houses, in order to ward off the spectre of a Henrician-type reformation in Scotland. The actual amount offered by Pius V was only a fraction of the amount needed to put an army in the field: his 20,000 *scudi* (about £29,850), of which only a fifth was actually paid, was nearly matched by the official gifts from France and England, totalling 14,000 *scudi*, for the baptism of Mary's son. Scotland might have been a 'special daughter' of Rome, but it necessarily ranked low in papal priorities: the pope had granted 55,000 *scudi* to the Emperor in 1565.[89] What was problematic was not so much Mary's intent as the ability of the papacy, without any prospect of French assistance, to meet the bill for a Scottish Counter-Reformation.

Lack of finance was the most serious but not the only defect in Mary's Catholic *risorgimento*. Yet however flawed the scheme was, it was dangerous enough to provoke a sudden escalation of Protestant violence, which in the capital had previously been generally muted, if never far beneath the surface of events. On the eve of Darnley's investiture in February 1566 an attempt was made on the life of John Black by a gang of Edinburgh Protestants and, a month later, he was murdered – on the night of Riccio's assassination. Both murders were acts of desperation; the Protestant activists amongst the nobility were, for a number of reasons, apprehensive of the coming parliament; and the reason for the involvement of more than a score of the Protestant party in the capital was the drastic slippage since 1560 in their position on the town council, to the point where only one still held office.[90]

The queen's policy continued after the Riccio murder, although it had lost some of its momentum. Knox, writing in May 1566, complained of the spread of the mass to 'all quarteris of the realme'; and it was reported that more Catholics than ever before, some 9,000 from Knox's own parish and the surrounding district, had attended Easter communion in the queen's chapel at Holyrood.[91] The Riccio murder which had taken place on the eve of the first Sunday of Lent, had, in turn, provoked a Catholic backlash – in the largest Catholic demonstration since the Reformation. A Protestant Lent, marked by a fast called by the General Assembly, gave way to a Catholic Easter.[92] The atmosphere in the middle of 1566 was sharpening and beginning to resemble that in France five years earlier. The increasing willingness of Catholics to attend the mass, together with a stricter Catholic attitude in defence of images (seen in Benoist's tract of 1565) was the backcloth for the ratification by the reformed church of the Second Helvetic Confession in September, to which it added a rider that its own explicit rejection of images and holy days, like Christmas and Easter, made it the purest of all the reformed churches.[93] Both Scottish churches were seeking to underline their own strict orthodoxy — a Catholic church 'under the cross' and a Calvinist church under siege. The real difficulty for both was that the task was great and the labourers were few; the Confession was endorsed by the ministerial elite of the reformed church, forty-one in all, who represented a further 200 ministers.[94] The active Catholic corps was a good deal smaller. Yet by December 1566 the General Assembly was appealing directly to Protestant nobles to check 'the open erecting of idolatry'. It is hardly surprising that the bishop of Dunblane predicted bloodshed in the summer of 1566, with Catholic blood being spilt first, or that the papal nuncio, who had seen the fruits of calculated Catholic violence in France, should draw up a death list as the answer to Mary's problems.[95]

Mary — whether because of her natural caution or her distaste for violence or a loss of nerve it is difficult to say — drew back from the increasing prospect of a war of religion, putting her trust in her ability to draw together her nobility on the same lines as had worked in 1565. The programme of legal reforms continued, with one of its inspirers, David Chalmers, now planted in the key post of common clerk in the capital, where he supplanted 'King' Guthrie, one of the leaders of the original Protestant caucus which had seized power in 1560. Further royal nominees were added to Edinburgh's town council in October 1566, consolidating the fall of the Protestant activists, yet there were some signs that the queen was beginning to overplay her hand in her interventions in the burgh's politics.[96] Studied concessions were made, not least to reassure the reformed church, which in October was granted, in the form of the small benefices, the most significant concession to it since 1560. The balance of the programme might have altered, but there was no sign as yet of its abandonment and, still less, of panic by Mary. That came only with her behaviour after the murder of Darnley in February 1567 and her third marriage, three months later.

The greatest of Mary's errors have, properly, been identified in this volume as the marriage with James Hepburn, earl of Bothwell, not least because it was by Protestant rites, and the precipitate flight to England after Langside in 1568.[97] No amount of concessions to individual nobles, burghs and the reformed church could stem the tide of opposition in 1567, even if it was largely directed at Bothwell rather than the queen. Even her closest Catholic advisers were divided by the marriage, and some of her sharpest critics were her Catholic nobles.[98] A limited defence of it can be made, in terms of Bothwell's political independence and his proven ability as an administrator, both as High Admiral and in the Borders; his hand can be detected both in some of the legislation of Mary's parliaments of 1563 and 1567 and in the publication of the printed acts of parliament. He was Protestant, but both his own scepticism (which prompted English observers to brand him 'of no religion') and the varied religious convictions of his clients indicated that he could operate in the flexible atmosphere which Mary's policy had since 1565 encouraged at court.[99] Mary may have put passion above all else. Or she may, as in 1562, have put dynastic politics above religion, believing that without the foundation provided by the former, the latter would founder. Whatever her motives, the marriage was a serious miscalculation. What Mary did not recognize, but which emerged clearly by the time of Langside in May 1568, was that a Stewart queen did not need the dubious support of a Hepburn marriage. The folly was all the greater because her policy up to that point in 1567 had indeed resecured the authority of the monarchy and brought a Catholic revival within sight. The greatest irony of the situation in early 1567 was that popular Catholicism was still on the increase; Mary's confessor reported, with unusual precision, that 12,606 had taken communion at Easter in her chapel and that he had, as Trent decreed, duly recorded their names.[100] But without the stimulus of what Knox called 'the holy water of the court' and lacking any tradition of ritual violence, as in France, ordinary Catholics were both leaderless and politically insignificant.[101]

There can be little doubt that Mary's policy from 1565 was, by a variety of means, directed squarely at encouraging a Catholic revival. It might be wondered if she miscalculated by putting so much trust in nobles rather than playing the populist card, especially in her capital. Only a fifth of its inhabitants had attended Protestant services *before* her return, and a deep vein of Marian feeling survived the crises of 1567.[102] There were major Catholic demonstrations at every Easter from 1563 onwards, some as an obvious reaction to Protestant harassment. Yet even if many of these Catholics found solace in Mary's own chapel, the queen had usually distanced herself from them. Even in the major demonstrations at Holyrood on Easter Sunday 1566 and 1567 the queen, despite the obvious political temptations, declined to exploit Catholic populist feeling; although in Edinburgh, she chose to stay in the Castle.[103]

Three times, in effect — in 1562, 1566 and 1567 — Mary refused others' invitation to the mass. Like her Protestant nobles in the revolt of 1559—60, the queen was at heart too politically conservative to risk the support of the mob.

Was then the attempt to reconvert her nobility over-ambitious or even naive? It was still Jesuit strategy, it might be noted, in the 1590s.[104] Arguably it had better prospects in the 1560s, for these were still times of great flux. Mary was surrounded at court by a variety of notables, churchmen as well as lay magnates, whose careers before and after 1560 had been distinctly chequered in their attachments to Rome and Geneva. Some of the nobles, as well as most of her bastard half-brothers, were still in her eyes churchmen, having held commendatorships; technically at least this was correct, for none of these commendators had married before 1560 without resigning their commend first.[105] There were grounds for thinking they might be enticed back to Rome by the offer of preferment. Some of the leading ministers, including three of the committee which had drawn up the Protestant *Book of Discipline* in 1560, had been very late converts to Protestantism; another, George Hay, was later still, delaying his conversion until mid-1561.[106] Late converts might well return to the fold, for the drift of opinion was far from being one-way traffic. Knox's old companion on the galleys, the lawyer James Balfour, seems by 1560 to have returned from Lutheranism to Catholicism.[107] This was a world of firm opinions which resulted in scepticism in some (like Bothwell) and frequent changes of mind in others — an apparent paradox, but only to the non-sixteenth-century mind. The earl of Cassillis was firmly Protestant in mid-1564; by mid-1565 he was attending the mass, with all the fervour of a new convert; and by the time of his marriage a year later to the daughter of the Protestant Lord Glamis he was restored as a more precise Protestant than ever.[108] Alexander Gordon of Galloway, one of the three conforming bishops of 1560, was actively considering a return to Rome in 1565—6, if only on the basis of the mutual disappointment he and the reformed church by now had in each other.[109] This was the atmosphere of the court on which so much of Mary's policy tacitly depended, and which John Knox rightly feared. Even if outright conversion might not succeed, liberty of conscience was, for Knox, an equally dangerous recruiting sergeant for the queen.

There would, however, have been an inherent difficulty for the Catholic revival, had it gone any further. It has been claimed, with some justice, that the reforms made by provincial councils of the Scottish church in the later 1540s and 1550s faithfully reflected similar provincial reform in both France and Germany as well as the first session of

Trent.[110] The Tridentine reform of the 1560s was rather different in its emphasis and at variance with much of the effort invested, in the meantime, by the Scottish church in vernacular literature and prayers. And Trent's disapproval of many manifestations of popular piety would have come hard to a society which had adopted the full panoply of a civic cult, in the form of occupational saints and the Holy Blood devotions, only over the course of the previous three-quarters of a century.[111] Just as the reformed church had after 1560 to de-Lutheranize as well as convert,[112] so the post-Tridentine Catholic church, which was faithfully reflected in the queen's own household, would have had in some respects to convince the faithful anew.

The personal reign also gives a number of important clues to the exile. It seems unlikely that Mary came to a real belief in Catholicism, as distinct from mere conformity to it, only in her last years.[113] Too much can be made of a deepening of her faith in captivity; both the character of her French confessors in Edinburgh and her library testify to a strict, if uncomplicated devotional piety in the 1560s. Her Catholic beliefs were already sharpening on matters such as images and devotions, as a direct reflection of the shift of mood after Poissy in the French church, which had anticipated the last session at Trent. There is also evident in the 1560s, as later, as Mark Greengrass points out, the same access to up-to-date and detailed information, both in the form of books and intelligence. Throughout her whole career in both England and Scotland — whether measured by her books, as John Durkan does, or by the concerns revealed in her correspondence in captivity, as examined by Peter Holmes, or by the bequests in her wills — her greatest interests lay in the courts and kingdoms of France and Scotland. The key to understanding Mary lies, not so much in seeing her as either an English pretender or a Guise, as in her real status as a Stewart and a Valois queen.

For how long did she aspire to the English throne? Her original claim, as Marcus Merriman demonstrates, was Valois rather than Guise in inspiration, going back to 1550 rather than 1558 or 1559. It was thus increasingly inappropriate in the prolonged crisis of the French monarchy which began while she was queen of France and lasted virtually throughout the rest of her lifetime. The evidence from her personal reign in Scotland, which tends to show that her own interest in the English succession receded from the time of the Darnley marriage, seems to confirm the evidence of her correspondence in captivity, which shows little reference to it.[114] Her claim to the English throne, while never conceded, was not pursued, at least by the queen herself, with any real urgency or seriousness after 1571, and perhaps even after

1565. During her imprisonment in England Mary was, at worst, a marginal plotter. The real difference between the two periods — the personal reign and the exile — is one of personnel. In France, as in Scotland, a new generation of politicians had come of age by 1574.[115] By then most of the leading figures of Scotland in the 1560s were dead — Moray, Lennox, Châtelherault, Knox and Archbishop Hamilton; in France the dukes of Guise and Montmorency and the king of Navarre were all dead by 1568 and the two Guise cardinals by 1578. Her council in France changed its character with its change of personnel after 1574. There were in these new circumstances no checks on the potential hotheads around her, like John Leslie; there were even less on new recruits like Thomas Morgan. For the last dozen years of the queen's life her supporters were more Marian than was Mary herself.

The Marian cause was taken up in the 1570s and 1580s by a *mélange* of committed individuals and special interests. Rarely did they pull for long in the one direction. Some groups, like the French Jesuits and the leaders of the English Catholic community, found that Marianism provoked serious internal divisions amongst themselves; the involvement of Henri Samier in Marian intrigues threatened the control exercised by the Jesuit General, Aquaviva, on the whole mission in France.[116] The involvement of Marians of this stamp exaggerated the conspiratorial image of Mary's cause and, at the same time, gave it a real fragility. Interest groups like these would, when it came to the brink, consult their own interests first and those of Mary second. Well before the axe fell in 1587 the queen had been abandoned, even by friends such as these. Mary was left at the mercy of young hotheads, like Parry and Babington. For the queen who had promised so much in the Valois and Scottish courts, martyrdom was a kinder prospect.

Notes

[1] I am grateful to Dr Merriman for drawing my attention to this point. See his ch. 2 n.18 below for references.

[2] G. F. Barwick, 'A sidelight on the mystery of Mary Stuart', *SHR*, xxi (1924), 121.

[3] Patrick Adamson (future archbishop of St Andrews), *Serenissimi ac Nobilissimi Scotiae Angliae Hybernie Principis Henrici Stuardi et Mariae Reginae* (Paris, 1566). I am grateful to Mrs Evelyn Stalker for her translation. Since Adamson was a client of Châtelherault, this may represent an early attempt by the duke, exiled to France in Dec. 1565, to rehabilitate himself; see Michel, *Français,* ii, 53n.

[4] See Labanoff, iv, 256, 390; *CSP Scot.*, v, 241, for portraits made of Mary in captivity for sympathizers in England and for Archbishop Beaton in Paris.

[5] A. Dufour, 'Le mythe de Genève au temps de Calvin', *Revue suisse d'histoire*, ix (1959), 498—518.

[6] Calderwood, *History*, iv, 3—18; Wright, *Elizabeth*, ii, 216. Despite denying it on oath 'before God and his angels', Melville took flight to England.

[7] See e.g. Fraser, *Mary*, 429; J. E. Phillips, *Images of a Queen* (1964), 54—63.

[8] *Warrender Papers*, i, 251.

[9] P. Adamson, *De papistarum superstiosis ineptiis* (Edinburgh, 1564). See I. D. Macfarlane, *Buchanan* (1981), 218, 229; J. Durkan, 'Native influences on George Buchanan', in *Acta Conventus Neo-Latini Sanctandreani*, ed. I. D. Macfarlane (1982), 36—7.

[10] Barwick, 'Sidelight', 115—18.

[11] Donaldson, *Queen's Men*, 79. Adamson published a second edition, in English, *A defence of the honour of Mary, Queen of Scots* (Liège, 1571), Michel, *Français*, ii, 52—3n.

[12] *CSP Scot.*, ii, 408.

[13] Barwick, 'Sidelight', 124—7.

[14] Printed in Forbes Leith, *Narratives*, 85—126.

[15] J. Durkan, 'James, third earl of Arran: the hidden years', *SHR*, lxv (1986), 163. See also Adams, ch. 6 below, for Randolph.

[16] Buchanan, a likely apologist as 'a man of Lennox', had limited room for manoeuvre in his account of 1565—6 to defend both it and Moray; Darnley grew in death to a stature he had not experienced in life as a result.

[17] See the important discussion in Donaldson, *Queen's Men*, 48—69.

[18] The household is given in Teulet, *Relations*, ii, 268—81; see also A. Lang, 'The household of Mary, Queen of Scots in 1573', *SHR*, ii (1905), 345—55; Michel, *Français*, ii, 31—2n.

[19] See ch. 8 below. The jointure's value must also take account of shifting exchange rates.

[20] *CSP Scot.*, iv, 505; W. A. McNeill, 'Documents illustrative of the Scots College, Paris', *IR*, xv (1964), 67. See also refs. in Durkan, ch. 4 n. 101, and Holmes, ch. 9 nn. 54, 75 below.

[21] See E. Finnie, 'The house of Hamilton: patronage, politics and the church in the Reformation period', *IR*, xxxvi (1985), 3—28.

[22] Donaldson, *Queen's Men*, 72.

[23] ibid., 62.

[24] As by Adamson, who hailed 'the eternal kingship, in the power of the Stewart family' in his poem on the birth, which also looked forward to 'the reign of Charles'; see n. 69 below.

[25] *CSPF 1566—8*, 59.

[26] *Diurnal*, 103—4. See also Durkan, ch. 4, app. 1, n.24, below.

[27] H. de la Ferrière-Percy, 'L'entrevue de Bayonne', *Revue des questions historiques* (1883), 505.

[28] Greengrass, ch. 8 below.

[29] H. D. Sedgwick, *The House of Guise* (1938), 46.

[30] Adams, ch. 6 below; Greengrass, ch. 8 below; Holmes, ch. 9 below, for Guise influence. Most of the Scots congregated and published in Paris; but the

Jesuit college at Pont-à-Mousson, founded in 1574 and attended by many Scots, was in Guise territory.

[31] D. Nugent, *Ecumenism in the Age of the Reformation: The Colloquy of Poissy* (1974), 17—36, 228; M. Greengrass, *France in the Age of Henri IV: The Struggle for Stability* (1984), 8—9.

[32] R. K. Marshall, *Mary of Guise* (1977); J. Wormald, *Court, Kirk and Community: Scotland, 1475—1625* (1981), 117.

[33] M. Lynch, 'The crown and the burghs', in M. Lynch (ed.), *The Early Modern Town in Scotland* (1987), 45—8.

[34] Melville, *Memoirs*, 222.

[35] See Donaldson, *Queen's Men*, 83ff, for the strength of the queen's party in the civil war.

[36] ibid., 51; M. Lynch, 'Scottish Calvinism, 1559—1638', in M. Prestwich (ed.), *International Calvinism, 1541—1715* (1985), 227—8.

[37] As well as sovereignty, which has rightly been given primacy in the forming of opinions during the reign (Donaldson, *Queen's Men*, 100), the great political issues, like relations with England, also changed minds. The Ayr Bond, which coincided with the queen's progress to the north in 1562, was a mild enough Protestant statement to allow some lairds from the Catholic Kennedy kindred an opportunity to protest at its involvement with Huntly and Châtelherault. Tactical voting is one of the pitfalls for those who take a fundamentalist view of subscription to such bonds or, indeed, to attendance at the Reformation parliament of 1560.

[38] The poet, Richard Maitland, had appealed to the queen to take a husband quickly to 'maintein our libertie' (*Maitland Quarto Manuscript* (STS, 1919—20), ii, 29).

[39] McRoberts, *Scottish Reformation*, 473; *Papal Negs.*, 4—25, 522—30.

[40] Donaldson, *Queen's Men*, 25, 160. NLS, MS Balcarres Papers, v, which is not included in the printed edition, *Foreign Corresp.* (SHS), contains much detail of various pensions and preferments. One such was the commendatorship of L'Absie to David Paniter, bishop of Ross.

[41] Durkan, 'James, third earl of Arran', 160.

[42] Wormald, *Court, Kirk and Community*, 214.

[43] Donaldson, *Scotland*, 113.

[44] Donaldson, *Queen's Men*, 74, 87, 100.

[45] See e.g. K. Brown, 'Much ado about nothing', *History Today* (Feb. 1987), 8.

[46] *CSP Spain*, i, 259. I am grateful to Dr Adams for advice on this point.

[47] By the poet, William Stewart; see *The Bannatyne MS* (STS, 1928—33), ii, 256, ll. 16—25, I am grateful to Dr A. A. MacDonald for this reference.

[48] I. B. Cowan, *The Scottish Reformation* (1982), 89—106; Lynch, 'Calvinism', 225—32.

[49] *CSP Scot.*, ii, 173.

[50] *Papal Negs.*, 522—5. The letter of 27 Dec. 1555 is now in Vatican Library, MS Barberini Latini 3616, fo. l; I am grateful to Dr Durkan for this information. See I. B. Cowan, 'Patronage, provision and reservation: pre-Reformation appointments to Scottish benefices', and J. Kirk, 'The exercise of ecclesiastical

patronage by the crown, 1560–1572', both in I. B. Cowan and D. Shaw (eds.), *The Renaissance and Reformation in Scotland* (1983), 92, 98–9, for crown patronage.

[51] Cowan, ch. 5 below; McRoberts, *Scottish Reformation*, 74.

[52] Lynch, 'Crown and burghs', 70, 72; Lynch, *Edinburgh*, 72; *APS*, ii, 482–91, shows much concern with prices and dearth, but no mention of taxation.

[53] *Exchequer Rolls*, xix *passim;* Donaldson, *Thirds*, xxv.

[54] The deficit of 40,000 *livres* by early 1567 (see ch. 8 n. 22 below) was compensated by the 25 per cent fall in the £ Scots 1561–7; Gilbert, 'Usual money of Scotland', 143, 146.

[55] J. Boutier, A. Dewerpe and D. Nordman, *Un tour de France royal: le voyage de Charles IX, 1564–1566* (1984), 218; Melville, *Memoirs*, 112.

[56] Boutier et al., *Tour*, 13–28.

[57] I. B. Cowan, 'The progresses of Mary, Queen of Scots', in P. McNeill and R. Nicholson (eds), *An Historical Atlas of Scotland, c.400–c.1600* (1975), 86–7, 198–9; E. Furgol, 'The progresses of Mary, queen of Scots, 1542–48 and 1561–68', *Procs. Soc. Antiqs. Scot.*, cxvii (1987). Cf. Boutier et al., *Tour*, 28, 54–7.

[58] Leslie, *History* (Bann.), 60–1.

[59] François II to parlement of Paris, 1 Mar. 1560, cited in Boutier et al., *Tour*, 286.

[60] *CSP Scot.*, ii, 247.

[61] Donaldson, *Queen's Men*, 62; Calderwood, *History*, ii, 572–3.

[62] Cf. the emphasis in Donaldson, *Mary*, 72, that Mary had succeeded by 1562 in 'bringing about a unity among the Scottish magnates hardly paralleled' since James IV.

[63] Adams, ch. 6 below; Donaldson, *Queen's Men*, 35.

[64] *RPC*, i, 290; J. McGrath, 'The Administration of the Burgh of Glasgow, 1574–1586' (Glasgow Univ. Ph.D., 1987), i, 22, 91.

[65] *CSP Scot.*, ii, 174. The oath of knighthood is given in Keith, *History*, ii, 288–9. See also Boutier et al., *Tour*, 258–9.

[66] A. H. Williamson, *Scottish National Consciousness in the Age of James VI* (1979), 111–16.

[67] Keith, *History*, iii, 287.

[68] Michel, *Français*, ii, 52n; Teulet, *Relations*, ii, 108; Keith, *History*, ii, 390n; *HMC Salisbury*, i, 325. Thirty-nine were created in France Aug. 1564–Feb. 1565, underlining its status as 'the extreme mark of honour of the French nobility' (Boutier et al., *Tour*, 258–9, 390n) although the awards were primarily desperate acts to avert royal bankruptcy. It was still considered sufficient inducement to offer to Moray in June 1567 if he defended Mary (*HMC Pepys*, 106). Its wholesale decline came later. I am grateful to Dr Greengrass for advice on this point.

[69] *Diurnal*, 103; Keith, *History*, ii, 485–6. The name is also confirmed in D. Chambre (Chalmers), *Histoire abbrégée* (Paris, 1579), pt. 3, fo. 219, as Chalmers had attended the baptism; I am grateful to Dr Durkan for this reference. Adamson's poem on the birth also looked forward to 'the reign of Charles'. The joint name also explains the inscriptions 'M.C.J.S.' and others on the windows of the great guest hall at Buxton, described in a diagram in *HMC Bath*

(1907), ii, 20. It is likely that 'Charles' was also cast in the imperial tradition of Charlemagne, which had permeated the iconography of Henri II's court; see Merriman, ch. 2 below, and V. Hoffman, 'Le Louvre de Henri II: un palais impérial', *Bulletin de la Société de l'Histoire de l'Art français 1982* (Paris, 1984), 7–15.

[70] *CSP Scot.*, ii, 247.

[71] Adamson's poem reflects both influences: its imagery of peace and Scottish kingship can also be seen in the work of Richard Maitland and Alexander Scott; its reference to the prophecy of Merlin of 'an age of gold' directly reflects the imagery used in the royal tour of Bayonne in 1565, see *Recueil des choses notables à Bayonne* (Paris, 1566), cited in Boutier et al., *Tour,* 323, 368n. See also Merriman, ch. 2 below, for Valois imagery of the 1550s.

[72] A. A. MacDonald, 'The Bannatyne Manuscript: a Marian anthology', *IR,* xxxvii (1986), 36–47. The ostensible date of its compilation, 1568, explains why the love poems are styled 'ballatis detesting of luve and lichery'; by then the reformed church was exercising stricter control of the printing press.

[73] Thomas Craig, *Henrici et Mariae epithalamium* (Edin., 1565).

[74] Stewart, b. 1540, was son of 4th Lord Innermeath and Elizabeth Beaton of Creich, aunt of Mary Beaton, the queen's maid of honour, to whom she willed books; another relative was Alex. Beaton, son of the cardinal and archdeacon of Lothian, the earliest known reader of Ariosto in Scotland. Montgomerie, b. c.1545, was related to the Lennox Stewarts through his mother; another client of Eglinton was the queen's almoner and book collector, Archibald Crawford. I am grateful to Dr Durkan for this information. Cf. R. Jack, *The Italian Influence on Scottish Literature* (1972), 54–89; also see Macfarlane, *Buchanan,* 227–34.

[75] Randolph considered Balfour and Chalmers 'as of none' in religion, but Bishop Leslie, surely in a better position to know, considered them Catholics; *CSP Scot.*, ii, 211; Forbes Leith, *Narratives,* 113. See further refs. at ch. 4 n. 22 below.

[76] There had been an edition of the acts of the parliament of 1563, printed in 1565 by Lekpreuik. He had also been granted a licence in Feb. 1566 to publish the collected acts, but it was revoked in June in favour of Edward Henryson, one of the Bothwell legal circle. It was the moving force behind the two editions, of 12 Oct. and 28 Nov. 1566, although the same, ultra-Protestant printer, Lekpreuik, was used. Both the contents of the first edition (which contained the old heresy laws) and the fears expressed as late as May 1567 of new laws against Protestant nobles probably stemmed from the control of legislative initiative and the printing press, still held by this circle in 1566–7. *RSS,* v, 1987, 2615, 2869; *HMC Pepys,* 103. See Durkan, ch. 4 below, for the circle, and Goodare, ch. 7 below, for the acts.

[77] Four are identified in J. Sharman, *The Library of Mary, Queen of Scots* (1889), 65, 102, 125; a further four in Durkan, ch. 4 below, at nn.73–6, 78–80.

[78] Nugent, *Ecumenism,* 196–200; A. Lynn Martin, *Henry III and the Jesuit Politicians* (1973), 59.

[79] Durkan, 'Native influences on Buchanan', 38, 42n. See also the references in Lynch, 'Calvinism', 245n.

[80] Knox, *History,* ii, 138, 140–1, 143, 150.

[81] R. H. Pogson, 'Reginald Pole and the priorities of government in Mary Tudor's church', *Historical J., xviii* (1975), 14.

[82] Forbes Leith, *Narratives,* 108.

[83] *Papal Negs.,* 492, 495; McRoberts, *Scottish Reformation,* 315; Knox, *History,* ii, 175.

[84] *Diurnal,* 104. The chapel's exact status is unclear, and it should be distinguised from the chapel royal at Stirling, which had its own links with the court milieu, such as provided by the poet–musician, Alexander Scott, and George Clapperton, sub-dean and poet. It may have been Holyrood that was in mind when the pope promised in Aug. 1565 to help fund 'a college' in Scotland (*Papal Negs.,* 487).

[85] *Papal Negs.,* 505.

[86] See Cowan, ch. 5 below: the *livre* was worth 10*s* Scots (Gilbert, 'Usual money of Scotland', 145).

[87] Details are given in Cowan, ch. 5 below. Cf. G. Parker, *Spain and the Netherlands: Ten Studies* (1979), 126, 129, 248n, where a conversion rate of ducats to *escudos* is also given; the *escudo* was worth 5*s* 10*d* sterling, or 32*s* 1*d* Scots. I am grateful to Dr Adams and to Dr R. Mackenney for their advice on exchange rates. See also Gilbert, 'Usual money of Scotland', 140, 142.

[88] See Merriman, ch. 2 below.

[89] *Papal Negs.,* 200, 210, 334. See ibid., 264n, and Gilbert, 'Usual money of Scotland', 142, for exchange rates of the *scudi.*

[90] Lynch, *Edinburgh,* 114–18.

[91] Knox, *History,* ii, 5; *Papal Negs.,* 496.

[92] Hay Fleming, *Mary,* 495; Knox, *History,* ii, 178; cf. Nugent, *Ecumenism,* 21.

[93] Knox, *Works,* vi, 546–50; see also Knox, *History,* ii, 3.

[94] In 1567 there were 850 clergy in the reformed church, but less than a quarter were ministers; most of the remainder, readers and exhorters, were ex-Catholic clergy, many being late converts; Lynch, 'Calvinism', 248; Cowan, *Scottish Reformation,* 162–5, 170.

[95] Knox, *History,* ii, 197; *Papal Negs.,* 278, 499.

[96] Lynch, *Edinburgh,* 117–18, 282.

[97] See Cowan, ch. 5, and Holmes, ch. 9, below.

[98] *Papal Negs.,* 520; cf. Forbes Leith, *Narratives,* 123, for Leslie's claim that he and Chisholm opposed the marriage.

[99] See H. Drummond, *The Queen's Man* (1975), 107; R.F. Gore-Browne, *Lord Bothwell* (1937), 213, 216–17, for two spirited defences; also *HMC Pepys,* 76.

[100] *Papal Negs.,* 520; see also ibid., 275, requiring the compiling of an 'index of virtuous persons and Catholics of each diocese'. The question of numbers taking communion in a small private chapel is critically examined in Lynch, *Edinburgh,* 188; the dimensions of the chapel are given in J. G. Dunbar, 'The palace of Holyroodhouse', *Archaeological J.,* cxx (1964), 245, but portable altars may also have been used. The large-scale Catholic sympathy of the capital's population is not in doubt, only its precise numbers.

[101] Knox, *History,* ii, 12; Greengrass, *France,* 4—6.

[102] Lynch, *Edinburgh,* 190, 200—11.

[103] Hay Fleming, *Mary,* 537, 542.

[104] J. Durkan, 'William Murdoch and the early Jesuit mission in Scotland', *IR,* xxxv (1984), 5.

[105] M. Dilworth, 'The commendator system in Scotland', *IR,* xxxvii (1986), 59, 60.

[106] Lynch, 'Calvinism', 229—30; J. Durkan, 'George Hay's *Oration* at the purging of King's College, Aberdeen, in 1569', *Northern Scotland,* vi (1985), 99—100.

[107] Durkan, ch. 4 below. See also Forbes Leith, *Narratives,* 103—4.

[108] Knox, *History,* ii, 143, 174, 189. Another earl, John Erskine of Mar, although apparently a resolute Protestant, had been in holy orders until 1555, and had a Catholic wife — another reason here and with others for hopes of changes of mind; *Papal Negs.,* 278; McRoberts, *Scottish Reformation,* 56.

[109] A. Ross, 'More about the archbishop of Athens', *IR,* xiv (1963), 30—7. Gordon's efforts to become superintendent of Galloway, which included, according to Knox, the arm-twisting of electors, coincided with Mary's plea to Rome for new bishops. Her subsequent attempt to have Gordon replaced by her own almoner, Archibald Crawford, is likely to have encouraged him to reconsider his position; H. C. Stewart, 'Two letters and poems of Mary Stewart', *The Stewarts,* viii (1947—50), 224—6; *Papal Negs.,* 185.

[110] McRoberts, *Scottish Reformation,* 337—41.

[111] D. McRoberts, *The Fetternear Banner* (1956), 16—17.

[112] Lynch, 'Calvinism', 233. The timing and motives for printing the first edition of *The Good and Godly Ballads,* of 1565, which contained a number of Lutheran traces unacceptable to the increasingly Calvinist doctrinal unity of the church, are unknown, but a more sceptical evaluation of its circumstances seems warranted. An edition of the 1565 version is being prepared by Dr A. A. MacDonald for publication by Scot. Text Soc.

[113] E.g. Fraser, *Mary,* 452—3; G. Batho, 'A prisoner's pursuits: the captivity of Mary, Queen of Scots', *The Historian,* xii (1986), 8.

[114] Holmes, ch. 9 below.

[115] Greengrass, ch. 8 below.

[116] Martin, *Henry III,* 158—9.

2

Mary, Queen of France

M. H. MERRIMAN

On 15 September 1559, François de Valois entered the city of Rheims, which had prepared itself for his coronation as richly as the recent funeral (13 August) of Henri II would allow.[1] Later that day his wife made her own entry. By midday on 18 September François was crowned king of France, the second of that name; thereby Mary, queen of Scots, became queen of France. But, on 5 December 1560, François died. It has always been too easy to view her brief reign of seventeen months as queen consort of France with hindsight and to see it purely in terms of sterility. In 1559, François was not robust but he was not dead yet. The traditional picture of the sullen, hypertense, genitally inadequate fifteen-year-old, doomed to die in a brief time, may well be true.[2] He was at a dangerous age for Valois children: of François I's brood, François the Dauphin had died at eighteen in 1536; Madeleine queen of Scotland at seventeen in 1537, Charles at twenty-three in 1545. Three of Henri II's other children had died, but they in that most vulnerable of time, infancy (Louis at age two in 1550 and the twins, Victoire and Jeanne at birth in 1556). The health of François II indeed was no worse than many another king and as Ivan Cloulas has written of 1559, François and Mary were 'dans le fleur de l'âge, semblaient assurés d'une belle postérité'.[3]

François loved to hunt and play the soldier; conversely he hated attending the privy council, was often visibly bored and had a quite short attention span. His adolescent personality was no more repugnant or unpromising than that of many another young king; he simply had not yet grown up, as Henry VIII did not do until well into his twenties. As for Mary, she acted the role of his consort with aplomb and deft skill until his sudden death, when she became queen dowager and like another of her predecessors (Queen Eleanor, François I's wife retired to Spain, and there died in 1558, a mortal year for Habsburgs) returned to the land of her birth. She thus would appear to have been a typical sixteenth-century wife: largely dependent upon the fortunes of her husband.[4]

30

There is much in such a negative and traditional assessment of Mary as queen of France for it is hard to discover one major innovation in policy during the reign of her husband which can be traced to her intelligence or will power. Some historians have painted François as slavishly under her spell to the extent of her selecting the Guise brothers to run the realm.[5] But who else was there to be the Wolsey, or indeed the Montmorency, for the new king? Of course the Guises were parvenus, but no more so — and indeed much less so — than other *arrivistes* on the European political landscape, witness David Beaton or Northumberland. But as with Northumberland's equally high-profile, and brief, dominance of the central stage of politics (the royal person), that of the Guises was utterly dependent on circumstances beyond their control (the king's health) and luck. To lay responsibility for the assumption of power by the Guises under François upon Mary is both to misstate her importance and to ignore the realities of contemporary politics.

The Guises did not arrive, much less rise, at the court of Henri II through Mary's betrothal to François; in that sense their case was very much different from the Boleyns with Anne's marriage to Henry VIII or the Seymours' advancement with the marriage to Jane. They had a solid basis of performance both in their father's and their own generation and François de Guise's marriage to Anne d'Este (a granddaughter of Louis XII) was arguably as important to the family as Mary's role before 1558. Moreover, with the eclipse of Anne de Montmorency when he blundered into the débâcle at St Quentin, they had few effective rivals. When François de Guise then returned with an army from Italy in the summer of 1557 and in January 1558 executed the recapture of Calais, Guise command of the central ground of political life was temporarily sealed. The marriage of Mary to the Dauphin in April merely celebrated this fact.[6]

Mary indeed was never as significant as a person as she was as a dynastic entity. However much she blundered or was defeated politically, she remained important, for she was still not only a queen, but a Stewart, a Stuart, a Guise, a Tudor (and a Valois in-law). Only death could destroy her. As well as being about inheritance, dynasticism is both about claims (such as Mary's to England) and fortune. Despite the famous fragility and vulnerability of the Stewart line, Mary, queen of Scots actually had reasonably good luck. She lived long enough to reproduce a surviving, legitimate son in 1566; something the ill-struck and usurping Tudors did for the last time in 1536. Ever since the birth of James V in 1512, the Stewarts were never more than three heartbeats away from the English succession. It is worth remembering that England was regarded in the sixteenth century as profoundly unstable and kinetic in dynastic terms by most of Western Europe. No man became king of France between the reigns of Hugh Capet and Louis XVI who, by Salic laws of succession, should not have done so — something of contrast with England after 1064. In the fifteenth century, there was a school of thought amongst French, as well as Scots, genealogists which maintained that the sons of David I and Queen Margaret had the better title to the throne of England, one that was further enhanced by James I's marriage to Joan Beaufort.[7] Indeed the charge sheets against Mary in 1572 and 1587 accused her of the treason of claiming the throne of England through a threefold connection: the Saxons, the Lancastrians and the Tudors.[8]

Rumours and Bruits

In 1528, Sir David Lindsay of the Mount, Scotland's premier court poet, recorded having heard a prolix and bewildering rumour, the 'prophisies of Rymour, Beid and Marlyng' which was apparently widely popular in the north of England and which had clearly by the 1530s spread southwards, where numerous Englishmen were tried for repeating it and even listening to it.[9] William Neville, who had clearly been told a version of this poem, was arraigned in 1532 for claiming that Henry VIII would not survive his twenty-fourth year on the throne (1533) and that furthermore Neville would become earl of Warwick and would be a 'beyr whiche had ben long tyde to a stake' who would not only arise and slay a 'darf dragon thynkyng to wyn Renowne', but would also 'make peace & Vnytie'. For these and many other foolish sayings, Neville was held in the Tower.[10] Neville's examination, along with those of so many others, demonstrates vividly just how frightened the Tudor regime was at the time and how much the normal reverence accorded the English monarchy had been eroded by Henry's momentous acts. Concern over this particular prophecy lay in the rich manner in which any one of its many themes might be used to denigrate the king. For example, at the great battle in which the future earl of Warwick bear-like defeats the dragon, there also participated an eagle who when faltering had its resolve rekindled by a 'fair Lady'. The eagle, it was widely believed, was Charles V, who 'shall spred his winges over all this realme and rule it all'; in future 'shall neuer bee king in [England], but all shalbe holden of thempoure'. The fair lady, of course, was seen as Queen Katherine (and after her death in 1536, her daughter Princess Mary).

But even seemingly innocent ingredients could be seen as sinister. In the epic, there reoccurs the appealing figure of a glorious 'Childe' who in one episode gains the keys to the city of Paris, then receives in Rome great honour from the pope before proceeding to Jerusalem both to battle manfully against the Turk and most gloriously to recover the true cross. On the face it, there would seem to be little that was seditious in such an entertaining tall tale, the stock-in-trade of a widely enjoyed legend of the Emperor of the Last Days. However, this popular apocalyptic tradition takes on quite a different dimension when one appreciates that the 'childe' could easily be and was interpreted to be none other than James V of Scotland.[11] What gives the prophecy particular bite for students of Mary queen of Scots is its opening scene.

> Over a lande forth I blynte
> A semely sight me thought I se —
> A crowned quene in verament,
> With a company of Angelles fre
> Her stede was grete & dappyll gray,
> her apparell was of silke of Inde;
> with peryll and perrye set full gay,
> her stede was of a ferly Kynde.
> So Ryally in her Arraye,
> I stode and mwsyd in my mynde;
> all the clerkes a live to day
> So fayre a lady colde none ffynde

There then suddenly appeared a fierce armed knight

> he shoke his spere ferselye in hand,
> Right cruellye and kene;
> Styfly & stowre as he wolde stonde,
> he bare a shylde of Sylver shene....
> A crosse of gowles therin did he;
> he carpyd wordes cruell & kene,
> And shoke a shafte of suer tree;

But no sooner had he growled defiance, than his adversary emerged, bearing on his crest 'A Rede lyon that did rawmpyng be' and who 'spake wordes cruell & kene to that other that was hym by'. This was too much for the 'crowned quene' who rode between the fearsome warriors.

> Right as fast as she colde hie,
> She saith, 'men what do you meane?

stente your Stryff & your follye,
Remember that ye be sayntes in heven;
and fro my dere son comen am I
to take this ffelde you [twoo] between.
wherever yt shall fall in burghe or bye'.

She said, 'Seint George thow art my knyght
oft wronge heyres have done the tene;
Seint Andrew yet art thow in the right,
of thy men if it be syldom sene.[12]

Can the crowned queen in this arresting tableau be none other than James V's yet unborn daughter, who would stay the knights' spears, end all war and bring peace to both the realms? Certainly that momentous vision would come to haunt the decades from her birth to her end.

Initially, of course, Mary's accession to the Scottish throne led to war and strife, the Rough Wooing, traditionally portrayed as the clearest case of English aggressive assault on Scottish independence to be found since the reign of Edward III. But Mary from the moment of her birth represented not only a golden opportunity for the brotherless Henry VIII — the traditional line — but also a threat to his dynasty, particularly given the precarious health of his only son. That is why such strenuous political, diplomatic and then military efforts were made not only to secure her for the future king of England, but even more to deny her to another.

The Exampill off Brytanny

On 14 August 1532, seated on the throne of the last duke of Brittany (François II, who had died in 1488), François de Valois, the Dauphin, was crowned Duke François III.[13] It was by all accounts a splendid ceremony, one of those public spectacles which the French monarchy did so well. The king's eldest son (his third child to survive) was now fourteen years of age and had thus entered his majority. Two days previously he and his father had made a magnificent entrée into the city of Rennes. Now, richly garbed in blue velvet, the ducal coronet on his head, the young new proprietor of the duchy was presented with the sword of state by the bishop of Rennes in an elaborate transaction whereby Brittany became definitively annexed to the crown of France. When François died four years later, his brother, Henri, now the Dauphin, also became 'duc titulaire'; on his becoming king in 1547, his eldest son

François assumed that title, amongst, of course, many others such as duke of Châtellerault.

In some respects, this story is quite unremarkable. Charles V had come, by gradual stages from 1506 to 1519, to inherit by (fairly) normal, accepted, legal dynastic practices the greatest empire Europe had seen since the time of Charlemagne. But note that the Brittany process was not immediate, but spanned three generations (François II, his daughter Anne, her daughter Claude and only then her son François III) and took some forty-six years.[14] None the less, that case history was most illustrative and contained potent lessons. One was to avoid if possible a female succession. But the statistical possibilities of only girls surviving the traumas of birth and early childhood were quite high and proof was amply provided in the sixteenth century, which was full of queen regnants and female regents. Secondly, as Gaston Zeller trenchantly remarked about the marriage by which Anne of Brittany became queen of France in 1491, 'A partir de ce moment , en tout cas, [Brittany] cesse de se poser sur le terrain de la politique internationale.'[15] Too sweeping, perhaps, it none the less reminds us of a powerful fact of dynastic life and death.

This story is also fraught with 'highsightism'; it is too firm, fixed, final. There is nothing more wooden and inflexible than the family trees which necessarily accompany any discussion of family succession. At the time, it was uncertain, shimmering, pregnant with potentialities not realizable until births and deaths worked out right. For every example of Brittany which did result in long-term consequences, there were hosts of 'failures', dynastic possibilities which did not materialize: the union of France and Naples, France and Milan, England and the Low Countries, not to mention that of France and Poland. Dynasticism was thus something of a great gamble, a contest between competing loins, indeed something of a lifespan horse race.

Donec Totum Impleat Orbem

To appreciate that contest let us turn our focus from Rennes in 1532 to Rouen in 1550. The coronation of François III at Rennes is but one example of the numerous Renaissance spectacles with which monarchies celebrated their various nodal points: marriage, births of offspring, victories. A similar sort of pageant, but a much more timely and immediate occasion to state the contemporary accomplishments and aspirations of the monarch, is found in what were known as royal entrées.

Just such as example of art and power in the sixteenth century, about which there now exists such a potent literature,[16] was being elaborately prepared for Henri II at Rouen for his stay in October 1550.[17] It was to celebrate not just the king, but his whole family, for all of them would be there. Henry's family in 1550 was somewhat extended, for he counted amongst his children the little queen of Scots, Mary, aged almost eight, 'ma fille propre' as he called her. To Rouen, moreover, was coming Mary of Guise. The two had not seen each other since Mary, queen of Scots' celebrated voyage from Dumbarton in August 1548. The reunion of Mary the mother and Mary the child must have been a delightful occasion for between them there existed a profound bond of love and warmth. Since their separation, the young queen had lived in the household of her future father-in-law.

The first ten years of Henri's marriage to Catherine de Médicis, had been embarrassingly barren, so much so that the future king's mistress, Diane de Poitiers, had insisted that he should spend more time in his wife's bed so as to secure his position and establish his royal race. It was sage advice and it worked. Beginning with the birth of François in 1544, fully ten children were born: Elisabeth in 1546, then her sister Claude the next year, followed by Louis in 1549 (to whom Mary of Guise was a godmother — her sister-in-law Anne d'Este deputized for her; the real boy died in Mantes a mere three weeks after the Rouen celebrations),[18] and Charles in 1550. More children would flow and it is noticeable that increasingly their names reflected the imperial pretensions of the king. Charles's second name was Maximilian; Henri, born in 1551, was given those of Edward (in honour of the king of England, then an ally and betrothed to his daughter Elisabeth) and Alexander (always a hero). A Margaret was born in 1553 to be followed in 1555 by another François, additionally christened Hercules.[19]

This made for a lively household full of playmates for the young queen of Scots and she clearly was very happy there, becoming particularly close to Elisabeth, future queen to Philip II of Spain, and to her betrothed, François. It was with this household that, having just re-covered from a serious bout of illness, she travelled to Rouen in September 1550 to see her mother again. They must have been reunited there on 25 September.[20] But Mary of Guise was not only there to see her daughter, but also to expose to a band of accompanying Scotsmen both their young queen and the power and the glory that was the France of her future husband.[21]

Henri II had begun his reign with a series of fêtes and entrées: in particular his fabulous entry into Lyons on 23 September 1548 and that into Paris in June 1549.[22] The Rouen celebration was to be his grandest for it conjoined the twin sucesses with which he trumpeted the commencement of his reign: the reconquest of Boulogne and the salvation of Scotland. These were not mere delights or extravagances; they were rooted in political reality. He was engaged in a projection of a royal and imperial image as 'le plus digne roi' France had seen in two centuries. Various aspects were stressed in the major spectacles of his reign so far. Some were obvious, traditional and almost mandatory: others were more immediate and personal. One highly salient ingredient was the popularization of the new king's *impresa* and his motto. Henri's — the crescent moon — was quite deliberately different from the salamander of his father. It rapidly appeared on the garments of his servants, his banners and his coins.[23] The moon, a symbol mysterious and far distant yet seen by all, each day ringed the world and played its lunar glow over all beneath it. His motto, *Donec totum impleat orbem*, emphasized the point to all. As one reporter of the great Rouen triumph versified,

Puisque Henri second du nom a pris
Pour sa devise un celeste croissant
Sans reins choisir de terrestre pourpris
C'est bien raison quen bon heur soit croissant
Tant que tout lorbe ait soubx sa main compris[24]

A Renaissance entrée was more than just a parade; it was a total assault on the senses, communicating through both science and the arts: set design, choreography, sculpture, music, poetry, costume, acting, mechanics, anthropology and even zoology (both actors naked as Brazilian natives and life-size model elephants from Africa were judged by those knowledgeable in such matters as 'non faintz'). The Rouen entrée fell into three main elements for the king on 1 October 1550. The first was a march-past of several thousand members of the town, the rear brought up by eighteen Roman gladiators, battling amongst themselves with two-handled swords. There were many *tableaux vivants* here of the king's recent successes and statements of his place in history and the aspirations for his future. Perhaps the most splendid was the first float: drawn by four winged horses, it was decorated with friezes of battles, heaped with spoils of war, draped with two dead warriors. At the front was seated a skeleton, but chaining death at the other end was the goddess of 'Renommée', fame, her wings spread, a trumpet to her mouth. Her message was crystal clear for all.

There then followed a caesarian procession. The first bands of soldiers displayed models of the forts taken in the Boulogne campaign of August —

September 1549, spoil, victorious laurels and bound prisoners of war. Six elephants with flaming vases on their backs lumbered past, followed by Flora's nymphs strewing flowers of celebration on the streets. There then came a chariot on which townsfolk represented the king all in splendid armour, surrounded by palm leaves, his head wreathed with a Roman victor's wreath. Seated at his feet were four of his children: Elisabeth, Claude, Louis and just born Charles. Above him sat a winged Fortune holding over the monarch's head an Imperial crown. From horseback the Dauphin, the betrothed of Mary, queen of Scots, proclaimed his own homage to his father.

The fourth group of soldiers, preceding the king's chariot, were dressed all in Roman costume and carried banners. Each represented places defended or captured by French arms far to the north.

> Voila Dondy, Edimpton [Haddington], Portugray [Broughty Craig]
> Ou Termes prist & Esse le degre
> Pour devenir chevalier de ton ordre [of St Michael]
> Tout le pays ou avoit ose mordre
> Sur l'escossois la nation angloise
> Est recouvert par la force françoise
> Apres avoir endure mainctz travaulx
> Sire, voyez ceste Ysle de chevaulx [Inchkeith]
> Voyez aussy le fort chasteau de Fargues [Fast]
> Voila aussy le fort pres de Donglas [Dunglass]
> Et plus deca ou est assis ce bourg
> Est le chasteau conquis de Rossebourg [Roxburgh]²⁵

However execrable the verse, its point is clear enough. France had added fame and renown by its labours far to the north and thus, as at Boulogne and at sea, inflicted exemplary vengeance upon England, 'si odeux nation'.

When Henri then left his viewing stand, he paused to view with heightened excitement an elaborate *tableau vivant,* for on a specially constructed meadow, replete with trees, huts and wild life were two tribes of totally naked ('sans aucunement couvrir la partie que nature commande') Brazilian women and men, who lazed, then battled viciously with clubs and arrows. When the king moved through a series of prophetic and instructive scenes erected on the bridge, he was arrested by a lively *naumachie* between a French vessel and a Portuguese one in which the French naturally triumphed (with a real ship actually sunk; another was despatched the next day for the queen), a reference to the competing claims over parts of Brazil between the two countries. Again the imagery was explicit: Henri aspired not just to the recovery of France, nor to the salvation of Scotland, but soon his empire would extend about the world. *Donec totum impleat orbem* indeed.

Among the many who beheld these sumptuous happenings were the great and not so great Scots who came with Mary of Guise. Scots abroad usually aroused comment and the English ambassador at Rouen characterized them as 'brawling, chiding and fighting as though they had lately come from some new Conquest'.[26] Indeed they had, for the year 1550 had seen Scotland humiliate England, emerging victorious, with powerful French support, from the Rough Wooing. But they also underscored one further reason Mary was so important: Henri had expended an enormous treasure to gain this moment of triumph and in that sense Mary represented a considerable investment.

How much the Scottish intervention cost France is impossible to determine with precision owing to the extraordinary chaos which plagued the financial departments of the army there, particularly in 1548. Some order had been achieved by mid-1549, but even so, creditable figures are hard to come by. The budget for 1549 had proposed 800,000 *livres tournois* to be spent in Scotland (£400,000 Scots or £100,000 sterling), but French war budgets were like any others: hopelessly out of touch. A figure of 2,000,000 *livres* for the period June 1548 to April 1550 may well be on the low side; England's charges for Scotland for July 1547 to April 1550 came to just over £600,000 sterling (or £2,400,000 Scots or 4,800,000 *livres*). Mary had thus already cost a queen's ransom and expenditure would continue owing to garrisons still remaining in Scotland, funds to Mary of Guise (she would be granted the revenues of the principality of Orange), pensions to members of the Scottish aristocracy (12,000 *livres* yearly to James Hamilton, second earl of Arran and now due de Châtelherault) and a range of other important charges.[27]

The great victories in Scotland were not an end in themselves. They fitted potently into the king's plan for his reign which was here being so elaborately projected. On 27 September, Henri addressed a long letter to the Grand Sultan at Constantinople. This remarkable missive, a grandiloquent propagandist celebration of the victories of his reign so far, was intended quite obviously to impress upon Suleiman the Magnificent the prowess and might of France. It makes extraordinary reading:

J'ai pacifié le Royaume d'Ecosse que ie tiens et possede avec tel commandement et obedissance que i'ai en France, ausquel deux Royaumes, j'en joint et uny un autre, qui est Angleterre, dont par une perpetuelle union, alliance et confederation, ie puis disposer, comme de moy-mesme, du Roy de ses subjects, et de ses facultez; de sorte que les dits trois Royaumes ensemble se peuvent maintenant estimer une mesme monarchie.[28]

This is just what the Rouen fête was putting across. Hence the triple crescents, for Henri now saw himself about to be thrice king: of France, of Scotland and of England. In one scene, Orpheus, Neptune and Apollo, supported by other of the deities, urged Henri to new valour; Neptune especially assured him an easy passage up the Thames. Apollo then chimed in to urge 'faire je veulx de deux une courounne' of England and France, so that 'Henri second' may become 'Henri le neufiesme'.[29]

Henri thus stood as the present reconquerer of Boulogne, the saviour of Scotland and the immediate controller of England. But beyond this the future heralded not only exotic Brazil, but all the world. In Ronsard's famous *Ode*, the intention is quite clear:

> Quand entre les Césars j'aperçois ton image
> Découvrant tout le front de laurier revêtu,
> Voyez, ce dis-je lors, combien peur la vertu
> Qui fait d'un jeune roi un César avant l'âge...
> Ce signe te promet, grand roi victorieux
> Puisque vif on t'élève au nombre des Augustes,
> Que mort tu sera mis entre les plus grands dieux.[30]

Many of the themes first outlined so clearly in Rouen in 1550 would be repeated over the years, particularly in 1558, when Estienne Perlin nicely caught the mood of French self-esteem over their participation in the salvation of Scots with this piece of rhetoric:

O bien heureulx te doibs tu estimer Royaulme d'Escosse d'estre favorées, nourry, entretenu, comme l'enfant sus la mamelle du trespuissant & magnanime Roy de France, le plus grand seigneur de tout le monde & monarque futur de toute la machine ronde: car sans luy tu feusse en cendre mis, & le pays gaste, & ruine les Angloys, du tout de Dieu mauldicts.[31]

But Scotland was not just to be suckled; the whole thrust of French policy had been to make her part of France as 'une mesme monarchie'. Henri's costly intervention had not only secured Mary for François, but it had also denied her to Edward VI. Henri sought to capitalize on this further by the betrothal of the English king to his eldest daughter, Elisabeth. However, that was aborted when Edward died and his loss was made seemingly catastrophic by the succession of Mary Tudor and even worse by her marriage to Prince Philip of Spain. That event more than any other explains the unseemly haste with which Mary was declared to be 'of age' in December 1553 and Mary of Guise made regent in February—April the next year.[32] This policy of ensuring that Scotland was as firmly under French control as possible was pursued with some striking effect during the period 1554—8, as can be seen by the large English force which had to be stationed on the East Marches during the summers of 1557 and 1558 and the near-hysterical panic over the security of Berwick in the wake of the loss of Calais.[33]

All this needs to be borne in mind when discussing Mary's role in France, for even before her arrival Henri had spoken of Scotland as part of his son's own, rather as Henry VIII had done in 1543 when calling Edward prince of Scotland; immediately afterwards she had been put on display as part of Henri's brood and as the future wife of the Dauphin.[34] In that sense, Mary was very much a Valois, if as a step-child, from as early as 1548. The queen of course was also an intimate part of a wider household, the king's court, and everyone made a pet of her, including Montmorency and Diane de Poitiers.[35] But she was also identifiably and quite firmly a Guise as well, a connection wonderfully caught by a small book by Jean le Féron, published in Paris in 1555: *Le simbol armorial des armoires de France, & d'Escoce, & de Lorraine* which clearly underscored, in a way which a sixteeth-century audience readily could appreciate, the clear interconnection of the three.[36]

Moreover, Mary remained a Stewart. Scotsmen definitely increased their presence in France during the 1550s. Not only was the 'conte d'harran' (Châtelherault's eldest son) often at court, he also attracted to his duchy numerous kinsfolk as well as ordinary Scotsmen, several hundred of whom found employment in his *regiment des gens d'armes*.[37] Mary and the Hamiltons were of course kinsfolk, and she took a close interest in his welfare, proposed marriages for him and may have helped him in other ways.[38] All sorts of Scotsmen flocked to her in France and indeed she and Darnley first laid eyes on each other there shortly after François's coronation.[39]

But it was Mary as a living queen and as a claimant to the throne of England that mattered most to Henri. This is neatly caught in one of her early public participations in a court masque, played out at St Germain-en-Laye. The twelve-year-old Mary, elaborately costumed as the delphic oracle Sybil, addressed her future husband (since 1547 duc de Bretagne) with this prediction, penned by the distinguished poet Mellin de Saint-Gellais:

Delphica Delphini si mentem oracula tangunt
Britanibus junges regna Britana tuis.[40]

Jam non sunt duo sed una caro
They are no more twain, but made one flesh
(Matthew: xix,6)

Few marriages in history have had their details so extensively reported by later historians as that of Mary and François on 24 April 1558.[41] The formal pre-nuptial betrothal, service and celebrations, which were spread over three days, were attended by almost everyone of note in French society and involved prodigious expense and lavish, elaborate processions, masques, balls and banquets. The rocking sailing ships, the revolving planets and the hyperbolic imagery need not detain us, but a number of points need to be stressed.

The marriage of course made Mary much more firmly a member of the Valois family, giving her title (dauphine and duchesse de Viennaise), an estate and considerable finances. 'La fille propre' was now a daughter-in-law. For François, he became a king, as Philip had done when he married Mary Tudor in 1554. From the moment of the marriage in Notre Dame, Henri referred to his son in all correspondence as 'le roi-dauphin' and by 5 May 1558, charters were being issued in Scotland styling the two as 'Rex et Regina Scotorum'.[42] The Scottish testoon of 1558 incorporated the FM monogram on the obverse and the legend JAM NON SUNT DUO SED UNA CARO on the reverse while the widely circulated wedding medallion (and other coins) supported the equally compelling message, FECIT UTRAQUE UNUM: 'He has made them one'.[43]

Scotland and Scotsmen were thus closely involved in these events. One member of the crowd before the great doors of Notre Dame was a Scot, perhaps a student, who translated the popular official version of the event, but also personalized it with his own account which then made its way back to his native country.[44] There, too, were celebrations, such as the 'fyris and processioun generall' ordered to be made in the burghs of Scotland early in the summer with Edinburgh putting on a notable display in July costing £183 9s 9d.[45] Lord Herries recalled in his memoirs, 'that the two kingdoms shall be unitt in one, and be esteemed as one nation in all tymes to come'.[46] George Buchanan contributed fulsomely to the poetic outpourings, as did Richard Maitland of Lethington who saw in the marriage of Mary and 'the gretest zoung prince in Christintie' a cause of 'greit blyithnes and Ioy Inestimable':

> Scottis and frenche now leif in vnitie
> as ze war brether borne in an cuntrie
> without all maner of suspitioun
> Ilk ane to other keip trew fraternitie
> defend ane other bayth be land and sie[47]

Thus France had now achieved what England had failed to bring to pass in the 1540s, the beginning of union with Scotland; the second step on the ladder (first betrothal, now marriage) had been accomplished. It doubtless would take years to bring full union to pass, but at least that process was in hand, as Scotsmen appreciated only too well. In 1559 the earl of Argyll put to several Islesmen,

the persuasion that the France ar cumin in and sutin down in this realm to occupy it and to put furtht the inhabitantis tharoff, and siclik to occcupy all uther menis rowmes pece and pece, and to put away the blud of the nobilitie: and makis the exampill of Brytanny.[48]

One cardinal aspect about Renaissance public life was that it was hard to escape allusions to the classics. One can catch this particularly nicely by turning to a meeting of the *parlement* of Paris on 8 July 1558. The court was then convened to register an edict of the previous month granting French citizenship to all Scots.[49] Its wisdom and probity were justified by the members of the sovereign court, as benefited their training, with fulsome references to Claudius, Tacitus and Virgil and the registration − as often was the case − became a mini-history lecture. The two countries had been ancient allies for over 500 years, both through 'actes solempnels' as well as through Scots, such as King David II at Crécy, 'qui venir en persone leur roy au camp de roy de France pour le secourir contre son ennemy'. More immediate for 'double raison et considéracion' was the fact of the marriage of Mary to François, 'à present faict par ce moyen roy d'Escosse'. Mutual citizenship was thus founded upon the past and the present.

But it also rested on the lessons of history. Here much was made of the differences between the Greeks and the Romans. The Athenians had always jealously restricted the rights of citizenship to a narrow circle with the result that 'leur empire a moings duré que pas ung des aultres' and, even worse, 'ils ont esté fort blasmés par les historiens'. The moral was thus plain:

Ce que saigement considérans les roys de France, pour perpétuer leur domination, laquelle compte desjà plus d'ans que l'Empire Romain, ont mieulx aymé laisser la rigeur des anciens Grecs et suyvre la doulceur et bénignité des Romains, de façon que avecques toutes personnes nous avons entretenu et célébré *jura commercii, jura hospitii, jura foederis.*

What we have here is a literary and legal manifestation of the political messages of the Rouen entrée and the marriage triumph. The lawyers waxed even more, concluding their verification with three lines (102−104) spoken by Juno from book IV of the *Aeneid*:

Communem hunc ergo populum paribusque regamus
Auspiciis; liceat Phrygio servire marito,
Dotalesque tuae Tyrios permittere dextrae

Dido, queen of Carthage is now 'ablaze with love and has drawn her passion through her frame' for the Trojan Aeneas. Ever devious Juno contemplates the possible consequences of 'what a realm will rise on such a union' with Venus: 'So then, let it be in common that we rule this people with equality of power/Let her be allowed to marry her Phrygian and be his slave/And let her, for her dowry, assign her Tyrians to your control.'[50]

But note how Michel de l'Hospital's wedding anthem spoke of a time when the 'gallant boys' of Henri II would each find a part of Europe's royal halls to grace: Gaul, Lombardy, Britannia, 'So shall one house the world's vast empire share'. But the key arch of this inviting edifice was Mary, for through her, 'without murder and war France and Scotland will with England be united'.[51] Joachim du Bellay's ode to the queen probably best captures the vision.

Ce n'est pas sans propoz qu'en vous le Ciel a mis
Tant de beaultez d'esprit & de beauté de face,
Tant de royal honneur & de royale grace
Et que plus que cela vous est encor promis.

Ce n'est pas sans propoz que les Destins amys
Pour rabaisser l'orgueil de l'Espagnole audace,
Soit part droict d'alliance, ou soit par droict de race,
Vous ont par leurs arrestz trois grans peuples soumis.

Ilz veullent que par vous la France & l'Angleterre
Changent en longue paix l'hereditaire guerre
Qui a de pere en fills si longuement duré.

Ilz veulent que par vous la Belle Vierge ASTREE
En ce Siecle de fer reface encor' entree,
Et qu'un revoye encor' le beau Siecle doré.[52]

What catapulted these fantasies into the stuff of politics was a further piece of luck, an upset in the race, when on 17 November 1558, Mary Tudor died without heirs of her body.

Franciscus et Maria
Rex et Regina Francor.
Scot. Angl. et Hiber.

It is well to remember just how contingent the negotiations at Cambrai and Cateau-Cambrésis were, for 'hindsightism' can operate in the field of international relations and war just as easily as in dynasticism. We now know that France (outside of Calais) was denied any advancement in Flanders, was excluded from Germany (outside Metz, Toul and Verdun) and had lost virtually all of its possessions in Italy. But before April 1559, France was still seen as powerful and England as under threat, particularly with the fall of Calais and Elizabeth's succession. As early as 18 November 1558, English statesmen were worried as to 'what the French pretend by the marriage of the Dauphin with the Queen of Scots'.[53] French pretensions, which seemed to accelerate almost as soon as Mary Tudor died, took various forms.

One form was the manner in which they styled themselves; another was the heraldry which they adopted at various public occasions. As early as in December rumours flew that Henri had approached the Holy See for confirmation of his daughter-in-law's entitlement.[54] On 16 January 1559 Francis and Mary termed themselves in a letter to Lord Fleming as 'king and queen dauphins of Scotland, England and Ireland'.[55] At the marriage of Henri's daughter Claude to Duke Charles of Lorraine on 22 January, Mary's arms were quartered with those of England and it may be this armorial device which was shewn to Norfolk later that spring.[56] Certainly during the negotiations for the general peace of 1559, French envoys argued that they could never surrender Calais to Elizabeth as that would impugn Mary's entitlement of England (and note the ingenious ploy suggested that should a daughter of Elizabeth be wed to a son of François and Mary, Calais might become part of the girl's dower lands).[57] During the mutual ratifications for Cateau-Cambrésis and its Scottish back-up Treaty of Upsettlington with England, François and Mary confined themselves to being king and queen of Scotland only.[58] But Granvelle asserted that when he received the Dauphin's ratification on 28 May, it was in the form 'François par la grace de Dieu Roy descosse, Dangleterre, et Direlande, Daulphyn de Viennois, Etc.'[59] At the great chivalric triumph at Paris which celebrated the treaty, Mary's arms were again linked to those of England over the king's stand. More intriguingly, when the heralds for the Dauphin appeared at the lists where Henri was to be mortally wounded, their coats also included the arms of England.[60] Such utterances clearly alarmed both Cecil and Elizabeth and very quickly (13 June 1559) they obtained a ruling by the College of Heralds as to the invalidity of Mary's claim.[61]

The accession of François II as king raised the issue even more vividly for the English, particularly with Nicholas Throckmorton settled as resident ambassador to the court, able to report each rumour and every occurrence. The critical issue in July was the form that François's formal style would take. There was then some uncertainty because he would not properly be proclaimed king until the moment of his father's internment at St Denis. But clearly the matter was much debated. A major participant in these debates was Anne de Montmorency. When shown a seal declaring François as king of all four kingdoms, he protested that a king of France could only be styled 'Dei Gracia Francorum Rex' as had been François I and Henri II, despite the fact that they had laid claim to 'Naples, Milan and diverse other important places'. Even the suggestion that his style remain of France only, but the arms include France, Scotland, England and Ireland he rejected.[62] On the day of Henri's funeral, the Valois Herald at Arms proclaimed François solely as 'Roi de France' and most instruments issued in France during his reign were in that style.[63]

But the issue is not clear-cut and indeed until a detailed study of the diplomatic history of both François and Mary has been exhaustively carried out, we are in confused waters with incidents of almost every permutation.[64] The most potent, and frightening to Elizabeth, of course was the famous seal with the two of them seated with the legend: FRANCISCVS ET MARIA D. G. R. R. FRANCOR. SCOT. ANGL. ET HYBER.[65]

The arms appeared almost everywhere, although in various forms. The coronation at Rheims saw the city's main gate decorated with the claim to England (Ireland's arms never appeared separately).[66] Something similar happened at most of the king's and queen's entrées.[67] Perhaps the finest example occurred on 24 November 1559, when François and Mary entered the city of Châtellerault where both the gateways were richly painted: to the right François as king of France, to the left Mary as queen of England, France and Scotland (the reported order in the list also varied, as one can see). Over one of the gateways verses proclaimed,

> Gallia perpetuis pugnaxque Britannia bellis
>   Olim odio inter se dimicuere pari.
> Nunc Gallos totosque remotos orbe Britannos
>   Unum dos Mariae cogit in imperium.
> Ergo pace potes, Francisce, quod omnibus ais
>   Mille patres armis non potuere tui.[69]

In a deliciously rambling letter on 18 November 1558, Doctor Wotton, aged, ill, dyspeptic and serving now the fourth sovereign in his lifetime, had considered, 'Which way are they to begin?'. Not through war in Italy, nor Germany: 'they are not so mad'.

What rests then but England and the Low Country? If they are content to leave Piedmont and what they hold in the Siennois and renounce Milan to keep Calais, who can doubt what their meaning is? It is not Calais but England and the Low Country which may countervail Savoy and Piedmont. Peradventure they think that the next [nighest] way to get Italy is to begin with England.[69]

Shortly afterwards, he was even more worried, especially about 'the Scottish queen's feigned title to the crown of England for having England, Scotland, and Ireland, they would look to be monarchs of almost all Europe'.[70] But French options, as Cateau-Cambrésis closed in on them, became extraordinarily limited and Mary suddenly became all they had to play with. Thus Wotton was by and large correct. His was a vision which Protestant Cecil shared. That is why the English were so hysterically determined that her claim to England must be abandoned and that is how Cecil convinced Elizabeth to intervene in Scotland in 1559–60.

However, it was one thing to demand and attain in the Treaty of Edinburgh a clause that François and Mary would henceforth refrain from using the arms of England in any way whatsoever; it was an entirely different matter to gain the ratification of that treaty or to snuff out the claim. When Throckmorton arrived at Orléans to be with the court on 4 November 1560, he found 'on every gate of this town' François's arms quartered with those of England, 'and here at the Court gate most notoriously'.[71] But by 5 December 1560, Mary was no longer queen regnant of France and thus faded the Franco-Scottish dynastic game.

Yet, still her claim remained. In August 1561, Lord James Stewart, Mary's bastard brother, wrote a long and thoughtful letter to Elizabeth, commending friendship and amity between her and Mary: 'tender cusines, boyth Quenes in the flour of your aages'. He saw clearly that it was Mary's claim to England which lay at the 'rote' of their dissidence and he wished that Mary had never allowed it to have been advanced. Having made this point, however, the future earl of Moray himself could not resist spelling out what he – and almost everyone – saw as the obvious.

Inconvenient wer it to provyde that to the Quene my souveraine her own place wer reserved in the succession of the Crown of England? Which your Majestie will pardon me, if I take to be next by the law of all nations, as she that is next in lawfull discent of the ryght lyne of King Hendry the sevint your grandfather — and in the mean time this isle to be united in perpetual friendship. The succession of realms come by God's appointment at his good pleasure, and no provision of man can alter what he has determined but it must neidis cum to pas.[72]

Mary was thus many things, perhaps too many. She was a highly complex dynastic prodigy, almost a monstrosity, related to, and a threat to, many families. But only one factor was and would be critical. As Camden remarked when writing of her towards the end of the century, it was her claim to the English succession from which 'flowed as from a fountain all the Calamities wherein she was afterwards wrapped'.[73] Thus can it be argued that in her beginning was Mary's end.

Notes

[1] L. Paris, *Négociations, lettres et piéces diverses relative au règne de François II* (1841), 112–26.

[2] The assessment of A. de Ruble, *La première jeunesse de Marie Stuart* (1891), 33, is one which most authors have followed, perhaps too slavishly: 'timide, bilieux, d'une intelligence due développée, incapable d'efforts suivis, n'avait rien de la vigueur exubérante de son grand-père, non plus que de la beauté de son père. Il ètait petit et mince et présentait aux courtisans, avides d'étudier sa physionomie, l'image d'un prince destiné à rester toujours enfant.'

[3] I. Cloulas, *Henri II* (1985), 598.

[4] Mary's life in France has attracted specialized studies as well as being treated within the wider confines of the many complete biographies. Most can still be read with some benefit. Agnes Strickland devoted considerable space in *Lives of the Queens of Scotland* (1850–9) and more detail in her *The Life of Mary Queen of Scots* (1873) but she mangled a lot of the facts as did Joseph Stevenson in *Mary Stuart: A Narrative of the first eighteen years of her life* (1886). Ruble, *Première jeunesse* made good use of his intimate knowledge of both printed and manuscript French sources and no one can ignore him. Jane T. Stoddart, *The Girlhood of Mary, Queen of Scots* (1908) gave a worthy and wordy account of the time to 1561 and one enlivened by her own Border girlhood and familiarity with many of the places in France associated with Mary before the ravages of the First World War and urban development blighted so many of them. Less prolix, but unfortunately very rare, is B. C. Weber, whose *The Youth of Mary Stuart* (1941) has never received the critical appreciation that it deserves, despite its faults. Of the general biographies both F. Mignet, *The History of Mary, Queen of Scots* (1851) and M. Philippson, *Histoire du règne de Marie Stuart* (1891) can still be read with effect. Of the modern works, Fraser, *Mary*, is fair enough. Both Jean Plaidy, *Mary Queen of Scots — The Fair Devil of Scotland* (1975) and R. Marshall,

Queen of Scots (1987) have some nice pictures in them, but Plaidy's text is awful. Studies of Mary of Guise must also speak of this time, as do R. Marshall *Mary of Guise* (1977) and E. M. H. McKerlie, *Mary of Guise-Lorraine, Queen of Scotland* (1931).

[5] 'Les sympathies de sa jeune femme, Marie Stuart, désignèrent à son choix les deux hommes qui devaient gouverner en son nom', E. Lavisse, *Histoire de la France depuis les origines jusqu'à la revolution* (1900−11), vi (i), 1.

[6] This is not the place for a detailed bibliography of the Guises and their myth, but H. Forneron, *Les ducs de Guise et leur époque: étude historique sur le seizième siècle* (1877) is still useful. Also see especially D. L. Potter, 'The duc de Guise and the fall of Calais 1557−1558', *EHR*, xcviii (1983), 481−512.

[7] I am grateful to Dr K. Daly for this information. See also *La vraie cronique d'Escoce; etc.*, ed. R. Anstruther (Roxburghe Club, 1847).

[8] *A complete Collection of State Trials*, ed. W. Cobbett and T. B. Howell (1816−98), i, 1169 *et seq.* and see below, n. 56.

[9] S. L. J. Jaech, 'The "prophisies of Rymour, Beid, and Marlyng": Henry VIII and a sixteenth-century political prophecy', *Sixteenth Century Journal*, xvi (1985), 291−9.

[10] G. R. Elton, *Policy and Police: The Enforcement of the Reformation in the Age of Thomas Cromwell* (1972); see ch. 2: 'Rumour, Magic and Prophecy', especially 50−1 and D. T. Etheridge, 'Political Prophecy in Tudor England' (University of Wales, Swansea, Ph. D., 1979), *passim*.

[11] Elton, *Policy and Police*, 54, 59, 66, 74 and Jaech, 'Prophisies', 297−8.

[12] *The Romance and Prophecies of Thomas of Erceldoune*, ed. J. A. H. Murray, EETS (1875), appendix II (52 *et seq.*), but reference should be had to the original: BL, MS Lansdowne 762, fos 75−88.

[13] R. J. Knecht, *Francis I* (1982), 242−3.

[14] ibid., 6−12 and see also R. Doucet, *Les institutions de la France au XVIe siècle* (1948), *passim*, and A. Dupuy, Histoire de la réunion de la Bretagne à la France (1921).

[15] G. Zeller, *Histoire des relations internationales, de Christophe Colomb à Cromwell* (1953), 92.

[16] The two books by Sir Roy Strong, *Splendour at Court* (1973) and *Art and Power* (1984), the second a considerable update of the first, are the best introduction to this vital subject.

[17] M. B. McGowan, 'Form and themes in Henri II's entry into Rouen', *Renaissance Drama*, i (1968), 199−252.

[18] Stoddart, *Girlhood*, 36.

[19] Cloulas, *Henri II*, 610−11, 78−80, 118−19, 128−9, 144, 299.

[20] *CSPF, Edward*, 57; Michel, *Français*, i, 472−4; Leslie, *History* (Bann.), 234−6.

[21] Donaldson, *Queen's Men*, 25−7, 160. More work needs to be done on this trip.

[22] McGowan, 'Entry into Rouen', 200−3. Note that a Scot was the reporter of the famous Paris entrée: *Le grand triumphe magnifique des Parisiens de la venue du tres chrestien roy Henry, 6 juin 1549 par Jean Stuart* (Paris, 1549); in the Latin edition he was described as a Scot in the collège de Presles.

23 See Strong, *Art and Power*, 25–6 and plates 10, 12.

24 McGowan, 'Entry into Rouen', 225.

25 ibid., 213–14. Both of Strong's books reproduce the drawings made of celebration rather better than McGowan: *Splendour at Court*, plates 27–33; *Art and Power*, plates 35–6.

26 *CSPF, Edward*, 51–4.

27 French records are widely scattered not only within the major national archives, but also provincial ones and some are to be found in Scotland. See BN, fonds François, 3140, fo. 76; 4552, fos 8–9, 30, 50; 18513, fos 171–2. Out of a budget for 1549 totalling 11,432,901 *livres tournois*, 822,405 *livres* were estimated for Scotland, just over 7 per cent. See Greengrass, ch. 8 below, for the jointure paid to Mary as dowager queen from 1561.

28 *Lettres et memoires d'estate des roys, princes, ambassadeurs et d'autres ministres sous les regnes de François Premier, Henri II et François II par G. Ribier*, ed. M. Belot (Paris, 1666), ii, 288–90.

29 See also Joachin du Bellay's ode on the victory of Boulogne (1549) where he spoke not only 'de joindre en bref l'Angleterre à la France' but also Henri soon to be 'en la Françoise terre/second du nom, neufième en Angleterre', *Oeuvres poetiques*, ed. H. Chamard (Paris, 1912), iii, 77. See Durkan, ch. 4 below, for the prominence of both du Bellay and Ronsard in Mary's library.

30 Cloulas, *Henri II*, 533.

31 E. Perlin, *Description des royaulmes d'Angleterre et d'Escosse* (1558), fo. 30v. Mary also had a work celebrating Charles IX's entry into Rouen in 1563 in her library; see Durkan, Ch. 4, app. 1, below.

32 Donaldson, *Scotland*, 82–4; M. Levine, *Tudor Dynastic Problems 1460–1571* (1973), 90–5.

33 *Acts of the Privy Council*, vi, 243–5; Teulet, *Relations*, i, 300; *History of the Kings Works*, ed. H. M. Colvin, iv, 609, 644–8.

34 *Lettres et Mémoires*, ed. Belot, ii, 150, 152; Ruble, *Premiére jeunesse*, 26.

35 The queen's life in the French court is widely discussed: Ruble, *Première jeunesse*, 32–146; Stoddart, *Girlhood*, goes on entirely too much with chapters on Mary 'in the royal nursery', the nature of 'the house of Guise in 1550' and 'the dawn of womanhood', but her final chapter, 'French Influences on the Queen's Character' (380–403) does have some nice finds. Fraser, too, says something of this period but is frankly a trifle leadenfooted.

36 *Le simbol* was 'dedié à vostres Royale Principauté [Mary of Guise was princess of Orange in 1555], non moins qu'a la futur Royale préeminence de vostre chere fille, que à son Tresillustre espoux futur' (fo. 3v). Queen Mary had a copy in her library; see Durkan, ch. 4 below, at n. 19.

37 Arran's time in France is nicely discussed in J. Durkan, 'James, third earl of Arran: the hidden years', *SHR*, lxv (1986), 154–66.

38 Labanoff, i, 40–5.

39 Fraser, *Mary*, 218.

40 Phillips, *Images*, 4.

41 All the sources cited in n. 4 above discuss it in detail.

[42] *RMS,* i, 1272 (*RSS,* v, 400); note that it was issued at Paris. See also *RSS,* v, 109 and 568, 597, 601—2, 608, 611, 623.

[43] P. F. Purvey, *Coins and Tokens of Scotland* (1972), 6 no. 66. See also H. F. Holt, 'Observations upon a "shilling" of Francis the Dauphin and Mary Stuart', *PSAS,* vii (1870), 280.

[44] D. Hamer, 'The marriage of Mary Queen of Scots to the Dauphin: a Scottish printed fragment', *Bibiliographical Society Trans* (1932), 420—9.

[45] *TA,* x, 365; *Edinburgh Records: Burgh Accounts,* ed. R. Adam (1899), i, 269—74.

[46] Herries, *Memoirs,* 33.

[47] Phillips, *Images,* 15; *The Maitland Quarto Manuscript,* ed. W. A. Craigie (1920), 19.

[48] *Mary of Lorraine Corresp.,* 427. The same worries of the 'ancient nobility' surfaced again in 1565—6; see Lynch, ch. 1 above.

[49] Teulet, *Relations,* i, 312—17.

[50] P. Vergili Maronis, *Aeneidas,* ed. R. G. Austin (Oxford, 1955), iv, ll. 102—4.

[51] Phillips, *Images,* 15.

[52] Du Bellay, *Oeuvres,* ed. H. Chamard, vi (Paris, 1933), 35.

[53] *CSPF 1558—9,* 3.

[54] *Papal Negs.,* 4—18.

[55] *CSPF 1558—9,* 91.

[56] *CSP Ven.,* vii, 29. This issue is not clear and the arms may have appeared earlier. They have been widely reproduced, e.g. Plaidy, *Mary Queen of Scots,* 62; Marshall, *Queen of Scots,* 45. See also *Collection de manuscrits, livres, estampes et objets d'art relatifs à Marie Stuart* (BN, 1931), plate 4. C. Wilfred Scott-Giles discusses Mary's various arms in *The Romance of Heraldry* (1929, 1957), 162—5.

[57] *CSPF 1558—9,* 131, 156—7.

[58] *CSPF 1558—9,* 220, 250, 290, 296.

[59] *CSP Scot.,* i, 156.

[60] *CSPF 1558—9,* 347.

[61] *CSPF 1558—9,* 314.

[62] *CSPF 1558—9,* 416, 447.

[63] *CSPF 1558—9,* 474; *Les funérailles du roy Henry II,* ed. L. C. Galembert (1869).

[64] So far I have found the following: Scotland; France and Scotland; Scotland and France; France, Scotland, England and Ireland; Scotland, France, England and Ireland; England, France and Ireland. Doubtless there are others.

[65] The seal is reproduced in Plaidy, *Mary Queen of Scots,* 69. See also *CSPF 1558—9,* 559, and H. F. Holt, 'On the great seal of Francis II of France and Mary, queen of Scots', *J. British Arch. Assoc.,* xxiv (1868), 349.

[66] *CSPF 1558—9,* 561.

[67] *CSPF 1559—60,* 56, 110, 145, 506, 598; *CSPF 1560—1,* 17—18.

[68] Phillips. *Images,* 19, 237.

[69] *CSPF 1558—9,* 4.

[70] *CSPF 1558—9,* 85.

[71] *CSPF 1560–1*, 392.

[72] *CSP Scot.*, i, 540.

[73] W. Camden, *The history of the most renowned and victorious princess Elizabeth, late queen of England* (1675), 34.

3

Queen Mary's Northern Province

ALLAN WHITE OP

When Queen Mary's galley docked at the port of Leith in August 1561 it was noted that she was accompanied by a small party of her French relatives together with a select group of courtiers and servants; the absence of a bodyguard impressed her subjects most of all. One of the queen's greatest talents was her flair for the dramatic gesture. Like her cousin, Elizabeth of England, she knew when to present herself as a vulnerable woman in need of protective consideration from those around her. It was this vulnerability disguising a shrewd and calculating intelligence, which served her in good stead when confronting the aggressively masculine tone of many of her nobles and officers. However, her discreet arrival impressed at least one of this latter group, William Maitland of Lethington, who spoke in admiring tones of how she had come 'to trust her person in our hands'.[1] The significance of Mary's gesture lay in its implicit assertion of her legitimate authority. Mary's sovereign authority was understood to be the principle of regulation and legitimacy which bound the various component parts of the community of the realm together: the community of the region, the community of the burgh and the community of the kirk. The religious changes of 1560 had challenged the accepted certainties on which the fabric of these social and political relationships had long rested, and also radically questioned the boundaries which marked these respective communities as distinct. By the time of Mary's return to Scotland the uneasy coalition which had pushed through the national revolution of 1559–60 was already showing signs of strain. The queen was well aware of the fragmentation which threatened in Scotland since she had in the spring of 1561 already received embassies from at least two of the various parties anxious to secure her support when she returned home. The policies she was to follow after her return had been evolved in France in response to these enquiries from home.[2]

In March 1561 Lord James Stewart, the queen's half-brother, embarked for France to acquaint her with the views of the provisional government on the attitude she should adopt on her return. The main drift of his advice appears to have been a counsel of moderation: she was not to ally herself with the French interest, she should seek closer ties with England and not seek to undo the work of religious reformation. Under these conditions she was to be allowed the free and private practice of her religion.[3] Lord James was not the sole visitor to the queen in France. According to John Leslie, later bishop of Ross, she also received unsolicited advice from the earl of Huntly, the chief conservative noble in Scotland and the acknowledged power in the north of the country. In his *History* Leslie claimed that he conveyed a message to the queen from the earl of Huntly asking her to land at the provincial capital of Aberdeen where they could then join forces so that the whole country could be reduced to obedience through their combined efforts.[4] Huntly's may not have been a purely private intitiative. Even before the death of François II in December 1560 a meeting of conservative peers had taken place at Dunbar with a view to co-ordinating opposition to the provisional government, which had held power, nominally in the queen's name, since the deposing of her mother in 1559. Leslie's embassy may have been connected with this conference.[5] Huntly's commitment to the anti-French and Protestant cause had always been suspect; he had been a late subscriber to the bond of the Congregation and had, at one stage, protested that the strength of feeling against the Reformation in the north-east prevented his closer association with the revolutionary party.[6] John Knox, a vivid if not always reliable commentator, regarded him as a 'bye-lyer' and totally untrustworthy.[7] Evidently this opinion was shared by Lord James and the earl of Argyll, the principal advocates of the Protestant cause during the Reformation crisis. After the Reformation parliament of August 1560 they had pinpointed Huntly as the chief threat to them and had determined on measures to limit his power and influence.[8]

Huntly himself was always suspicious of any moves towards friendship with England, believing that an association with France still presented greater possibilities for the preservation of national independence as well as for the support of religious conservatism. By April 1561 Randolph, the English ambassador in Edinburgh, reported that the French sympathies of the two great territorial nobles — the duke of Châtelherault, leader of the extensive Hamilton family interest and a great power in the west, and Huntly, the great power in the north-east, were becoming more pronounced.[9] Châtelherault, however 'precise' a Protestant he was, was also a political weathercock whose chief interests were the preservation of his own family fortunes, in France as well as Scotland,[10] and the security of his claim to the Scottish crown, whereas Huntly's reservations about the drift of Scottish policy were based on the realization that alliance with Protestant England would mean a policy of religious conformity and the end of the conservative cause.[11] In the event, Mary chose the political option presented to her by Lord James Stewart. Her rejection of Huntly's offer was a definite refusal to risk the turmoil of civil war, but it also ensured that should she continue to pursue an anglophile policy then some kind of reckoning with the earl of Huntly would ensue with drastic consequences for the stability of the regional polity of the north-east, which depended on the strength of Huntly to maintain it. Mary avoided a civil war, but the risk she ran was the potential destabilization of her most Catholic province.

The Gordon earls of Huntly had established themselves in the north-east in the fifteenth century, building up their patrimony through the cultivation of royal favour and the pursuit of a judicious policy of advantageous marriage and prudent family alliances. By the mid-sixteenth century a pattern of considerable stability and continuity had been laid down with the earldom of Huntly as one of the few great territorial lordships of Scotland. Through the enjoyment of longevity and without the interruption and territorial fragmentation consequent upon the chief threats to the fortunes of a great house, female succession or forfeiture, the Gordons had become almost indispensable to the exercise of royal power in the region.[12]

However, by the time the fourth earl succeeded to the title in 1524, the landed expansion of the Gordons had largely ceased. The fourth earl's interest extended towards the extension of his 'affinity' by the conclusion of bonds of manrent with local noble and gentry families, together with the acquisition of honours and titles which would demonstrate the power and prestige of his lordship. Between 1536 and 1541 the fourth earl signed eight bonds of manrent with prominent local families including the Leslies of Balquhain and the Gordons of Strathavon, together with northern clansmen like the Mackintoshes and the Macleans of Duart. Between 1543 and 1560 a further twenty bonds were signed with Lord Lovat, the earls of Argyll and Crawford, and a series of local lairds, such as Grant of Freuchie and Meldrum of Fyvie.[13] Such bonds offered a double advantage to the earl, weaving him more tightly into the web of local landed society, creating an affinity and following, which in turn made his function as guardian of the north easier to fulfil.

Throughout the century before the Reformation the Gordons were establishing patterns of power and patronage, all the time operating within the traditions of good lordship. Since in many ways they were of recent pedigree in the north-east their aspirations to prove themselves of ancient lineage, expressed in a desire for offices and titles as well as an increase in the circle of clientage, were all the stronger. It was in the earl's interest to see that his family association was seen as part of the customary order handed down from the past. In this regard his endeavours to prove his good lordship were intense, stretching even to providing for the spiritual welfare of his tenants. He manifested his concern and piety as well as his wealth by beginning a project to establish a collegiate church on his lands.[14] On a number of occasions in the 1540s and 1550s the fourth earl was called upon to fulfil the terms of his implicit contract with the crown by curbing the men of the north and the isles. He failed in his trust only once and it was precisely then, in 1554, that the queen regent imprisoned him and declared him forfeit, albeit temporarily. It is a tribute to his own loyalty and his acceptance of the terms of the relationship that he did not contest her action but accepted it.[15]

Inevitably one of the significant strands running through the Gordon quest for land and titles, and their concern for constructing a complex of personal relations with the lesser families of the north-east, is the contemporary understanding of honour.[16] In Gavin Douglas's *Palice of Honour,* honour holds court in a chamber amongst his special intimates, the princes clad in golden armour set with precious stones.[17] The assumption underlying this image is that ancient lineage and noble blood were inextricably linked with honourable behaviour. The third and fourth earls of Huntly owed their positions in northern society to their special relationships with the sovereign. The function of nobility in terms of government and display was their particular concern, for it bound them into a corporate code of behaviour and underpinned their exercise of the royal commission. Their position of honour rested not simply on royal favour but also on its acceptance by lesser contemporaries.

The earl of Huntly's understanding of his role and power are clearly reflected in the accounts of the estate centred at Strathbogie Castle. When Mary of Guise visited the earl in 1555 it was alleged that his princely style and lavish way of life aroused the disquiet of some of Mary's French advisers who propose that the earl's power be curtailed. When Randolph accompanied Queen Mary and her half-brother to the north in 1562 he was able to describe the splendours of Strathbogie as the finest house in the country.[18] The existence of a fine house was indispensable for any magnate who wished to maintain any significant regional connection; he had to enjoy a place which could act as the centre of the country and be the location of his household.[19] By the time of the Reformation Strathbogie had become, like many English castles, less a place of defence and more a showcase for the power and prestige of its lord. Its lack of defensive credibility is seen in the ease with which it was taken after the battle of Corrichie.[20] The conspicuous consumption of the Gordon court at Strathbogie and its lavish display were not the arrogant expressions of the independence of an overmighty subject but the proper fulfilment of the responsibilities of one of the natural counsellors of the sovereign and one of the chief pillars of government. It is in this connection that Huntly's first attempt to give counsel to the queen whilst she was still in France should be understood. Huntly's traditional understanding of the role and function of the territorial princes in Scotland formed the background against which his final confrontation with the queen was played out.

The return of the queen in August 1561 did very little to satisfy conservatives like the earl of Huntly. Almost immediately upon her arrival Mary began manoeuvring around the subject which was to prove closest to her heart, at least until 1565, the succession to the throne of England. This was the cornerstone of her international and domestic programme during the first years of her reign and was to condition her relationships with her most powerful subjects, not all of whom were committed to her dynastic ambitions. In this regard Mary's choice of councillors after her arrival proved something of an unpleasant surprise in the north-east of Scotland. Before her departure from France Throckmorton, the English ambassador in Paris, had assumed that she would ally herself at home with those who shared her religious opinions and that chief amongst these would be the earl of Huntly.[21] In fact she chose exactly the opposite course, in the belief that by distancing herself from her Catholic subjects she would promote her campaign for the English succession. Thus she was attempting to prove that her succession to Elizabeth need not involve a religious or political revolution, and that she was prepared to be guided by even the most Protestant of advisers. In this regard her assiduous cultivation of the Lord James and her consequent rejection of the earl of Huntly make perfect sense. Huntly's fall was brought about by his inability to believe that the alliance between Lord James and the queen was anything but a temporary coalition. In many ways his fate was sealed in the first few months after Mary's return to Scotland and it became more certain as negotiations with England proceeded in the autumn and winter of 1561.

Mary's determination to secure the promise of the English succession can be seen clearly in her dispatch of her secretary, Maitland, to London to discuss the question soon after her landing at Leith.[22] In retrospect her attendance at Protestant ceremonies and her acceptance of the existing settlement may seem opportunist, but no more so that was the behaviour of many of her subjects. The prospect of the succession appeared sufficiently promising in September 1561 to warrant such an attitude. How immediate the question was, and how close Mary was to the English throne became obvious when Elizabeth was struck down with smallpox in October 1562.[23] Throughout the winter of 1561 and the following spring Mary invested considerable energy in arranging a meeting between the two queens. Her domestic policies were tailored to suit this grand design and to prove to Elizabeth her good intentions. Scotland for Mary was only a sideshow in the far more exciting arena of European dynastic politics.

The debate on the future direction of Scottish policy was continued enthusiastically by the Protestant leaders of the provisional government who had been confirmed in office on the privy council on Mary's return. A month later, in September 1561, Mary also confirmed Huntly as a member, recognizing his authority and attempting to secure a broad spectrum of representation.[24] He proved to be an outspoken and, to the queen's mind at least, indiscreet advocate of the conservative cause. In October 1561 a public dispute between the earl and Lord James took place in her presence, with Huntly offering to set up the mass in three shires if the queen commanded it.[25] Huntly's offer was an advertisement that the queen's attitude would determine not only the success or failure of the Catholic cause, but also the survival or otherwise of the balance of relationships which had existed between the crown and the principal magnates of the kingdom for the previous three decades. Mary's attitude to Catholicism and to the English sucession entailed a decisive political shift involving the outflanking of the territorial princes on whom the crown had traditionally relied. Mary's intention to raise the Lord James even higher and her contemplation of such a shift in the governing of the realm were obvious to both the Spanish ambassador in London and the English ambassador in Edinburgh.[26] Meanwhile Huntly was seen as the principal opponent of the English association and his rallying cry was taken to be the restoration of the mass.[27] However, even Huntly's rallying cry showed the confusion into which the various communities of the realm had fallen. The earl's much vaunted Catholicism was a desperate attempt to prove some relationship or shared vision with a queen who seemed determined to undermine his role in the local community by excluding him from the national community. His appeal to the language of commission, the religious language of the community of the old church, was almost an admission of failure and despair rather than a proud boast. Not even the old religious certainties moved a young and politicially radical queen, whose radicalism, some thought, might extend to a change of faith should such a move seem necessary.

The English bias of Mary's policies inevitably alarmed the French who, casting about for a suitable spokesman to voice their disquiet, fixed on Huntly as the only credible leader of a loyal opposition. They prevailed on him to use his good offices to prevent any meeting between Elizabeth and Mary.[28] Unfortunately for them Huntly's influence was waning by the hour and, by the beginning of 1562, stood at a very low ebb. In January of that year Mary sealed her bond with Lord James by secretly conferring on him the earldom of Moray, which had been administered for some years by the earl of Huntly and whose historic territories fell well within the accepted sphere of Gordon influence.[29] Mary's gift signified her determination to evade alliance with Huntly and marked the opening shot in her campaign against the Gordons.

The agreement in principle to a meeting between the two queens was given by the Scottish privy council in May 1562, and early in June Elizabeth consented to a meeting at Nottingham at some date between July and August.[30] Huntly had been a consistent attender at the privy council since his appointment. Apart from an absence of a few weeks in November and December 1561 he was present for the majority of the meetings in the early months of 1562. He did not, however, attend the meeting of 19 May which approved the prospect of the conference at Nottingham; neither did he appear at the council again.[31] His decline from favour coincided more or less exactly with the increasing likelihood of a meeting with Elizabeth. Randolph was able to report to London in June, when the meeting seemed certain, that Huntly held no credit with the queen and that France was very disturbed at the prospect.[32]

It was the conspiracy of international events and the foolhardy impetuosity of his third son, Sir John Gordon, which was to seal Huntly's fate more than any other factor. A reckoning with Gordon power may have seemed inevitable to Lord James and Mary at some point in the future but it was brought decidedly closer by the religious troubles which erupted in France in June and July 1562. Elizabeth's abandonment of the proposed meeting was a direct consequence of the growing crisis in France; a result which admirably suited Huntly and Châtelherault who, for very different reasons, had been consistently working to undermine the meeting between the queens.[33] Elizabeth's interests at home dictated that she prove her distance from such association with a member of the house of Guise and her independence of action. News of the postponement of the meeting, conveyed to Edinburgh in July by Sir Henry Sidney, brought the queen and Lord James intense disappointment.[34] It was in the wake of this setback that Mary decided on a visit to the northern parts of her kingdom. The recent escape from prison and flight northwards of Sir John Gordon provided her with the opportunity to use the expedition to show the force of royal justice and her determination to exercise it against all those who opposed her. Gordon had originally been confined for engaging in a street fight with Lord Ogilvie and some members of his family over a question of inheritance. The offence was serious enough but hardly of such gravity to warrant a full-scale military expedition to the north. Nevertheless it provided a convenient occasion for the queen to accomplish her purpose.

The project to visit the north had long been in the queen's mind. The burgesses of Aberdeen had been 'suirlie informit' in the early part of 1562 that the queen intended to visit the burgh at some point between that Easter and the Easter following. The burgesses had even agreed that the prodigious sum of 2,000 merks should be set aside for the decoration of the town in preparation for the queen's arrival.[35] Since the plans for a meeting between Elizabeth and Mary had caused the post-ponement of the projected visit to the north, it came as a great surprise to the burgesses that Mary was at the gates of the burgh a few short weeks after the collapse of plans for a meeting with Elizabeth.[36] Yet Queen Mary's progress to the north and her abortive visit to Nottingham were linked: the precipitate decision to journey north stemmed from her own disappointment but was also intended as an earnest of her good intentions towards Elizabeth.

One of the chief threats to the current trend of Mary's policy had been the possibility of a coalition between the two most discontented nobles in the kingdom, Châtelherault and Huntly. Both had refused invitations to come to court during 1562, Huntly because of a sore leg and Châtelherault because of a sore arm. The prospect of a coalition against closer ties with England looked less remote towards the end of 1562. Knox remarked, possibly unreliably, that Huntly had sent his second son, Lord Gordon, to the west, where recent Catholic demon-strations had taken place, in an attempt to co-ordinate a joint rising against the queen's pro-English advisers.[37] In response to this threat from the west the minister, George Hay, subsequently commissioner for Aberdeen, in company with Knox himself, began a preaching camp-aign in the region which was supported by the Protestant Bond of Ayr.[38] The queen's journey to the other focus of opposition to her policies, the north-east, was a signal that she was prepared to distance herself from France and the conservative cause by sacrificing a northern earl who had become too powerful. Lord James, newly created earl of Moray, had a personal interest in the region and success there would overawe the rival to his own power, the duke of Châtelherault. The expedition to the north was primarily a demonstration to Elizabeth who was troubled by her own conservative north and powerful northern earls. In order to ensure that the message got through to London and that Elizabeth was fully apprised of the progress of events Randolph, the English ambassador, was brought along to report.[39]

Huntly was treated with considerable coolness from the outset of Mary's visit to Aberdeen; she refused to visit him at Strathbogie and signalled by her attitude that he had fallen from favour.[40] The irresponsible behaviour of Sir John Gordon, and the refusal of the Gordon-appointed keeper of Inverness Castle to yield it to her, provided the queen with sufficient grounds for beginning the offensive against the Gordons.[41] Huntly seemed reluctant to enter into open revolt against the queen and hoped instead to intimidate her by the size of his forces. Randolph reported that on the road to Inverness Huntly had planned to engage the royal army at the Spey with 1,000 horse and foot, but Mary was not intimidated since her own forces amounted to 3,000 men.[42] Her confidence in her own victory and her unwillingness to compromise are well illustrated by her public naming of Lord James as earl of Moray at Darnaway Castle, the historic seat of the earls of Moray.[43] Despite all the evidence to the contrary, Huntly appears to have hoped for some means of reconciliation with the queen. He and his wife believed that one of the factors recommending them to Mary was their shared Catholicism. When Maitland of Lethington mounted a surprise raid on Strathbogie Castle in the hope of catching Huntly unawares he managed to gain easy access to the castle. Although the earl was absent, the countess took pains to show him the apartments which would be made available to the queen should she accept the earl's invitation to share his hospitality. Amongst the rooms awaiting the queen was the chapel sumptuously furnished for the celebration of mass.[44] Huntly's stress on their shared faith made it all the more important to Mary to demonstrate that she could not be moved by any such claim. The queen's acknowledgement of a shared religious community with Huntly would have undermined her credibility in the eyes of her supporters, and entirely subverted her purpose in making an example of the earl. Huntly was not brought down despite his Catholicism but precisely because of it.

The queen's implacable hostility to Huntly goes some way towards explaining the most striking failure of 1562, the dramatic disfunctioning of the formidable Gordon alliance system. With the approach of battle the earl's local support dwindled alarmingly. On 28 October Randolph reported that Huntly had the support of 700 men, consisting mainly of his friends, tenants and their servants, most of whom deserted him before the battle of Corrichie.[45] The majority of his supporters came from amongst the Gordon lairds, twenty-eight of whom were named in the remission which was finally granted for the rebellion in February 1567;[46] the most important lairds refused to support him. One reason for this failure was the clause in all bonds of manrent entered into by the earl since 1534 which included a reservation of loyalty to the crown. In the event of rebellion against the sovereign Huntly was unable to rely on his clientage to defend him.[47] It was precisely the support of his affinity that the earl needed if he was to overawe the queen and show that not only was the force of his authority recognized but so also was his honour. His visits in great state to Aberdeen and his display of strength were designed to convince the queen of the advisability of accepting his counsel and allying with him. Her refusal to co-operate with his view of the appropriate constitutional relationship between crown and magnate had undermined his standing with his supporters. They were not prepared to risk all in what appeared to be a lost cause, neither were they agreeable to being drawn into a fight to save Gordon honour. The power and prestige of the monarchy had conventionally been increased by the success of its regional agents and magnates; yet the events in the queen's progress of 1562 showed that royal power, when personally represented, could function successfully even in the face of opposition from its principal local agent.

The accepted relationship between crown and magnate was paralleled and reflected in the ideal relationship between magnate and client. Just as the sovereign was the focus of loyalty within the kingdom so was the territorial lord expected to be the same in his lordship. However, the various ties of kinship and clientage were not only vertical, converging in the person of the earl of Huntly, they were also lateral extending into a network of alliances between the earl and local lairds, and the local lairds and the more prominent burgess families of Aberdeen and other important burghs. Thus there existed a kaleidoscopic pattern of concerns which did not form one single thread linking the various sectional interests within the Gordon association. The client families of the earl of Huntly and the web of kinship enjoyed by the lairds had plainly grown in independence and assurance over the decades before Corrichie. The county gentry had achieved status and experience as administrators, ensuring a measure of order in the locality. Powerful nobles depended on the co-operation of lesser families to make their authority real within the bounds of their lordship. The frequent absences of successive earls from their territorial power base had devolved more influence on the lesser lairds. That this power was generally exercised in the maintenance of order is clear from the activity of Leslie of Balquhain in 1560. His defence in concert with earl of Huntly of the ecclesiastical patrimony of Aberdeen and Old Aberdeen in 1560, although it may have been mo-tivated by a sense of religious conservatism, was also informed by a sure sense of responsibility.[48] Successive Leslies had acted as sheriffs-depute for the earl of Huntly and it was therefore incumbent upon them to ensure good order.

The Reformation parliament of 1560 had been attended not only by the earl of Huntly and his son, but also by his sheriff-depute and two Gordon lairds.[49] The appearance of more than a hundred of the gentry, which is often taken to signal the general phenomenon of increased participation by the lairds in the direction of national affairs, was prompted by their increasing involvement in local affairs. The lairds were becoming the social cement which bound the locality together, in the north-east and elsewhere. Their influence crossed the boundaries dividing town and country and linked them both to the aristocracy, represented by the earl of Huntly, and the urban aristocracy embodied in the burgess elite of Aberdeen. Their connections with the burgesses gave them an enviable influence in the burgh through marriage ties. By contrast, the earl of Huntly had often sought direct political influence over the burgh but had persistently failed to achieve it. It could be argued that it was not the queen and the earl of Moray who defeated Huntly in 1562 so much as the lairds and burgesses of Aberdeen who refused to support him.

Mary's defeat of the earl of Huntly in 1562 did not only rid her of a powerful obstacle to her English plans, it also administered a severe shock to the traditional polity of the north-east. Her victory called into question the constitutional balance within the realm as it had developed over the previous century. It is clear from her actions in the north that she failed to understand the long-accepted relationship between crown and nobility which had been thought necessary for peace and good government. Huntly was broken not because he was an over-mighty subject but because he was powerful and in the way; his ruin was accomplished *pour encourager les autres*. In November 1562, shortly after Huntly's collapse at Corrichie, Maitland wrote to William Cecil claiming that he and Queen Elizabeth should have no fear of Mary showing favour to Catholics should she be accepted as the heir to the throne of England, for her behaviour in the north and her distancing herself from her Catholic subjects had proved her to be free of any such partiality.[50]

By bringing about Huntly's downfall and laying claims to direct obedience from the localities Mary was cutting across the various forms of aristocratic leadership, kinship, clientage and local influence upon which the crown had not only relied in the past but actively sought to increase and support.[51] A good example of how different her understanding of sovereignty was can be seen in her treatment of the unfortunate keeper of Inverness Castle. His refusal to surrender his charge to the queen without the authority of his kinsman and her officer, the earl of Huntly, should not be seen simply as an act of open rebellion but a result of the unutterable confusion into which her direct and autocratic actions had plunged the region.[52] Moreover, the castle itself was largely the work of Gordon investment. The third earl had been appointed sheriff and keeper of Inverness, with power to garrison and add to the fortifications of the castle, in 1509. At the same time he was ordered to build a stone hall, kitchen and chapel within the ramparts at his own expense.[53] Whilst the castle was undoubtedly the crown's it had been built largely by the Gordons and entrusted to their care for over fifty years.

Huntly's fall left a vacuum in the north which Mary did not think about filling, least of all by encouraging the ambitions of her half-brother. Ironically her inactivity, far from threatening local conservative opinion, insulated it from further threat for some years to come by taking it out of the sphere of national politics; equally, Moray's boast of bringing the north-east to Protestantism failed to materialize. Mary's ambition proved too great and her sense of governmental reality too small. She did not comprehend that the honour of her estate rested on that of her nobles; the craggy independence and rough counsel she experienced from them seemed too much like disobedience. When she was powerless to confute them she sought to outflank them, and what should have been astute diplomacy occasionally appeared more like government by whim.

The expediency and opportunist nature of Mary's policy in the north-east became clear in the aftermath of Corrichie; no consistent attempt was made to dismantle the infrastructure of Gordon power. The complex of relationships symbolized by the earl's collection of bonds of manrent remained intact if severely strained. However, the obligations which were not fulfilled in 1562 were not shirked some years later during the civil war, fought between supporters of the deposed queen and her young son, James. In 1568 a large number of northern lairds joined the fifth earl who had been appointed queen's lieutenant in the north, in subscribing a bond for her service at Huntly Castle.[54] Amongst these were three of the Gordon lairds who had so conspicuously failed to follow the fourth earl in 1562. The prospect of serving for the queen and not against her dramatically altered their interpretation of loyalty owed to the head of their kin. Amongst the other signatories of this bond were John Grant of Freuchy, whose father had signed a bond of manrent with the fourth earl in 1546;[55] Lachlan Mackintosh, the chief of Clan Chattan, who had also signed a bond with the fourth earl, and Duncan Forbes of Monymusk, one of the prominent Protestant burgesses of Aberdeen who had subscribed a bond of manrent in 1560. It was fortunate for the queen that she did not dismantle the network of the Gordon affinity after Corrichie, for, when it was reactivated and used for her service, it proved to be the real locus of the Marian cause during the civil war.

The queen's failure to make any long-term political provision for the government of the north in 1562 suggested that she had no particular purpose in ruining the fourth earl of Huntly other than making an example of him to please Elizabeth and further sealing her alliance with the earl of Moray. However, her impetuosity and unpredictability failed to ensure that the power vacuum in the north-east was adequately filled. In effect the political life of the region was only marginally affected in the years after Corrichie; in many areas of life there was no significant change. Lack of any real support from the queen for his personal ambitions and the absence of a significant power base prevented Moray from establishing any real authority in the area. Indeed it was the expression of Moray's irritation and frustration in the abortive coup which resulted in the Chaseabout Raid in 1565 which prompted the restoration of the Gordon position in the north. After Chaseabout Mary rapidly freed Lord Gordon from the prison in which he had been confined since Corrichie and restored him to favour as fifth earl of Huntly. Her confidence that the new earl would act as a useful counter-balance to the earl of Moray was not misplaced since the 'whole force of the north' was soon marching to her assistance.[56] The restoration of the fifth earl to his lands and titles was easily accomplished and he soon fitted into the space left by his father as chief spokesman for the conservative sympathizers within the country. Henceforth the north-east was to be the stronghold of all those who supported the queen against her enemies.

Although the fifth earl immediately resumed his father's former position as leader of the conservative opposition it was unclear whether, in his exercise of that role, he was motivated more by religious concerns or by a simple hatred for Moray. One of the facts of political life in the north-east was the widespread survival of Catholic belief and practice. The fifth earl of Huntly, although tolerant of Catholicism, was by no means personally committed to it. In February 1566 he refused to take part in the queen's Candlemas celebrations, although Darnley, Lennox and Atholl were prepared to do so.[57] Similarly in June of the same year Killigrew, the English ambassador in Edinburgh, wrote to Cecil describing his attendance at a sermon in St Giles, in company with Huntly, Argyll, Mar and Crawford.[58] The fifth earl was a dubious Protestant whereas his father had been an idiosyncratic Catholic; the former was supported by his Catholic clients whereas the latter was not. This raises the question of the allegedly paramount role exercised by the earls of Huntly in the survival of Catholicism in the north-east. If the relationship between magnate and affinity was one of counsel and consent then it cannot be the case that Catholicism survived through the unrestricted exercise of authoritarian influence from Strathbogie Castle. The earls of Huntly were likely to remain Catholic sympathizers because their power was largely derived from Catholic supporters. Catholicism was built into the regional structures of social and political life and it was to prove a long time before they could be dismantled.

The earl of Huntly loyally exercised his office as queen's lieutenant in the north until the end of the civil war. Although he was a conservative with Protestant associations acting for a Catholic queen he did not always rally to his cause the other important conservative power-brokers in the region. The affinity constructed by the fourth earl stood firm and remained on the whole loyal to its patron. Yet the fifth earl, like the fourth, had always found it difficult if not impossible to create any strong party within the burgh of Aberdeen. Control of the burgh with its busy port and network of trading contacts with northern Europe was absolutely vital to the survival of the queen's cause in the north. Theoretically there should have been a substantial identification of interest between the queen's party and the burgesses of Aberdeen. The town was dominated by a burgess aristocracy engaged in investing their surplus capital in rural estates and busily founding dynasties by marrying into the local gentry families.[59] Many of Aberdeen's chief citizens were also Catholic sympathizers personally involved in maintaining a covert Catholic way of life.[60] This religious and political conservatism did not overcome their determination to maintain their hard-won burghal independence by entering into an alliance with the earl of Huntly.

A constant stream running through the political history of Aberdeen during the first half of the sixteenth century had been the regular attempts of the earls of Huntly, together with their gentry clientage, to secure the domination of the burgh. Throughout the various conflicts between the local nobles and the burgh over the previous century the burgesses had often relied on the crown for protection, but the outbreak of civil war robbed them of such a shield. When the central authority was weak they were deprived of the protection necessary to maintain their independence. The resurgence of the queen's party in July 1568 presented the earl of Moray with a strong challenge to his authority as regent,[61] and it also threatened a number of Scottish burghs which had been seen to take the regent's side against the queen. Dundee and Perth were faced with assault by the earl of Huntly and his men[62] whilst Aberdeen too fell victim to a Gordon attack. In August 1568 one of

Huntly's lieutenants, John Leslie, besieged the house of Thomas Menzies, the provost of Aberdeen, and forced the town to yield to the earl.[63]

Leslie's involvement in the business was itself indicative of the swiftly changing patterns of alliance in the north-east since only a few months before the provost of Aberdeen, together with Leslie and many other leading Catholic gentry in the area, had banded together to protest at the earl of Moray's order that the lead be removed from the great cathedral of St Machar in Old Aberdeen.[64] Aberdeen and its leading burgess families were coerced into co-operating with the earl of Huntly and the queen's party. When Moray reasserted his authority in the north in 1569 he showed by his very different treatment of Huntly and the burgh of Aberdeen that he saw the advantages in accepting the burgh's plea of co-operation through coercion. Whereas Huntly was forced to pay such 'compositions as never were taken before', a discharge was granted to the burgh which recognized that any assistance furnished to the earl of Huntly had been wrung from it through fear and compulsion.[65] It was to Moray's advantage to be understanding and conciliatory towards Aberdeen, for a more rigorous policy might have driven the burgesses closer to Huntly. With Aberdeen as a potential enemy at his back Huntly would be forced to divide his forces to secure the burgh and its port. The wisdom of Moray's policy became clear during the second phase of the civil war when Huntly had to find considerable numbers of men and large sums of money to keep the burgh for the queen's party.

Throughout the civil war years the north remained the queen's province because of the power and energetic loyalty of the fifth earl of Huntly. In 1562 Mary had broken with the convention of royal govenment by acting decisively and directly against a magnate in a region which had hitherto shown total loyalty to the sovereign. By achieving her purpose she had run the risk of undermining the foundations of royal power as it had been consolidated over a century. Fortunately for her the habits of loyalty developed by the earls of Huntly had proved difficult to break; without the support of the earl of Huntly Mary's cause would not have remained so vigorous for so long after she had been deposed. One of the mainstays of the society in which crown and magnate were bound together was a regard for lineage and veneration of the 'true blood'. In such a society bonds of kinship and patronage coalesced with loyalty to the crown. The subtleties and confusions of 1562 when the earl of Huntly was virtually forced into rebellion against the crown were absent during the civil war when the Gordons were unequivocally for the 'true blood' represented by the queen. However, the northern province which they aspired to rule in her name was a coalition of interest groups and not all of them shared magnatial ideology with the same intensity. The wild card in the political game was always that played by the burghs. In 1562 Aberdeen, regional capital of the north-east, remained loyal to the crown, distanced itself from the earl of Huntly and remained untouched by his fall. At the outset of the civil war its role was much more finely judged, drawn towards the queen by ties of natural sympathy and to the earl of Huntly by a shared conservatism. In 1568 it reserved its position and independence of action, to emerge battered but comparatively unscathed when the conflict was ended. It was this move towards independence of action which was to strengthen the tendency towards regional fragmentation rendering the function of the Gordons as royal agents increasingly difficult to execute. Mary and the Gordons needed each other, the one to remain with some chance of retaining royal authority and the other to sustain regional supremacy. Despite all the efforts made on her behalf by Huntly and his affinity, the north did not remain the queen's province. The failure of the fifth earl to maintain the internal political coherence of the north-east during the civil war did not signify the end of Gordon power in the region by any means, but it showed that it could never be what it once was.

Notes

[1] *CSP Scot.*, i, 544—5.

[2] See Cowan, ch. 5 below, for the policy decisions of 1561.

[3] Donaldson, *Queen's Men*, 49.

[4] Leslie, *History* (Bann.), 294.

[5] *CSP Scot.*, i, 498—9.

[6] ibid., i, 438.

[7] Knox, *History*, i, 309.

[8] *CSP Scot.*, i, 478.

[9] *CSPF 1561—2*, 71. The Hamilton interest, concentrated in Lanarkshire and Renfrewshire, also extended into Ayrshire and West Lothian, see E. Finnie, 'The house of Hamilton: patronage, politics and the church in the Reformation period', *IR*, xxxvi (1985), 11.

[10] See Merriman, ch. 2 above, also Lynch, ch. 1, for Hamilton interests in France.

[11] See Adams, ch. 6 below, for the marked Protestant emphasis in the policy of amity with England.

[12] A. J. White, 'Religion, Politics and Society in Aberdeen, 1543—1593' (Edinburgh Univ. Ph.D., 1985), 191—4.

[13] *Spalding Misc.* (Spalding Club, 1849), iv, 207, 210, 205, 217—19, 214—15, 223.

[14] SRO, GD 44/15/3/1.

[15] *Records of Aboyne, 1203–1681* (New Spalding Club, 1894), 455.

[16] M. James, 'English politics and the concept of honour', *Past and Present* suppl., iii (1978), 6–7.

[17] The *Palice of Honour,* in *The Poetical Works of Gavin Douglas* (STS, 1874), i, 72. I am dependent on Mr Mervyn James for the interpretative basis of the concept of honour and its application to the north of Scotland.

[18] *CSP Scot.*, i, 649–50.

[19] M. E. James, 'Obedience and dissent in Henrician England: the Lincolnshire Rebellion, 1536', *Past and Present,* xlvi (1970), 44.

[20] *Records of Aboyne,* 467.

[21] *CSPF 1561–2,* 122–3.

[22] *CSP Scot.,* i, 548.

[23] W. Ferguson, *Scotland's Relations with England: A Survey to 1707* (1977), 84; see also Adams, ch. 6 below.

[24] *RPC,* i, 157.

[25] *CSPF 1561–2,* 353–4.

[26] *CSP Spain,* i, 217; *CSPF 1561–2,* 372, 391–2.

[27] *CSP Spain,* i, 222.

[28] *CSPF 1561–2,* 457.

[29] *Records of Aboyne,* 460.

[30] *RPC,* i, 206.

[31] ibid., i, 204. The last recorded appearance of Huntly at the council.

[32] *CSPF 1562,* 82.

[33] *CSP Scot.,* i, 641. See Lynch, ch. 1 above, for the repercussions of this joint anti-English stance.

[34] *CSP Scot.,* i, 635–6, 641.

[35] *Council Register of Aberdeen* (Spalding Club, 1844), i, 339–40.

[36] ibid., i, 347.

[37] Knox, *History,* ii, 54.

[38] ibid., ii, 55.

[39] *CSPF 1562,* 273–4.

[40] *CSP Scot.,* i, 649–50.

[41] Knox, *History,* ii, 58.

[42] *CSPF 1562,* 359.

[43] *CSP Scot.,* i, 654–6.

[44] ibid., i, 654–6, 657.

[45] *CSPF 1562,* 399.

[46] *RSS,* v, pt.2, 3298.

[47] *RPC,* i, 220.

[48] G. M. Fraser, *Historical Aberdeen* (1905), 94; J. Davidson, *Inverurie and the Earldom of Garioch* (1878), 145.

[49] Donaldson, *Queen's Men,* 101.

[50] *CSP Scot.,* i, 666–8.

[51] J. Powis, *Aristocracy* (1984), 62; J. M. Brown, 'The exercise of power', in J. M. Brown (ed.), *Scottish Society in the Fifteenth Century* (1977), 52–4.

[52] *CSP Scot.*, i, 651.

[53] *RMS*, i, 3286.

[54] *Spalding Misc.*, iv, 156–7.

[55] ibid., iv, 214–15.

[56] *CSP Scot.*, ii, 221.

[57] ibid., ii, 254. See Lynch, ch.1 above, and Goodare, ch. 7 below, for the Candlemas celebrations of 1566.

[58] *CSPF 1566–8,* 93.

[59] White, 'Religion, Politics and Society in Aberdeen', 14.

[60] ibid., 153–63.

[61] *CSP Scot.*, ii, 476.

[62] *CSPF 1566–8*, 523, 527–8.

[63] *CSP Scot.*, ii, 470.

[64] *RSS*, vi, 566.

[65] *CSP Scot.*, ii, 660.

4

The Library of Mary, Queen of Scots

JOHN DURKAN

In May 1573 when Peter Young, as Genevan-trained preceptor to the young James VI and his future almoner and librarian, sat down at Holyrood with his royal master's paper work-book, he set himself to estimate how its blank pages were to be utilized.[1] He left eight pages for entering items from the dispersed library of the exiled Queen Mary, to take account of whatever was available in Edinburgh itself, or detained by successive regents and others, the information to be gathered with the help of accessible inventories.[2] These, formerly in the hands of the acting keeper of Holyrood, Servais de Condé, who had fled to Flanders, were now with his 'guidsoun', Benoist Garroust, 'passementier' or cloth-braider, who lodged with him.[3]

No systematic account of Mary's library, based on the fullest information taken from Young's record as well as what can be garnered from the 1578 castle inventory or from authentic surviving items from her book collections, has so far appeared. To be useful, any such account must take note of the presence of inherited volumes; it needs to consider not only Mary's personal tastes but the climate of opinion in her immediate circle, including her French relatives and associates with views on how a Renaissance monarch should be nurtured, her tutors and any who might have the leisure to read to her such as the royal almoners as well as courtiers, foreign visitors and aspiring authors presenting or dedicating their various productions. Most were concerned with pressing her to read along certain definite lines.

Young's central concern was not monitoring the return of Mary's books so much as building up a library for the studies of the juvenile king; his 'Index of the King's Books', begun in 1574, was finished by the end of 1575,[4] but the recovery of Mary's own collections proved painfully slow.[5] The regent's help was invoked by Young in amassing Mary's lost volumes, but the salvage operation could only come up

71

with a wreck of a library. The first items surrendered in July 1573 were in the hands of a former member of her household staff, Benoist Garroust, who, as a craftsman in cloth may have been, along with the queen's embroiderer, involved in velvet casings, unhappily a style of binding that was far from durable. It has been the accepted view that no stylish French leather bindery existed in Edinburgh before 1580.[6] Yet one such binder, Jhonn du Moullings, died there in March 1567, when Garroust was appointed as his executor dative and Sebastien Davelourt, commissariot clerk, described at one point as Mary's secretary, was given as surety for delivery of the 'warklumis' and 'bukis' of this Jean du Moulin. How long he had resided in Edinburgh can only be guessed at, and it is a tantalizing question whether he is identical with, or younger kinsman to, the Rouen bookbinder of the same name who bound for English clients and is thought to have provided the model for the mill device employed by Scotland's first printer, Andrew Myllar. For the first time the possibility can be entertained that some of the Regent Moray's and Mary's leather bindings are assignable to Edinburgh rather than to France.[7]

After the defeat of the Marians in Edinburgh Castle in 1573, an order went out for the recovery of the queen's household stuff. The first compelled to disgorge was James Sandilands, Lord Torphichen, holder of an ecclesiastical barony that Mary had secularized, and the tale he told was one of change and chaos. About 1565, when captain of Linlithgow Palace, he had intromitted with the palace gear, as an inventory of 1569 had recorded. He was reported to have lost his post as chief chamberlain to the queen on Darnley's arrival,[8] but on the latter's death, and while Mary was in her Lochleven prison, she wrote to Moray and the council on behalf of the diseased Sandilands, who had been assigned a room in Holyrood by de Condé's wife and Garroust. This room had been specially fitted up to contain all the small moveables 'appertenand to the grand priour, hir unkle', François de Lorraine, Grand Prior of France, who had accompanied Mary on her journey to Scotland in 1561, and who before his death in 1563 was a colleague of Sandilands abroad as a knight of St John. The sick man also had access to items in Mary's library for which he had acquired a taste in sunnier days in Malta — light literature in French, Italian and Spanish. With the plague creeping near the gates, Servais cautioned him to remove his belongings home to Torphichen, but not without surrendering a receipted inventory which Young seems to have seen. At Torphichen, one of his servants testified to remarking three or four volumes with the armorial stamp of François and Mary.

After the briefest of intervals, however, the rival Hamiltons seized and transported Sandilands, his servants and gear into custody at Hamilton Palace, where for four months he was held till the queen again interceded. The chamberlain of Hamilton took 'na compt of the keping' of the books, and on Sandilands regaining freedom, the books suffered from 'harling thame on sleddis throuch the foule muris' and consequently were 'all disparit, dismemberit and spilt be thair sogeouris' on the convoy back to Holyrood.[9] Though he handed over several books in October 1573, several absent volumes were noted by a disappointed Young, including Italian tragedies and comedies that a more precise Protestant might have disdained. The celibate knight of the reigns of Mary's father and mother had married in the first flush of the Reformation the young Janet Murray of Polmaise, but had deserted her by 1571; the book she gave in 1575 perhaps came from her less as husband of Torphichen than as friend of Young. Indeed when in 1560, the Protestant lords sent him to France for royal ratification of the Reformation parliament, Mary twitted him with the fact that the news of his marriage could be bad news at his order's headquarters in Malta. The fate of the remainder of Mary's books still with Sandilands at his death in 1579 is obscured by the complicating factor that, in the absence of Lady Torphichen, his goods were interfered with by Dundas of that ilk, whose sons read Italian. In any event, Morton detained what Sandilands surrendered, although the king's library did not receive the last of them till 1578.[10]

Not all the young king's subjects were as prompt to restore borrowed items as was Sandilands. Some ninety or so volumes had already been received by the earl of Moray, signed for by his secretary, Mr John Wood of Tillydovie, son of the laird of Largo, who, however, had evidently borrowed some items he did not sign for: less than half of these were returned,[11] Young noting some specially desirable items not yet to hand by 1578. Wood as vicar of Largo had accompanied Moray to the schools in France in 1548, and his relations with Mary and the kirk fluctuated with the interests of Moray; he 'flattered her not in her danceing and other doinges'.[12] A few of the Wood books were poached by Sandilands during Moray's occupancy of Holyrood, though Wood's assassination, like his master's, followed close on the inventory.[13] In dividing her library between her maid of honour, Mary Beaton, and St Andrews University in the testament made during the alarms of 1566, Mary assigned the Greek and Latin tomes to the latter. Something of that preference is evident in the high seriousness of Moray's selection contrasted with the Mediterranean flavour with a dash of religious polemic in what remained, though six titles taken by Moray are not listed except as 'vj syndrie bukis'. Moray made his own generous donations to the university both before and during his regency, and it was as his successor as prior of St Andrews and not as bishop of Caithness, that Robert Stewart returned some of the books including uninventoried Italian items.[14] Some concealment by French officials during the spoliation in the summer of 1567 is to be presumed, though Mary's library, unlike her jewels, was not exposed for sale in London; and from Lochleven, Mary ordered Servais to release 'grayth' from her cabinet to Robert Melville, including a book that Moray impounded, which ended up in the custody of George Douglas, brother of the laird of Lochleven.[15]

About 300 books are known as belonging to Queen Elizabeth during her long reign, begun at a more mature age than that of Mary. The Marian inventories of 1569 and 1578 contain respectively 103 and 104 entries,[16] that is, 243 volumes were accumulated during a short personal reign; they were less of a ragbag than Elizabeth's collection, which, moreover, paid little attention to foreign literature. Many of Mary's books were surely presentation copies (though not at all in the elaborate style expected at the English court of which nine items presented by Garter King of Arms came to light recently in Hampshire). Few volumes are dated early enough to be inherited from other than her mother. If the fine Frescobaldi Ptolemy of 1490 was really a presentation copy by one of that banking firm, as is arguably the case despite its sitting a little uncomfortably in its present casing of *c*.1580 and despite the disputed date at which the Marian gold-tooled stamp was added, then it may be an inheritance from her grandfather, a thanksgiving gift from Girolamo Frescobaldi whom James IV considered a good friend.[17] The Pierpont Morgan library also holds her father's de luxe printed-on-vellum copy of John Bellenden's translation of Hector Boece, which miraculously survived the English raids of 1544. As to inheritances from her mother, the size of that collection is a big question mark, the single item linked with her being a fifteenth-century Latin Book of Hours at Fort Augustus.[18] However, the dedication implies her ownership of Jean le Feron's heraldic 'recueil' *Le Simbol Armorial des Armoiries de France et d'Escoce et de Lorraine* (Paris, 1553).[19]

Of James VI's preceptors, Buchanan and Peter Young, we know something, but of Mary's little. About 1553 there is a letter from Claude Millot, her tutor from 1550, sent from Meudon to Mary's mother, claiming that his charge grew daily in stature, virtue, beauty and good grace; nothing there about the young queen's intelligence, yet, on the word of her governess, by 1554 she was demonstrating knowledge and good judgement as she moved on from the vernacular to Latin.[20] In the company of Catherine de Médicis some tincture of

Italian was requisite, while the literature and history of France's Spanish neighbours also demanded attention, and one way of mastering foreign languages was to use them as cribs in learning Latin, just as Latin could later be useful as a crib for Greek. It surely would be hard in the French Renaissance court, so lately associated with the Hellenist, Guillaume Budé, and now harbouring Jacques Amyot and Pierre Danès, not to attempt Greek or a smattering of Hebrew. All this was part of the heavy, even unreal demands conventionally made of most royal persons; both Lancelot de Carle, tutor to the Guises and Amyot, later almoner to Charles IX, stressed the need for them to be read to by virtuous and erudite courtiers. Music, painting and architecture filled the very buildings where Mary moved as the court itself moved. The king's mistress, Madame de Valentinois, otherwise Diane de Poitiers, was a patron and inspirer of these triumphal arts, a lover of fine bookbindings if not of books, and a devotee of the young queen from Scotland; with her as with Mary one is made conscious of woman's central role in the Renaissance court.[21]

At court a window into Millot's schoolroom is provided by a surviving exercise-book in Mary's juvenile hand, comprising brief Latin epistles in reasonably accurate prose, her ordinary correspondent being her fellow scholar Elisabeth, Henri II's daughter and future wife of Philip of Spain. It shows a conventional Renaissance schooling on the Erasmian pattern, with Aesop's Fables, Cicero, Plato's *Laws* and his *Phaedo* dialogue on immortality, Latin comedy in the form of Plautus (Terence is strangely missing), but above all, as citations attest, Plutarch, inclusive of the *Septem Sapientum Convivium* of which Edward Henryson had lately proffered a French crib. Erasmus had advised close attention to Greek and Roman moralists in whom glimpses were afforded of the workings of the divine among the hearts of good pagans. The young queen adverts also to three of the Erasmian colloquies. Her other correspondents included the duke of Guise, the Dauphin, and (surely a letter never posted) Calvin too, the last claiming that pagan thinkers were familiar with purgatory even if he was not. In the main, though, she gathered instances of illustrious women as a run-up to her Latin oration of *c.*May 1555 on this favourite theme, an oration praised with courtly extravagance by the young Ramist rhetorician, Antoine Foquelin. This could be 'Ane Oratioun Buik in write' as noted in the inventory.[22]

Even at an early age Mary's role in government had to be envisaged, initially by feeding her on simple political maxims as the aperitif to a more substantial diet. The absence from the inventories of Machiavelli is less astonishing than that of Budé's *Institution of a Prince*, which wrestled with the abstractions of virtue with the aid of famous virtuous men, stressing moreover how vital to a contemporary monarch's success was language study in Latin, Greek and Hebrew, an idea already accepted by Mary's mother.[23] Erasmus's own *Institution* was to hand in anthologized form in Francesco Patrizzi's *Book of Human Policy*, a compendium edited by Gilles d'Aurigny. Patrizzi, a fifteenth-century Sienese, highlighted the need for strong constitutional sense in the ruler whose Aristotelian virtues would be topped up by Christian ones. The Platonic undercurrent in Patrizzi would be fortified by Louis Le Roy's French version of selections from the *Republic*, demonstrating that justice and the personal interests of the powerful need not go hand in hand. The aspect of Synesius of Cyrene that Mary was likely to appreciate most was his passion for the hunt and that least his section assailing the imperial policy of hiring foreign troops, which was too painfully reminiscent of Mary's own mother and more likely to please Buchanan who presented a copy (this one?) to the young King James. Machiavelli had broken the mould by his equation of power and virtue, and minor writers like Guillaume de la Perrière called for a royal paragon of moral responsibility while Pierre Boaistuau and Jean Maugin extended this requisite to the nobles as well.[24] On the few facts available to him, the popular Antonio de Guevara created the imperial antidote to the weak Arcadius in his largely fictional Marcus Aurelius, the imperial paragon who preferred peace to conflict and justice to tyranny. Like Budé, he extolled the prime need for early training and the role of learned counsellors, but what if their learning was in Machiavelli? The cardinal of Lorraine suspected that some wished to set up republicanism in Scotland, and Knox pointed to Plato as a man prepared like himself to put up with a regime he did not personally approve.[25] Mary's inventory listed an *Institution of Patience* which has not been identified, though a copy credited to her was held in London in 1874.[26] But the ultramonarchist on the French scene and its conviction politician most resolutely in favour of recentring all theory around France's local customs, the 'municipal' as against the international laws, was Charles du Moulin whose notions tended to absolutism.

Mary's moderate position was stressed by an Italian Protestant, Pietro Bizzari, who visited her in the spring of 1564. Then, before he found it expedient to adhere to the subsequent official English view, Bizzari confessed himself impressed by her prudent and courageous government, reining in the forces that exploded into religious warfare elsewhere. When he presented her with the manuscript of his *Peace and War*, it appealed to her Erasmian antipathy to brute force, and she responded with the gift of a gold collar. Was he not reflecting the contacts he had made at the Scottish court: the earl of Moray whose defeat of Huntly he celebrated, William Maitland of Lethington, George Buchanan and even the young Andrew Melville? To Maitland he dedicated his *Pro L. Virginio contra Ap. Claudium*, the contemporary lesson of which was that the good ruler should be firm in restraining the evil passions of wicked men. What would he later make of the panic folly of the Bothwell marriage? Even as late as 1568, Mary was still for Bizzari a queen 'extolled by all as a miracle of nature' and, apart from Bothwell in whom he saw her alienating her whole nobility, he judged remarkably positively her role in the Riccio and Darnley affairs.[27] In 1616 Bishop James Montague indicated that Mary herself had composed a French verse treatise on the 'institution' of a prince, the cover of which she personally embroidered, a royal manuscript that James considered a 'most pretious Jewell'. Composed perhaps in the 1570s, these were *Tetrasticha ou Quatrains* addressed to her son, gifted to Edinburgh University after James's death by Drummond of Hawthornden but now missing.[28]

Of more immediately practical moment was a work on the administrative styles of the French chancery, though on fiscal policy there are only the French ordinances of 1540. She naturally owned Jean du Tillet's defence of her husband's succession to the throne, confronting the opponents of the French monarchy's link with the 'foreign' Guises. Her attachment to the Guise family and her desolation at the duke's death at Orléans in 1563 found an echo in her ownership of one of the few vernacular, as distinct from Latin, commemorations of that event. The private quarrel involving her friend Damville, later constable of France, naturally engaged her interest as did the statutes of the French order of St Michael, conferred on Huntly in her girlhood days and latterly on Darnley himself.[29] Besides the acts of her father's parliaments, her English aspirations necessitated the possession of the first acts of the English parliament of the Catholic Mary Tudor.

The legal content of Mary's extant inventories is meagre and hardly does her justice. The year 1566 saw a cluster of distinguished lawmakers (some of them also law-breakers) seeking her attention at court – Thomas Craig with a wedding hymn; Edward Henryson, John Leslie, David Chalmers and James Balfour, all on the royal comission for printing the acts of parliament and Bothwell himself as patron of Chalmers and Balfour and president of the Admiralty Court.[30] In that year too Chalmers addressed to her his manuscript dictionary of Scots law, a volume that must have been hers. However, Moray soon snapped it up for its leather covers are inscribed in gold lettering, 'Erle James of Murray regent to our soveran'.[31] Before attaching himself to Bothwell, Chalmers, a beneficed man, provost of Crichton and chancellor of Ross as successor to his uncle, had been present in Rome for Pope Paul IV's election in 1555, and had probably been an alumnus of Aberdeen before his higher studies at Paris and Louvain. His dedication shows his attachment to the 'municipal' laws; as a senator of the College of Justice he made use of Lethington's 'Practicks'. The Bothwell—Chalmers—Balfour axis horrified the English who saw the trio as men of 'no religion', that is, in the code-language of the time, uncommitted sceptics. Although Balfour, it is said by Knox, then followed Martin's opinion of the sacrament, this means the opinion of his orthodox uncle Martin of St Salvator's College, not of Martin Luther of whom he was a one-time disciple or of Knox even if he 'did rowe in a gallye'.[32] Other legal works were the *Various Lessons* of the Lutheran, Johann Oldendorp, and the treatise on primogeniture of a Bartolist precursor of the 'French method', André Tiraqueau, whose work was dedicated to Henri II. Luther's initial depreciation of law raised questions and Oldendorp aimed at a fresh understanding of the links between theory and practice, and, in the tradition of Melanchthon, employed Aristotelian categories to re-establish natural law and thus foreshadowed dimly the work of Grotius. Tiraqueau was remote from Du Moulin whom he helped to condemn, but Paris custom was important for him too, though he did not wish to shatter the fabric of traditional theory.[33] The work of Henryson, Balfour and Chalmers was more as gatherers of the monuments of law, however, than as scrutinizers of its interpreters, ancient and modern. As a feudalist, Craig was to be more in the Tiraqueau line of succession.

As a queen, Mary's importance would lie in being a patron of poets rather than as a poet herself; she certainly was no Ronsard. Budé, great Greek zealot though he was, fought also for the vernacular, and Claude Millot may have awakened its appreciation in Mary who, as his grateful student, left a pension to his brother.[34] Here is the largest vernacular collection known in Scotland up to her time, though precious little of it in Scots or English. Both in France and Scotland, Brantôme had seen her touched to tears as she read from Ronsard and Du Bellay and also from Maisonfleur, whose history was obscure till the discovery of a manuscript gathering of rhymes in Brantôme's hand last century. Like his friend, Jérome Lhuillier, Maisonfleur was a soldier-poet attached to Guise, and as such he commemorated Mary's farewell to France with an elegy of 330 lines.[35] An aid to her Latin versification was her copy of the 'tables' of Joannes Murmellius, an early humanist propagandist. Brantôme had a high opinion of her verse compositions, but, if the suspect sonnets are excluded, there is little to go on, though she did attempt sonnets in French and Italian. Alexander Scott, the poet-musician, could have visited the court in France and familiarized her with his poems in Scots years before his 'Ane New Yeir Gift to the Queen Mary quhen scho come first Hame 1562', a present not recognizable in the inventory unless as part of a presumed first version of the Bannatyne Manuscript; possibly it was in the unidentified 'Gadderingis of Rymes and Peces'. Scott's masters, the Erskines, were close to Mary, and John Erskine, prior of Inchmahome, presumably read to her as her almoner. 'Alexander Scottis sone' (misread as 'Scothsone') presented English psalms to James in 1575, perhaps those of his father.[36]

Mary's interests reflected the interest still shown by Budé's disciples in philology as a programme for living, highlighted in the interplay between the texts of antiquity and the language of the present. The same conviction also applied to Du Bellay's famous *Defence* of his native French vernacular, that brought about the birth of the poets of the 'Pléiade' movement. Their aim was less to uproot themselves from their French past than to imitate antiquity in order to transform the present, both by exploring new poetic forms (like the sonnet) and by the reappraisal and domestication of all the classics. The current mood of religious reformism encouraged their recovery of neglected classics like Plato and post-classical writers of a strong Platonic colouring like Petrarch. The resultant overspill from philology into the whole cycle of learning helps explain a significant section of Mary's library. The *Epistles*, in French, of Ovid, who still lacked a scholarly French editor, were probably those translated by Octovien de St Gellais. Another admirer of Ovid was Henri II's moralizing court poet, François Habert, and it is likely that it was his Christian pastoral allegory and not the *Pantagruel* of Rabelais that Mary owned.[37] The volume inventoried as 'The triumphe of Pallas' is likely to be his *New Pallas* which celebrates the birth of Henri and is very free with the Pallas of myth whom it Christianizes in orthodox evangelical style. Habert's master was Clément Marot, not yet outdated by the new school of poets; apart from his *Works*, Marot was generously anthologized in the *Recueil de tout soulas*, while there were strong evangelical overtones in Marguerite de Navarre.

Olivier de Magny was certainly among the new men but his courtly sonnets needed music to set them off and another courtier poet owing much to Petrarch was Marc-Claude Buttet. Alongside such minor metrical virtuosi was one whose work is shot through with Platonism, Pontus de Tyard, a newcomer to the Pléiade, in whom we find that ideal Petrarchan mistress beloved of later sonneteers in Scots. However, Mary, as the introducer of the sonnet, at least of the French sonnet, into Scotland, found better models to hand in Du Bellay's own *Olive* in its second augmented edition which had twice as many sonnets as the first.

'The Frenche Sonnatis in Writ' were probably the manuscript offerings of the unfortunate Chastelard, executed after his second expedition to Mary's bedchamber. One of Du Bellay's final little allusive epigrams printed in Aubert's *Elegy* was composed for New Year's Day 1560 punningly rendering 'Stuart' as a combined 'stoa' and 'area', a dual reference to the traditional Scots courage in action and to Mary's patronage of the Muses and the arts of peace.[38] But her favourite was the poet who above all celebrated her delicate air and laughing eyes, Pierre de Ronsard, who hopefully, and dangerously, saw her as queen of the sister lands of England, France and Scotland, dividing her time unequally each year between them, devoting six out of twelve months to France.

At the Scots court Sandilands was one of those who shared Mary's tastes, and who could also be at home in the French court where, on 25 November 1575, there is a precept from Henri III to his grand chamberlain to receive 'milord St Jehan escossois' as gentleman-in-ordinary of his chamber.[39] Sandilands likewise longed to see the sunshine of Italy, sharing Mary's devotion to its civilization, as indeed did Elizabeth who had attempted a version of Petrarch. Though we have no such index as to Mary's competence in the other Romance languages, she can scarcely be faulted for her good taste in Italian books. As to how this competence was acquired we are in the dark since she left no surviving grammar such as the French–Italian one of Darnley.[40] Letter-writing models, however, were available in a famous anthology, while her Italian crib to Ovid's *Metamorphoses* was there to guide the steps of a child learner. Dante she had as well as Boccaccio, but the former was less highly regarded in her century than in ours, while Petrarch remained a central Renaissance interest. One of the themes touched on in his *Triumphs* was the Carthaginian war episode of Sophonisba; as reworked by Giangiorgio Trissino in the first modern tragedy on antique lines it was a theme adopted in her son's time by David Murray, a post-Castalian, in an extended versified piece. One is curious regarding the 'ferses, masking and other prodigalities' of French origin that Knox complained of, the equivalents, it seems, of items not recovered from Sandilands, the unspecified comedies and tragedies in Italian. She owned Bandello's tales, one of them the source of Shakespeare's *Hamlet,* but that was in its French version, though *Il Pecorone,* a source for *Romeo and Juliet,* was the Italian original. She also relied on the French of Matteo Boiardo's *Orlando in Love,* a heroic adventure story of the days of Charlemagne, to which her copy of Ariosto would prove a brilliant and more sophisticated sequel. Less striking was the quota of Spanish books, Spain's golden age of literature being still some distance away. Though it is doubtful if the ownership note is Mary's autograph, it is contemporary, and a Spanish crib to Virgil's *Aeneid* would be useful to tutor and pupil, on a par with her Spanish–Latin dictionary. A major early chivalric romance was the *Amadis de Gaula* cycle, which includes Amadis being presented at the court of Languines, mythical king of Scotland.[41] The work of Jorge de Montemayor influenced English poets like Sir Philip Sidney with elegant pastoral fiction set against an idealized backdrop, while the colourful 'first fruits of Pallas', a seven-play collection of Bartolomé Torres Naharro, treated the chivalric theme of honour with a Renaissance flavour. Mary's German probably, like Elizabeth's, was minimal, though Jan van der Noot disagreed with Sir James Melville about the latter.

In those days history was still a treasure house of ancestral good examples and Budé was not alone in seeing it as the best guide to modern government. In his encounter with Elizabeth in 1564, Sir James Melville drew her attention to Mary's leisure hours when 'sche red upon gud bukis, the historeis of dyuers contrees, and somtyme wald play upon lut and virginelis.'[42] *The lives of illustrious men* in the Italian of Petrarch set the pattern. Universal history was provided for by the *Chronicle of Chronicles,* the *Mer des histoires* and the confused world history of Diodorus Siculus. There was Greek history, if not Thucydides; Roman history without Tacitus but with an antiquarian study of ancient religion by Du Choul;[43] lives of the popes; a Catholic history in response to Sleidan's Protestant compilation; an account of the contemporary battle of Rhodes and another in German of the war of the Swiss Confederation with the Emperor Maximilian; a Spanish compendium, patently Collenuccio's on the kingdom of Naples;[44] a plethora of French history beginning with Froissart; English history, but without Polydore Vergil; and Paradin's chronicle of Savoy of which the queen's copy is now in its stamped binding at Barnbougle.

Among books annexed by Sandilands was also a manuscript Scots chronicle. There is now in Edinburgh a Fordun-Bower *Scotichronicon,* unhappily rebound later, but probably removed from the library at Holyrood before the inventories were made.[45] It was definitely in Scotland earlier in the century, though by 1567 it had fallen into the hands of a certain Mr Robert Fournier, a kinsman, it appears, of Guy Fournier, Mary's comptroller clerk. The manuscript is best explained as a victim of the spoliation of the summer of 1567, as a letter-fragment insert in the binding, addressed 'My Lord' (probably Archbishop James Beaton, then resident in Paris), actually uses that word.[46]

Mary appointed Archibald Crawford, parson of Eaglesham and vicar of Kilmarnock, as her almoner at Joinville in October 1560. Originally a client of the Eglintons, Crawford had succeeded Jean Fournier as grand almoner to Mary of Guise in 1548 and had been able to produce testimonials fron Anet, residence of Diane de Poitiers.[47] His appointment was a significant one, for the almoner's duties were light enough to be combined with reading to his royal employer and some tuition.

How well read was Mary in dialectic and philosophy? John Knox, brought up on the logic of the John Major circle, mocked her with the taunt that she should leave dialectic to her secretary, Maitland.[48] Yet even if Mary had not mastered the art of demonstrative reasoning, it is likely that she had had some schooling in France in the dialectic of Peter Ramus, who had enjoyed the patronage of her uncle, the cardinal of Lorraine. Further conclusions, drawn from the marginalia on her books and ascribed to her almoner, seem generally valid but these were not in fact in Crawford's characteristic angular hand.[49] Like him, Mary owned the *Complete Works* of Plato, though his were in Latin translation and hers the folio Greek as possessed also by Henri and Diane de Poitiers. The folio commentaries Mary used are said to be in Greek also, evidently those of Proclus in the great Basle folio. The whole slant is towards more rhetorical approaches as the prominence accorded to Plato and Cicero makes clear, as does the attention to the *Topics*, while the general Ciceronianism is reflected in the choice of Bembo. Louis Leroy's French versions of the *Symposium* and *Timaeus* dialogues were certainly refreshing initiations into the world of ideas, though philosophy as consolation, an evergreen medieval theme, assured that the work of Boethius, of a slice of which Elizabeth had made a tolerable translation, continued to be a book for all seasons.[50]

The stress on civic virtue is illustrated by the lives of the great and the wise in Plutarch, Xenophon and Diogenes Laertius. The code of gentlemanly conduct could be learnt from the first five books of the *Ethics* of Aristotle as rendered by a gentleman of the household of the third earl of Arran, Philippe le Plessis-Prévost, who reappeared six years later heralding the triumphal entry of Mary and her husband at Chenonceaux.[51] Judah Abrabanel, otherwise Leone Ebreo, a Portuguese Jew who resided in Italy, wrote original Platonic-style dialogues on the intellectual love of God, inspiration of Michelangelo's sonnets. Stoicism was inculcated by Guevara's pseudo-Marcus Aurelius, an emperor whose world-wide rule was won by patient suffering, and indeed the Scots queen's fate would make many demands on her reserves of Stoicism as her treatise on 'Adversity' shows. The circle of Sandilands included Robert Wedderburn, another student of Guevara.[52] More traditional cosmology still circulated in the *Sphere* of Joannes de Sacrobosco, of whom George Buchanan too was an addict. He was indeed 'a stoik philosopher mekle maid accompt of in other contrees', as Melville of Halhill wrote.[53] After dinner each day in the spring of 1562 and under

Buchanan's supervision, the queen read 'somewhat of Lyvie.' One day her Livy lesson included an oration of Cato on the Oppian Law, a piece of Roman sumptuary legislation directed against women's finery. Side-stepping the anti-feminist tone of much of Cato's harangue, Mary astutely settled on a point both she and her tutor could agree on. This was a Latin phrase implying that it was safer to go along with a law already in existence than to try to bypass or repeal it, doubtless a reference (since Randolph thought it an incident worth passing on) to the Reformation laws enacted in Scotland before her arrival.[54]

One thing Mary's tutors would see as their primary responsibility was her training in public speaking. So much schooling was in Latin that the possibility of being addressed in Latin was always there, and Elizabeth replied effectively, if briefly, to the Polish ambassador on one memorable occasion. Yet when in 1562 Mary was subjected to a Latin appeal by the Jesuit papal envoy, de Gouda, she quickly interrupted to point out that, while she could readily follow what he said, she preferred to answer in French or Scots.[55] Dictionaries, grammars and intro-ductory handbooks would have preceded the great Latin and Greek orators in her education. The inventories are so vague that much more detective work needs to be done on the precise editions employed. The rhetorical exercises of Aphthonius, edited by Marsilio Ficino and Pietro Angelio, needed to be supplemented by the French *Garden of Pleasure*, with an art of rhetoric by a certain Jourdain attached to an anthology of works by Villon and others. The Greek *Deipnosophistae* was a useful repertory of information, but Budé's commentaries were at too ac-ademic a level for young scholars and the anonymous French rendering of *The Praise of Folly* more appreciable but still over-subtle. Mary had two editions of Lucian, one the Greek folio which included Philostratus as well. That the Greek orations of Isocrates, in selected passages at least, were considered a sound preparation for effective speech-making is plain from the task that Elizabeth set herself of translating them in part, but the *Dialogues* of Lucian drew frowns in some circles as their cynicism over pagan superstition might fortify permanent questioning and so corrode religious faith. Some volumes could correspond to those owned by Henri and Diane de Poitiers like their four-volume Homer, their Athenaeus, Hesychius and Demosthenes. Some are entered as folios which are clearly not, such as the *Tragedies* of Sophocles. Ronsard's abridgement of prosody arrived too late when schooldays were past; besides generalities about invention, disposition and elocution, it offered expert words on rhyme and metre. The traditional Latin poets were well represented, but neo-Latin works were thin on the ground. Pre-sumably it is the first edition of Buchanan's *Psalms* that she had, dedicated as they were to herself and prefaced by that lyrical masterpiece on the

Caledonian 'nymph' that featured in all subsequent editions. This was
the kind of training which lay behind Mary's 'painted orison', made in
the Edinburgh Tolbooth in 1563, which nauseated Knox but which for
many represented 'the voice of Diana'.[56]

Mary's leisure pursuits are well documented — the royal hunt, heraldry, chess and firework displays, such as that at the baptism of her
son.[57] Yet they are only sparsely represented in her library. The *Cynegetica*
of Pietro Angelio of Barga may have attracted her by its echoes of the
fun of the chase and reminders of that passionate lover of the hunt,
Synesius. But there was also Antonio Massa's attack on the practice of
duelling. Twenty-five prints are listed of the heraldic bearings of herself
and her mother, who, as former duchess of Longueville, was interested
in the varieties of its coats of arms, but Mary's interest did not really
extend to the heraldry of the marquis of Elboeuf as a scribal error might
make us believe, the 'larmes', for the tears of a funeral elegy, having
been carelessly misread as 'les armes'.[58] A Turkish book of painting is
the sole item on painting, while architecture is totally absent, though its
advanced practice is shown on the Italianate doorway to the queen's
lodge at Edinburgh Castle surmounted by her carved initials in monogram with Darnley's. The final inventory at the time of her death listed
two lute-books as well as two lutes. The antiphonary that her almoner
Crawford accepted on 11 January 1562 is not found on a subsequent
inventory of 1567 of gear delivered by him to Moray; much disappeared
in the summer of that year and six mass-books were summarily burnt
by the earl two years later.[59] Thus the three music books still there in
1578 were presumably of secular music. Three royal composers she
undoubtedly knew were Guillaume Belin, Clément Janequin and her
tutor's brother, Nicholas Millot. Four-part arrangements by Belin were
indeed attached to the sacred paraphrases of the Guisard Lancelot de
Carle, while the works of Marot found in the same inventory could
have been Psalms in oblong format, with music for four voices, by
Janequin, perhaps dedicated to Mary in 1559, when he, formerly of the
Guise household, was, like Belin and Millot, a composer to the French
chapel royal. If so, Mary's Holyrood chapel, the furnishings of which
appear drastically simplified, had grown accustomed to hearing plain
settings of Marot psalms rather than sacred echoes of polyphonic *chansons*.[60]

Turning to scientific works, we find an equally thin harvest. The
uncategorizable *Lessons* of Pedro Mexia are placed here for the few
scientific inclusions they have. The others in the library all contributed
modest advances in mathematical instrumentation, cartographical techniques, simplified astronomical tables and general theory. For this school
cosmography was more mathematical than descriptive geography, while

astronomers were still expected to be astrologers too. Knox himself was anxious to credit the two-headed calf that Mary's mother scoffed at, not to mention a strange fire (comet) of 1558 that attacked the harvest of that year.[61] Petrus Apianus, or Bienewitz in German, was official astronomer to the emperor Charles V. Claude de la Boissière's *Principles* rendered the views of Renier Gemma Frisius. Johann Stoeffler constructed an improved astrolabe (as used for navigation before the invention of the sextant) and published regular tables. The breakthrough in astronomy had not yet come, so Ptolemy was still the basis. The medieval *Sphere* treatise, on which Alessandro Piccolomini leaned heavily, was still standard teaching. The work of Jean Pierre de Mesmes was basically the same with importations from Melanchthon's *Physics*. However, Mesmes was appreciative of Copernicus as a 'second Ptolemy', though dismissing his heliocentric theory out of hand. He was also attached to the verse of Buchanan which he collected in manuscript.[62] Ramusio, for his part, went out of his way to correct Ptolemy regarding Africa and south Asia. The strange *Hodoeporicon* of the half-Dutch, half-Italian Ugo Favoli, was a relation in hexameter verse in three books, not four as the inventory has it, of a journey of 1545 to Constantinople, and, while Marco Polo's was an old tale, that told by Gonzalo Fernandez was not, for it was a pioneer natural history of the West Indies in the New World. James Bassantyne was a Scot who inhabited Lyons for a time, so that his *Astronomical Discourse* is a fine piece of Lyonnese book production of which Mary had a splendidly bound copy.[63] 'Hippocrites in Frenche' sounds rather splendid, but was probably the brief *Prognostics* or 'presages', first rendered into English in 1597 by the Glasgow surgeon, Peter Lowe. The *Rule of Health* appeared with that title at the press of Jean Saugrain in Lyons, a popular work of which there were English editions, by the physician to the French kings.[64] The gardens of Holyrood may have benefited from the medicinal herbs in Dietrich Dorsten's picture-book as much as from the distant model of Diane's gardens at Anet.

Religious literature weighed down the library shelves. Apart from the Isaiah edited by Sebastian Munster, a Creek-Hebrew commentary consorting ill with the bulk of her books and apparently reflecting an aspiration of her tutor and almoner more than her own (for Crawford owned two Hebrew volumes), there are five categories: old-fashioned left-overs from a traditional upbringing; biblical works; Greek and Latin Fathers; Reformers; and Counter-Reformers. Here more than elsewhere one is conscious of gaps in the survivals: no Latin or vernacular bibles and only two Latin Fathers with two Greek, sets seemingly broken up, though the Augustine includes the key Reformation issue of nature and grace. Her religious training, and this may have been its strength, reflected her girlhood's sheltered world broken only by the learned teasing of Erasmus's *Colloquies*. There was a simple spiritual regime of Latin masses and psalm-centred prayerbooks, with familiar standbys like the *Life of Christ* of Ludolph of Saxony, and in the saints' lives a continuing sense of supernatural kinship with the company of heaven such as her almoner, Crawford, would show in his final will.[65] Eyebrows might be raised at Amerval's sensationally named *Book of Devilry*, but this is no more than verse dialogues of self-justification by Satan to Lucifer, his master, bragging of conquests among all classes of humankind, clerical and lay.

Not a single bible is listed, but Mary could have used a plagiarized and Catholicized Genevan one, such as her confessor, René Benoist, later published in Paris. Biblical guides included the Lutheran Andreas Osiander's harmonized gospels, a splendid piece of book-making, curiously popular with the presses in Paris, as well as *Figures of the bible,* her copy of which seems to have been retained by the laird of Lochleven.[66] Other items personally annexed by the earl of Moray were an English catechism, unidentified psalm commentaries, the psalm themselves interspersed with prayers and a prayerbook, all in Latin. It is worth recalling that her mother's almoner, Jean Fournier, when given two pamphlets by Nicolas de Bris, reader to the cardinal of Lorraine as presents for the queen regent, was also promised another book still in the making, which would be an onslaught on the very notion of a bible or even prayers in the common tongue.[67]

Mary's almoner in France, John Erskine, prior of Inchmahome, soon joined the Reformation party, although members of his family were still suspect papists.[68] His replacement, Archibald Crawford, was an Erasmian enthusiast to whom the pro-dialogue policies of the publicists, George Cassander and François Baudouin, influential proponents of the Colloquy of Poissy, must have appealed: and the visits to Scotland of such supporters of dialogue as the French bishops, Jean de Montluc and Paul de Foix, along with that friend and editor of Buchanan, Charles Utenhove, associate of Ronsard, would fortify Mary's expectations. Prominent exponents of opposition views like Beza and Peter Martyr were also given a platform. Randolph, the English ambassador, lost no time in presenting Mary with a copy run off the native presses of Beza's oration, but it is absent from both inventories, though the reply of her uncle, the cardinal of Lorraine, features in the castle list. Beza's *Confession of Faith*, Italian version, has Mary's late bookstamp and was the gift of Melville of Halhill, acquired abroad, possibly during a visit in 1563 to Venice and Rome; this work too is uninventoried.[69]

The Reformers' works range from Luther onwards, though they are not especially representative. For instance, the only Calvin is his defence against Servetus of the Trinitarian doctrine common to all Christians, and of Martin Bucer only the letters in the Catholic tract of Matthieu de La Lande, Guisard preacher in Metz. There is nothing here so redolent of Zwingli as the Oecolampadius volume, one of three signed in the crabbed Gothic hand of Knox.[70] Of Counter-Reformation literature the selection covers a wide variety of contested points of doctrine, though not all are works of substance. Friedrich Staphylus as a recruit from Lutheranism was a capable battler for orthodoxy, yet his work looks like a present from another such recruit, James Balfour, who owned a Staphylus work himself. Cardinal Stanislas Hosius had a European reputation, and his work on the 'express word of God' was translated by Carle who had close links with Guise.[71] Mary, of course, knew Ronsard, whose *Discourse* in its two parts carried enormous weight internationally, though less for the quality of its theological debate than for his poetic renown.

By this time, after Poissy and Trent, argument was hardening into ideology: Mary's uncle was now the 'tiger cardinal' and Trent a council of blood. Mary's two copies of the printed canons of Trent were the gift of Pope Pius IV himself, in 1564.[7] 'An certane Freir' translated the letter of her French confessor, René Benoist, to John Knox and this is presumably identical with the otherwise unidentifiable item by 'Regier Brontanis' in the castle list. She had some friars about the court, John Black, Andrew Abercrombie and John Roger, all of them represented in *Early Scottish Libraries*, the last owning a work with the name of Andrew Duncan on it, 'servant of the queen'.[73]

Unlike Johann Eck and Gabriel Dupuyherbault, whose tracts on papal primacy and penance figure in the lists, her confessor, Benoist, was not scholastic but Platonist in outlook having edited Marsilio Ficino. Like Ninian Winzet he brought no heavy artillery to bear on the debate, but was a sharpshooter, an untidy but not unlearned pamphleteer. The stream of Catholic verbal sallies in manuscript and print emanating from the queen's household was sufficiently disturbing for the printing press to be seized and Benoist and Winzet encouraged to leave Scotland.[71] Benoist had also had some impact as a preacher; Randolph condemned a 'foolish sermon' in defence of the mass and saints which, according to Argyll and Lord James, caused broken heads and bloody ears amongst the chaplains at Holyrood.[75]

There were at least half a dozen pamphlets of Benoist in the castle list, and Benoist, as both confessor and controversialist, helped to confirm the queen's stand on disputed doctrines. 'The Maner to tak

away the Contrauersie of Religioun be Renatus Benedictus' is not quite
the title as 'translatit in Scottishe be Ninian Winzet' and published in
Paris in 1565. Benoist's Latin original was ready in December 1561, and
it is possible that John Scott printed in Edinburgh a friar's Scots version
soon afterwards; after all even the Winzet Paris book survives in one
lone copy. Here, echoing Erasmus, Benoist, as he turns on the savage
beast of religious discord, claims that Christians are called 'nocht
disputers be reason of thair disputing: bot faithful be reason of thair
faith and beleuing'. He ends with a call to public repentance, a striking
foretaste of the challenge taken up in the sensational public penances of
Henri III. His *Triumph of the Faith* is said likewise to be an Edinburgh
production, completed on the eve of his departure in August 1562.[76]

The pamphlet debate that can now be associated with Mary's household reflected both her own position in Scotland and changing circumstances in France. The Holyrood masses in that 'idolatrie chappell'
offended the Protestant kirk session of Edinburgh's Canongate even
more than the immoral conduct of palace servants or the scandal of a
priest, John Scott, who had the queen's letters of protection.[77] Although
Randolph complained that the queen's 'poore soule' was so troubled for
the preservation of her 'syllye mass' that she did not know where to
turn for its defence, such a defence did emerge in 1564, explicitly
dedicated to her. It took the shape of French version of an alleged
treatise of Proclus, fifth-century patriarch of Constantinople, which
with modern hindsight we know to be a late forgery, but which
Benoist accepted as genuine under the title *The Evangelical Sacrifice*.[78]
The debate was also affected by the profound change that had come
over French Catholic opinion after the second attempt and failure, at
the Colloquy of St Germain-en-Laye in January 1562, of a conciliation
policy. By now the prospect of a 'Third Church', neither Catholic nor
Calvinist, had small appeal to either party. The new Catholic opinion,
scandalized by the furious storm of Huguenot iconoclasm after this
second colloquy, was accurately reflected in 'The four Homoleis' in the
castle list; these must surely be Benoist's own three, together with those
of John Damascene and Theodore the Studite in defence of the Catholic
position on images. Benoist's letter to Calvin also reflected this live
issue, one soon to affect Holyrood's own church and private oratory
when their altarpieces were smashed in 1567.[79] In that year an augmented
edition of the *Enchiridion Precationum* of Simon Verepaeus appeared,
which was rendered in French by Benoist in 1568, and appears to be
the 'Supplement of Devotion' in Mary's list.[80] Circumstances in France
had more impact on Mary's position in Scotland than her apparent
neutrality in its domestic policies would indicate.

Mary's educated awareness of present events and their historical background is also illuminated by the large slice of French history in her reading programme.[81] Besides Jean Lemaire des Belges, Paolo Emilio and Guillaume Paradin, Lorraine history is touched on by Charles Estienne, while the prevalent idea that the dukes there had imperial origins as descendants of Charlemagne gave the Elie Vinet life of that legendary hero instant relevance. Mary thus was thinking of more than France's current ruler, Charles IX, when she had her son christened as Charles James. Guillaume des Autels was a Guise apologist defending their non-foreign status as Lorrainers in France, his harangue like Ronsard's holding up the glass to the civil disorder after the death of Henri II, when the Calvinists had become more numerous, public and demanding.[82] Estienne Pasquier's call to the princes of the blood and the nobles also opened up the perils of a disunited France. Mary was as conversant with pan-Catholic politics in the 1560s as in exile, during the 1570s and 1580s. She knew of the emperor's insistence that the reconvened Council of Trent should not overlook German demands for clerical marriage and lay communion under both kinds. She was also aware of the objections of the estates of Burgundy to the royal edict of pacification of 1562 allowing Calvinists free exercise of their religion.

Light-hearted entertainment was available in illustrated books attractive to Mary's strong visual sense. In 1569 she was visited by an Englishman, Nicholas White, who related how the queen broke the tedium of a winter's day embroidering with threads of many colours. As White went on to evaluate with her the relative merits of carving, painting and needlework, her instant verdict was to give first place to painting. In her prison, however, she was compelled to settle for engraved prints, though she taught Elizabeth Hardwick, countess of Shrewsbury, to work into her embroideries devices especially from the animal world including the 'byrd from America', the toucan. Her models were from Claude Paradin's *Heroic Devices*, and works by Pierre Belon, Conrad Gesner and Gabriele Faerno. The date of all these publications was early enough to have been forwarded from Scotland along with her apparel.[83] That she already felt drawn to picture-books is clear from her ownership of Guillaume Rouillé's *Promptuarium*, the second part of which featured herself, and the work of the author-engraver, Enea Vico, picturing Caesars and empresses taken from gold and silver Roman coins. A particular favourite would be an engraver from Lorraine, P. Woeriot, employed for the tableau ('pinax') of ancient grave-scenes originating with Lilio Gregorio Giraldi. This obsession with colour and materials soft to handle has not aided historians of her library looking for ownership indications on book covers once they were, like Elizabeth's, embroidered in silk and velvet whose durability does not compare with leather. A missal cover claiming to be the work of the queen herself was, however, on view at the Peterborough exhibition. Even leather covers have been needlessly replaced, though a note of Marian ownership might be entered in a later hand, as may be true of the Dublin Trinity College Sallust.[84] But so-called 'traditions' have to be guarded against where palpable forgeries have been so common, even extending to signatures and marginalia. Fresh study is needed of Mary's gold-tooled leather bindings, not all of which need be assigned to French binderies. A particularly thorny problem concerns books tooled with François-Mary monograms where a Greek 'phi' represents the first element, a type associated both with the Benedictine convent in Rheims and the Scots College in Paris, but a bookstamp used long after Mary's death. This is too large a problem to settle in a small space: an interim personal conclusion would be that it was first adopted by the queen's scholars (as distinct from others who also sought her support, but who had existed for centuries maintained by revenues from a farm called Grisy), and continued after their absorption in the Paris college of 1603 in order to sustain a claim of patronage by the French crown.[85]

Though for all practical purposes the books inventoried after the queen's departure for England are all that we know of her library apart from some uninventoried survivals, it is beyond doubt that she continued to build up a collection in custody, even if her gaolers thought her books trash and made no precise inventories. Sir Amyas Paulet particularly resented Catholic prayerbooks. In 1585 he himself confessed that she had so much apparel and so many books that four carts would be essential for their removal. A final list recorded merely 'a greate number of bookes', though they included 'large history books containing engravings, and others'.[86] From the English histories, she declared, she had learnt that 'this realm was used to blood.' Soon after her capture, her keeper brought her a volume on the 'art of magic', taunting her with the news that the author was a prominent Catholic; but the revelation, duly transmitted to Beaton in Paris, left her unmoved in her Catholic conviction. It could be that Benoist's treatise on the reprehensibility of magic has some connection with this incident.[87] Gifts from abroad were liable to interception by officials, as happened when a gift to Maitland by Nicholas Sanders was confiscated in London. A certain George Fitzwilliam, who had been granted access to Mary in June 1571, brought away her letters to Philip II of Spain as well as a 'book of gold' for the duchess of Feria, and an old Latin service book on which Mary had written, 'Absit nobis gloriari nisi in cruce Domini nostri Jesu Christi'. In January 1573, Shrewsbury wrote about a little black-velvet covered book enclosed in a box casing and sent from the duchess of Guise, perhaps the matins books with gold clasps in the list of 1586, yet pointing out how annoyed she was to find Randolph selected to convey it.[88]

The view that no books could have been specially bound for her in her prison days cannot be upheld, as John Leslie's autograph manuscript of 1573 is precisely such a book. Tooled with her initials and crown on its covers, it is a work of Christian Stoicism on how to retain peace of mind in adversity. After Ninian Winzet was discovered secretly acting as her confessor and forced to free in 1571, she felt acutely the need for a priest, noting bitterly than when she asked for one, the only consolation she got from Elizabeth was a defamatory book by the 'atheist, Buchanan'. She complained that both her Latin and her devotion were going rusty, but grieved even more for her non–Latin speaking domestic servants.[89] Consequently when in 1574 she acknowledged the acquisition of a Book of Hours of the Pius V revision, the Tridentine edict banning the vernacular prompted her to ask if the ban applied solely to public prayer, and whether she might follow up the Latin Hours with private devotions taken from a French manual. Meantime she was restricted to reading the sermons of François le Picart, a zealous if old-fashioned preacher, scorned by Calvinists though tremendously popular with the Parisians. The provision of new books was apparently regular enough up to November 1577 when increased surveillance provoked the suggestion that Beaton might use them for communications he wished to keep secret by employing alum and gall–nut to write invisibly betwen the lines.[90]

Cornered in her hopeless situation, Mary was increasingly at the mercy of exiles and others exploiting her for political ends. Two such correspondents were the French Jesuits, Emond Auger and Henri Samier, of whom the Scots members of the order, Edmund Hay and William Crichton in particular, were highly critical. However, her correspondence with Auger, which may go back to 1574, reads harmlessly enough, though she may have heard echoes of the conflict over Auger's use of new-fangled devotions, which involved Benoist, now 'pope of the market-place' in the greatly frequented Paris church of St Eustache. There is an undated letter, assigned to 1578, requesting a book by Auger whose receipt through Beaton she anxiously awaited, at the same time adding that he should compile another, an order of service for household use on solemn feasts and times of special need. She also asked that Auger approach her Paris scholars at the college of Clermont there requesting prayers for their royal benefactor.[91] Her old ally, David Chalmers, who enjoyed a pension on her dowry as her Master of Requests, in 1579 printed a defence of her cause in Paris; as her regular correspondent, he must have forwarded it on. Whether out of prudence or timidity, her Scots almoner, Crawford, had kept his distance since Langside, even though he was summoned after it for mass-saying.[92] Mary Seton, one of her maids-in-waiting, left to become a nun at Rheims and in 1583 sent a book from there through M. de Courcelles of the French embassy in London, a prayerbook that later aroused the suspicions of Paulet, who also found his suspicions confirmed that Mary's new 'reader', Camille du Préau, was really her priest-almoner.[93] Samier had not tarried long with her, though his foreign news service, in competition with Cecil's, kept her in touch under various aliases like Jacques La Rue and Girolamo Martinelli. More dangerous still, as the mood of English Catholics swung from compromise to resistance, was the huge delight with which Mary accepted from Cardinal Allen his treatise of 1584 with its onslaught on British injustice.[94] It was under Allen that at last a Catholic English version of the New Testament was issued at Rheims in 1582, a copy of which the queen evidently acquired.[95] Among religious books Sharman failed to identify 'The Institution of Lentren', but once her devotion to Benoist is established, it clearly emerges as his 1564 pamphlet on the dominical institution of the Lenten fast.[96]

A further difficulty with the inventories is that titles were written down to dictation, and hence Michael Ritius becomes Regius and Heliodorus was heard as Diodorus. It is modern transcription that renders an answer *to* Ronsard as an answer *of* Ronsard. Ronsard questioned the authenticity of the Casket Letters and Mary read him avidly even in captivity, rewarding him handsomely in 1583 with a vase inscribed to to him as 'Apollo of the Muses' well'. Thus, even in her last years of captivity, Mary read other than religious literature.[97] In 1570 when Leslie was compiling as volume of songs and ballads, the author of 'The Nobility of Women', William Barker, supplied one for which mary wrote from Chatsworth to thank him.[98]

The library assembled during her personal reign can now be seen to hold about 300 volumes. It confirms a high view of her native intelligence and width of interest, comparable only in Scotland with Bishop Henry Sinclair's.[99] Her love of 'the arts of Pallas' was celebrated by Michel de l'Hospital before his initial regard turned to alienation. Even after Langside, the Englishman, Sir Francis Knollys, could maintain that 'this ladie and prynces is a notable woman.'[100] As absence from the centre of power lengthened, infidelity grew; this was reflected in some of her circle of *literati* and apologists. In 1571, John Gordon had written a manuscript defence of the queen, which had disturbed Cecil and earned him a pension from Mary's revenues; he somehow also acquired the estate of Longorme in the duchy of Estampes. Yet his conversion to Catholicism, on his wife's own testimony, proved a politic pretence and his *Manes* of 1587 reverted to what had hardened as the official English version of Mary's life.[101] Such conversions in a time of flux were not uncommon, and it has been argued that temporary shifts of religious opinion even affected Mary herself. The refusal of Huntly and Bothwell to attend Mary's mass in 'this triumphal time' of honeymoon with Darnley was something Randolph found astonishing, convinced as he was that Bothwell was 'of no religion'. The ebb and flow of religious questioning even touched this man, often pictured as a pirate king or Epicurean, as well as his legal circle. One who had handled pleas in Bothwell's courts was Edward Henryson, who dedicated his French version of Plutarch's onslaught on the contraditions of Stoicism to Mary and Darnley, while his associate, Balfour, had turned his back on an earlier Lutheranism.[102] Another in this circle was David Chalmers, who as yet could not bring himself to query the sacrifice of the mass or accept justification. His career after 1568 continued as chequered as before: after spells as a Marian pamphleter in Paris and as a spy for Walsingham, he returned from France to Scotland, acquired a family and re-acquired his lost benefices.[103]

Mary found Sir Amyas Paulet no sympathetic keeper, but, when Elizabeth enquired why he had not found a way to shorten her life, Paulet was appalled at being required to do an act that conscience forbade. Thus he was relieved at ridding himself of her gear to her French servants; hence there is no need for surprise if they turn up in Avignon or Niort.[104] Of the collection held in Scotland most went to James VI, laying an early basis for the literary revival of his 'Castalian band'. Yet by then the easy companionship of chivalric and Renaissance ideals, Giron le Courtois as well as the Pléiade, no longer held. In the 1560s the movement was still young and vibrant, containing its tensions, humanism still in its triumphant time and not yet a tired orthodoxy. For Alexander Scott as for Bannatyne, the great collator of Scotland's late medieval poetry, their predecessors were not yet archaic. Mary had also courtiers like Sandilands who enjoyed Mediterranean culture as much as she, and some such volumes may have been presentation copies such as the traditional 'estrennes' or Ne'erday gifts. The Latin *Strena* of James Foulis for James V was one such offering and it is likely that Scott presented not just the verses we know of but a whole bookful of them. How she shelved them all is far from clear, but seemingly in her personal quarters. Remnants of earlier monarchs may also have been lodged in the library room which Patrick, son of Peter Young, revisited in 1628. Since none fell into the hands of interested descendants like the cardinal of York, it can be assumed that catastrophe overtook the bulk of them when part of Holyrood's west quarter suffered a fire while Cromwell's troops were in occupation in 1658.[105]

Notes

Main Bibliography: Julian Sharman, *The Library of Mary, Queen of Scots* (1889), prints the inventories with identification of authors and editions, useful, but needs correction; additional books in G.F. Warner, 'The library of James VI' (*SHS Misc.* (1893), i, xxxi−lxxv).

[1] BL, Add. MS 34275; see fos 10−14.

[2] Sharman reprints the only two surviving ones, of 1569 and 1578, from T. Thomson, *A collection of Inventories and the Records of the Royal Wardrobe* (1815) and J. Robertson (ed.), *Inventaires de la royne Descosse, douairière de France* (1883).

[3] *TA*, xii, 216; *CSP Scot.*, iv, 173. Garroust was also 'commess' of Servais, Thomson, *Inventories*, 187.

[4] *TA*, xii, 347.

[5] Young left fos 10−14 for Mary's books, but they are interspersed with some items from the king's own index, as fos 1−2, 19−20, were taken up with personal notes, and fos 4−9 by items culled from European publishers by Andrew Melville or from catalogues of Young's uncle, Henry Scrimgeour, who had recently died in Geneva (BL, Add. MS 34275, see fo 6v). Young placed a cross against items suited for classroom use.

[6] W. S. Mitchell, *A History of Scottish Bookbinding* (1955), 69; Warner, 'Library of James VI', xxxi.

[7] M. Wood, 'The domestic affairs of the burgh', *Book of the Old Edinburgh Club,* xv (1928), 20; C. Davenport, *Cameo Book-Stamps* (1911), 168−9; G. D. Hobson, 'Parisian binding 1500−1525', *The Library,* 4th ser., xi (1931), 416. He is not to be confused with two contemporaries, both sieurs de Moulins, both Scots, one Thomas Straton, the other John Heriot.

[8] Robertson, *Inventaires,* 153; *Protocol Books of Dominus Thomas Johnsoun 1528−78* (SRS, 1920), no. 839; Wright, *Elizabeth,* i, 204.

[9] Thomson, *Inventories,* 187, 190. Mary's letter is dated 7 Oct. 1567: SRO, Torphichen Writs, GD 119/46.

[10] Warner, 'Library of James VI', xxxi−xxxiii, xliv, lvii; I. B. Cowan, P. H. R. Mackay, A. Macquarrie (eds), *The Knights of St John of Jerusalem in Scotland* (SHS, 1983), lii−liv; *CSPF 1561−2,* 293, 302; SRO, Edinburgh Commissariot Records, xvi, unfoliated (dated 25 Feb. 1587), CC8/2/16: G. W. T. Omond, *The Arniston Memoirs* (1887), 1−2; his son, Walter, owned *Lettere volgari di diverse nobilissimi huomini* (Venice, 1544), a copy unfortunately rebound, which had belonged to the queen's banker, Timotheo Cagnioli. Other owners were Jean Piat of Lyons and Alexander Dundas.

[11] Robertson, *Inventaires,* 179; Warner, 'Library of James VI', xxxiii, xxxvii, xlix, li.

[12] NLS, Adv. MS 15.1.19, Sir J. Balfour's Papal Deeds, no. 26, shows that Pope Paul III appointed him on 7 Cal. Oct. 1539; R. K. Hannay (ed.), *Acts of the Lords of the Council in Public Affairs* (1932), 576; Knox, *History*, ii, 86.

[13] The following were returned by the Regent Morton on behalf of Sandilands: Bassantyne, Heliodorus in French; by Sandilands himself, Charles Estienne on Lorraine and Flanders, and by his wife, *Le parangon de vertu*. Wood was killed in Apr. 1570.

[14] Robertson, *Inventaires*, 124; Warner, 'Library of James VI', xxxvii—xlix (Wood), xliii—xliv, l (Caithness), li (where Wood's brother's name is cancelled); D. W. Doughty, 'The library of James Stewart, earl of Moray, 1531—1570', *IR*, xxi (1970), 17—29.

[15] Robertson, *Inventaires*, cxlviii—cxlix; *CSP Scot.*, iv, 616. Mary's almoner, Crawford, surrendered chapel gear to Moray in Nov. 1567.

[16] See Sharman, *The Library of Mary*, who confuses the reader by placing the 1578 inventory entries before those of 1569.

[17] G. F. Barwick, *A Book bound for Mary, Queen of Scots* (1901); *Letters of James IV*, ed. R. K. Hannay (SHS, 1953), nos. 153—4.

[18] H. M. Nixon, *Sixteenth-century Gold-tooled bindings in the Pierpont Morgan Library* (1971), 23 (Bellenden), 252 (Mary); there is a MS of Bellenden also (M527), but this has been rebound. Re Fort Augustus MS A2, M. Dilworth, 'A book of hours of Mary of Guise', *IR*, xix (1968), 77—81; N. R. Ker, *Medieval Manuscripts in British Libraries* (1977), ii, 850—1.

[19] *Foreign Correspondence with Marie de Lorraine*, ed. M. Wood (SHS, 1925), ii, 188.

[20] NLS, Adv. MS 29.2.4, fo. 67; A. de Ruble, *La première jeunesse de Marie Stuart* (Paris, 1891), 281; *Foreign Correspondence*, ii, lv, 253.

[21] R. E. Halliwell, 'Prince humaniste ou prince chévaleresque: a French Renaissance debate', *Kentucky Romance Quarterly*, xxi, suppl. 2 (1974), 173—83; G. H. Bushnell, 'Diane de Poitiers and her books', *The Library*, ser. 4, vii (1926—7), 283—302; J. Porcher, 'Les livres de Diane de Poitiers', *Les trésors des bibliothèques de France*, ed. R. Cantinelli and E. Dacier, vii (1926), fasc. xxvi.

[22] See, on these manuscript 'themes', Paris, BN, MS Lat. 8660; A. de Montaiglon, *Latin Themes of Mary Stuart* (Warton Club, 1855) and Mrs P. Stewart Mackenzie, *Queen Mary's Book* (1907). Foquelin, or Fouqelin, influenced the standard Ramist textbooks of rhetoric.

[23] J. Durkan, 'The royal lectureships under Mary of Lorraine', *SHR*, lxii (1983), 73—8.

[24] C. Bontems et al., *Le prince dans la France des XVIe et XVIIe siècles* (1965); D. Bigalli, *Immagini del principe* (1985); also for Guevara, A. Redondo, *Antonio de Guevara et l'Espagne de son temps* (1976).

[25] *CSPF, 1561—2*, 392; Knox, *History*, ii, 14.

[26] H. M. Nixon, 'Binding forgeries', *Sixth International Congress of Bibliophiles 1969* (1971), 69—84.

[27] G. F. Barwick, 'A sidelight on the mystery of Mary Stuart; Pietro Bizari's contemporary account of the murder of Riccio and Darnley', *SHR*, xxi (1924), 115—127; Pietro Bizzari, *Varia Opuscula* (Venice, 1565), including: 'De bello et

pace' (Item 2); 'Pro L. Virginio' (Item 5); 'Poemata varia', fos 93 (Moray), 109v (Andrew Melville). See also Lynch, ch. 1 above, for strictly contemporary opinion of Mary during her personal reign.

[28] *Work of James VI* (1616), preface; R. H. MacDonald, ed., *The Library of Drummond of Hawthornden* (1971), 226.

[29] Se Lynch, ch. 1 above, for the significance of Darnley's investiture in Feb. 1566; also Goodare, ch. 7 below, for its circumstances, coinciding with Mary's invitation to some nobles to return to the mass.

[30] *APS*, i, 29. The printed acts of the Admiralty Court do not cover beyond 1561, but both Chalmers and Balfour were clearly associates of the High Admiral, Balfour, according to a lost treatise of David Kintore, Bothwell's deputy; see *Acta Curiae Admirallatus Scotiae 1557–1561* (Stair Soc., 1937). See Lynch, ch. 1 above, and Goodare, ch. 7 below, for the legal circle and the printing of the acts in 1566.

[31] BL, Add. MS 27472, Dictionary of Scots Law.

[32] *CSP Scot.*, ii, 211, 218; *HMC Salisbury*, ii, 46; Knox *History*, i, 93, also 219, 'brought up in Martines' opinioun', i.e. Martin Balfour's, the latter being Catholic provost of St Salvator's College, SRO, Bell Brander Writs, no. 37. See Lynch, ch. 1 above, for the Catholic sympathies of Balfour and Chalmers.

[33] An edict of 1546 in the Paris *parlement* inaugurated the debate about 'noble status' which Tiraqueau took up, M. Greengrass, *France in the Age of Henri IV* (1984), 167. The view that humanist law was a symptom of a transition from theological commitment to independent secular learning may not be wholly valid, but some such climate of opinion may explain the outwardly anarchic conduct of lawyers like Balfour and Chalmers.

[34] Teulet, *Relations,* ii, 278. Nicolas Millot was a composer whose music the queen must have known at first hand.

[35] BN, MS n.a. fr. 11688. See *CSPF 1572–4*, 307–8; J. Lavaud, *Un poète de cour au temps des derniers Valois: Philippe Desportes* (1936), 123–6, for his subsequent career after he converted to Calvinism.

[36] On Scott, see J. MacQueen (ed.), *Ballattis of Luve* (1970), xxxv–lxvii, and for career of John, prior of Inchmahome, W. Fraser, *The Red Book of Menteith* (1880), i, 528, but Ruble, *Jeunesse*, gives no Christian name or precise date, except between Jan. 1549 and Dec. 1553 (John followed Robert as prior in 1547/8). An 'Alexandre Schot', son of the poet, is Mary's attendant in 1573, and died, before his father, in 1581 (A. Lang, 'The household of Mary, Queen of Scots', *SHR,* ii (1905), 355; *CSP Scot.*, v, 227, 248, 304; vi, 101.) For other, French 'gatherings' of poetry, see Sharman, *Library of Mary*, 97, 113.

[37] Cf. Warner, 'Library of James VI', lxiii, *Les songes de Pantagruel*.

[38] M. Smith, *Joachim du Bellay's Veiled Victim* (1974), 97; this also prints the elegy on the poet.

[39] M. C. Smith, 'Ronsard and Queen Elizabeth I', *BHR*, xxix (1967), 93–119; SRO, Torphichen Writs, GD 119/54.

[40] *ESL*, 185.

[41] *Los Doze Libros de la Eneida de Vergilio* (Antwerp, 1557), in GUL (unfortunately, rebound). This inscription is now believed to be certainly the young Mary's.

[42] S. Cowan, *The Last Days of Mary Stuart* (1907), ii, 307–12 gives specimens of her Italian and Spanish mottoes; Melville, *Memoirs*, 124–5.

[43] Not in the inventories: Guillaume du Choul, *Discours de la religion des anciens Romains* (Lyons, 1556) in Lucius Wilmerding sale, part II at Parke-Bernet, 5–6 Mar. 1951, lot 221 (black morocco, eight gold-tooled M's with crowns on both covers, nine on spine).

[44] This cannot be the *Compendio* of Estevan de Garibay (Sharman, *Library of Mary*, 56) as that did not appear till 1571 when Mary was out of Scotland.

[45] In Edinburgh, Scottish Catholic Archives; Ker, *Medieval Manuscripts*, ii, 522–4.

[46] The letter was from James Curle, b. 1517, witness to the marriage of James V in Paris, in France until appointed custumar of Edinburgh in 1560; after 1567 he returned to Paris, with Beaton in the college of St Jean Lateran. He is sometimes confused with his son, James. Another son, Gilbert, was Mary's secretary in captivity; a daughter, Janet, was wife to her Italian banker, Cagnioli and another, Elizabeth, attended the queen in her final days. *RPC*, i, 547, 555, 559; *CSP Rome*, ii, 218–19; *RSS*, v, 807, 1928; *CSP Scot.*, ii, 514; v, 74; Fraser, *Mary*, 550.

[47] B. 1512 (SRO, Barony Papers, RH11/32/1/1); d. 1593, according to tomb excavated on site of Glasgow collegiate church of which he was provost (*Glasgow Courier*, Feb. 1794). Held office in Glasgow University before studying in Paris; carried corpse of queen regent back to France in 1560; D. Baird Smith, 'Archibald Craufurd, lord of Session', *Juridical Rev.*, xlv (1933), 166–78; *Diurnal*, 64; J. Paterson, *History of the Country of Ayr* (1852), ii, 196. For his books, see *ESL*, 84–5; also n. 65 below.

[48] Knox, *History*, ii, 96.

[49] The Crawford Plato has been rebound, so Smith's conclusions based on binding are nullified and the underlinings of the *Republic* cannot safely be assigned to him; the former Baird Smith Erasmus has the original Crawford binding, however, and is now in EUL.

[50] A proper account of Elizabeth's books awaits the publication of T. A. Birrell's Panizzi lectures. C. Pemberton, (ed.), *Queen Elizabeth's Englishings of Boethius, Plutarch. Horace* (Early Eng. Text Soc., 1899), foreword; L. Bradner (ed.), *The Poems of Queen Elizabeth* (1964).

[51] Cf. Warner, 'Library of James VI', xlix; *Les Ethiques d'Aristote a son fils Nicomache: nouvellement traduittes de grec en francois, par P(hilippe) L(e Plessis) gentilhomme de la maison de Monsieur le conte d'Aran* (Paris, 1553); Philippe le Plessis-Prevost, *Les triomphes faicts a l'entrée du roy a Chenonceau* (Tours, 1559). With Book vi, the more theoretical and 'contemplative' section begins, the first books concentrating on the Renaissance ideal of 'civic virtue'.

[52] R. Wedderburn, *The Complaynt of Scotland*, ed. A. M. Stewart (STS, 1979), xiv, xviii, xxvii.

[53] Melville, *Memoirs*, 262. Sotheby's sale, 8–11 Apr. 1919, lot 170 is the Lyonnese type calf-bound copy of 'Bassantin', with Mary's crowned 'M's.

[54] *CSP Scot.*, i, 615; Livy, *Ab Urbe Condita*, Book xxxiv, 4.

[55] *Papal Negs.*, 132.

[56] Knox, *History*, ii, 77–8.

[57] J. Vincent, *La pyrotechnie ou l'art de feu* (Paris, 1556). See W. Barclay, *De regno et regali potestate adversus Buchananum* (Paris, 1600), 81, for a description of a highland hunt.

[58] R. Belleau, *Larmes sur le trespas de marquis et marguise d'Elbeuf, Ensemble le tombeau (du) duc de Guise* (Paris, 1566).

[59] NLS, MS 6135, fo. 34; Robertson, *Inventaires*, cxli, cxlix.

[60] F. Lesure, *Musique et musiciens francais de XVIᵉ siècle* (1976), 185−6, assigns Janequin's death to 1558, the date of his Catholic-style will, and G. Turbow, 'Mary, queen of Scots, patroness of the arts of France,' *Scotia*, iii (1979), 18−33. But the lines signed by Janequin in the 1559 edition of *Octante-deux Pseaumes par Marot et autres,* addressed to 'the queen of France' suggest he was still alive then, cf. F. Lesure and G. Thibault, *Bibliographie des éditions d'Adrian le Roy et Robert Ballard* (1955), no. 59. Verses by Janequin, addressed in 1559 to 'the most high, most excellent and most illustrious Princess, the Queen of France', are printed by M. Cauchie, 'Les psaumes de Janequin', *Mélanges de musicologie offerts à M. Lionel de la Laurencie* (1933), 47−56.

[61] Knox, *History*, i, 124.

[62] J. Durkan, 'George Buchanan: some French connections', *The Bibliotheck,* iv (1964), 66−72.

[63] Favoli's book, *Hodoeporici Byzantini libri tres* (Louvain, 1563) eluded identification, for which I have to thank Mr M. Sinclair.

[64] J. Goeurot, *L'entretènement de santé* (Lyons, 1559).

[65] Dated Aug. 1584, though he did not die till 1593, SRO, Edinburgh, CC8/8/25, fo. 346.

[66] Gueroult, *Figures de la Bible* (Lyons, 1563), ded. to Catherine de Médicis; Warner, 'Library of James VI', xlix.

[67] *Foreign Correspondence*, i, 77−8.

[68] Fraser, *Menteith*, i, 524−7; *CSP Scot.*, i, 486, 555. In 1560 three French almoners are recorded, one of whom came to Scotland as a chapel clerk, L. Paris, *Négociations relatives au règne de François II* (1841), 747.

[69] D. Nugent, *Ecumenism in the age of the Reformation: The Colloquy of Poissy* (1974), 23−5, 117, 152; *CSP Scot.*, i, 560−1; i.e. the French *Harangue* (s.1., 1561), then being translated for the Scots printer, Lekpreuik. The book signed by Melville was Beza, *Confessione della Fede Christiana* (Appresso Fabio Todesco, 1560), gold-stamped on the covers 'Maria R. Scotorū'. For his Italian visit, Melville, *Memoirs*, 97.

[70] J. Oecolampadius, *Commentarii in libros Prophetarum* (Geneva, 1558), now untraced, but autograph reproduced in T. F. Dibdin, *A Bibliographical Tour in the Northern Counties of England and in Scotland* (1833), ii, 541.

[71] See Warner, 'Library of James VI', xxxxii and n. 6. Balfour owned his *Defence against Melanchthon* (1559) in AUL. S. Hosius, *Traité de l'expresse parole de Dieu* (Paris, 1562).

[72] P. Ronsard, *Discours des miseres de ce temps* and *Continuation du discours* (Paris, 1562); *Papal Negs.*, 187.

[73] D. Ferguson, *Tracts* (Bannatyne Club, 1860) prints the tract and Benoist's Latin original, which is somewhat longer; *ESL*, 66, 76, 139. See Lynch, ch. 1 above, for the preaching of these friars.

[74] E. Pasquier, *René Benoist. le Pape des Halles 1521–1608* (1913); R. Dickson and J. P. Edmond, *Annals of Scottish Printing* (1890), 155–7.

[75] *Papal Negs.*, 491–2, 517–21; *Bref discours sur la sainte confession nécessaire a chacun chrestien presentée (sic)a Marie Stouard, royne d'Ecosse* (Paris, 1587); *CSP Scot.*, i, 675.

[76] *The Necessar and Assurit Way to pluk awa al discord in religion* (Paris, 1565) is Winzet's translation of Jan. 1565, the Latin of Benoist having appeared in Paris in 1562; the former is in a Scolar Press reprint of 1979.

[77] *The Buik of the Kirk of the Canagait 1564–7*, ed. A. B. Calderwood (SRS, 1961), 8, 56.

[78] It opens with a 50-page treatise by Benoist, followed by the pseudo-Proclus.

[79] Nugent, *Colloquy of Poissy*, 190–200; Benoist, *Traité catholique des images* (Paris, 1564) and, dedicated to Charles IX, *Epistre à Jean Calvin* (Paris, 1564); *Papal Negs.*, 520.

[80] *Bref et utile discours avec le manuel de dévotion* (Paris, 1568), dedicated to the Bourbon princesses. Cf. Sharman, *Library of Mary*, 64, 93.

[81] See Greengrass, ch. 8 below, for Mary's continuing knowledge of French affairs after 1568.

[82] Vinet, author of *La vie du roy et empereur Charles le Maigne*, an adaptation of Eginhart (Poitiers, 1564), was a friend of Buchanan; G. des Autels, *Harengue au peuple français contre la rébellion* (Paris, 1560); D. Chambre, *Histoire Abbrégée* (Paris, 1579) has 3 parts, dedicated successively, to Henri III, Mary and Catherine de Médicis; the third part on the lawful succession of women is dated 21 Aug. 1573. For James's name, pt. 3, fo. 219; further refs. in Lynch, ch. 1 above.

[83] *HMC Salisbury*, i, 400; M. Swain, *The Needlework of Mary, Queen of Scots* (1973), 65,78, 84, 96, 107. In 1562 and in 1567 her staff included Jean de Court, painter, not given in M. R. Apted and S. Hannabuss, *Painters in Scotland* (SRS, 1978), but cf. J. Guiffrey, *Artistes parisiens du XVIe et XVIIe siècles* (1915), 20, and Teulet, *Relations*, ii, 273, in the former of which he is given as Mary's 'ordinary painter', He may be identical with an enameller of Limoges, 'Jehan Court dit Vigier', who produced a painted cup for Mary in 1556, but certainly is with the painter to Charles IX who succeeded F. Clouet and who wrote from Paris in July 1570 for a passport allowing him to portray the queen again for the French king: *CSPF 1569–71*, 292, 404. L. Dimier, 'About Mary Queen of Scots' portraits', *SHR*, iv (1907), 135–43.

[84] Canvas and satin were also common materials for book covers. *Peterborough Catalogue of the Tercentenary of Mary, Queen of Scots* (1887), no. 120. I am indebted to Dr D. Caldwell for drawing my attention to this and similar catalogues. TCD, Sallust, *Opera* (Lyons, 1523).

[85] G. D. Hobson, *Les reliures à la Fanfare* (1935), 73–5; Nixon, *Sixteenth-century Gold-tooled Bookbindings in the Pierpont Morgan Library*, 21–3, 252. The

Book of Grisy (in Scottish Catholic Archives) has a bookstamp proper to the Grisy scholars incorporating their own motto. I am grateful to Mr J. Morris of the National Library for access to his file of bindings.

[86] *CSP Scot.*, viii, 170; Labanoff, vii, 246, 272.

[87] *CSP Scot.*, ix, 106; *CSP Ven.*, vii, 430; R. Benoist, *Petit fragment catechistic d'une plus ample catechese de la magie et des magiciens* (Paris, 1579); 2 years later Benoist addressed a work *Ad pios et Catholicos Scotos*.

[88] J. B. Wainwright, 'Selected letters and papers of Nicholas Sander', *Miscellanea* (Catholic Rec. Soc., 1926), xiii, 7—8; *CSP Scot.*, iii, 598; Wright, *Elizabeth*, i, 457.

[89] BL, Add. MS 48180, 'Tranquillitatis animi preservatio', whose genuineness supports the possibility that the attribution to Mary of a printed work of Leslie now in EUL may not deserve the doubts cast on it in Mitchell, *Scottish Bookbinding*, 42; Labanoff, iv, 4.

[90] Labanoff, iv, 129, 214—15; v, 10. F. le Picart, *Les sermons et instructions pour tous les jours de caresme* (preface by Benoist, 1563) (Paris, 1566).

[91] A. Lynn Martin, *Henry III and the Jesuit Politicians* (1973), 57, 62 (the work deals with Auger and Samier at some length); Labanoff, v, 74; *Journal of the British Archaeological Association*, xxx (1874), 312—13.

[92] *CSP Rome,* ii, 398; Labanoff, v, 177, re. a cipher for him. For Crawford, Pitcairn *Trials,* i, pt. 2 (ii), 29.

[93] Fraser, *Mary,* 441; *Calendar of Shrewsbury Papers* (1966) MS 705, fo. 33. Camille du Préau is found first in 1584, *State Papers and Letters of Sir Ralph Sadler,* ed. A. Clifford (1809), ii, 437—8.

[94] J. H. Pollen, 'Mary Stuart's Jesuit chaplain', *The Month*, cxvii (1911), 11—24, 136—49; T. F. Knox (ed.), *The Letters and Memorials of William Cardinal Allen* (1882), 243. See Holmes, ch. 9 below, for the mood of English Catholics in the 1580s.

[95] S. Jebb, *De Vita et Rebus Gestis Mariae Scotorum Reginae* (1725), ii, 616; when the earl of Kent protested it was unreliable as a 'papist version', Mary declared it was 'by a learned and good man' (Gregory Martin).

[96] Sharman, *Library of Mary*, 178, recklessly thought it might be the grammar of Scipione Lentulo, but it is clearly R. Benoist's *Traicte de sainct jeusne de caresme* (Paris, 1564). Similarly Sharman, 73, for strange identifications for *Le Livre de l'institution chrestienne* (Antwerp, 1557).

[97] Checked with originals in SRO, Exchequer Records, E 35/1 and 10; Smith, 'Ronsard and Elizabeth', 10.

[98] W. Bercher, *The Nobility of Women 1559* (Roxburghe Club, 1904), 20—1.

[99] *ESL*, 49—60; T. A. F. Cherry, in *The Bibliotheck*, iv (1963), 13—23.

[100] M. de l'Hospital, *Oeuvres complètes* (1825), iii, 332, celebrating her beauty, gravity, majestic appearance, devotion to the 'arts of Pallas' and unusual prudence; *CSP Scot*, ii, 428.

[101] D. M. Quynn, 'The early career of John Gordon, dean of Salisbury', *BHR*, vii (1945), 118—38; *Mémoires-Journaux de Pierre de L'Estoile* (1876), iii, 22, gives the 1587 text of *Manes*; *CSP Scot.*, iii, 541; the duke of Etampes, de Brosse, was a friend of Benoist and Mary. For his father's pension from Mary's dowry, *CSP Scot.*, iv, 505.

[102] *HMC Pepys*, 77; J. Durkan, 'Henry Scrimgeour, Renaissance bookman', *Edinburgh Bibliographical Soc. Transactions*, v (1978), 1–31, esp. 20.

[103] Calderwood, *History* iii, 706–7, 737, 739, and iv, 2; SRO, CC8/8/25, fo. 134v, CC8/8/25, lists his wife, Christian Ross óf Balnagown, and children, Elspeth, Christine and William; *CSP Scot.*, viii, 222; *CSP Dom., Eliz., Addenda 1580–1625*, 290.

[104] The Paris BN *Liber precum* was in Avignon, the Blackwood *Book of Hours* in Niort. Firmain Alezard, Mary's goldsmith, came from Orléans and returned there, W. Fraser, *Memorials of the Earls of Haddington* (1889), ii, 412.

[105] *Sir William Alexander. The earl of Stirling's Register of Royal Letters* (1885), i, 311–12; *Royal Commission of Ancient and Historical Monuments. Inventory of the City of Edinburgh* (1951), 145. I have to thank the Very Revd. L. E. Boyle OP, Prefect of the Vatican Library, for access to the as yet uncatalogued collection of the cardinal of York.

Appendix I

Pre-1568 books not in Sharman *The Library of Mary, Queen of Scots*. Places and dates of publication are approximate.

1 Vico, E., *Le imagini delle donne auguste* (Venice, 1557).
2 Giovanni, Fiorentino, *Il pecorone, nel quale si contengono cinquante novelle antiche* (Milan, 1558).
3 Dante (unspecified).
4 Petrarch (do.).
5 Quintus Curtius, *De' fatti d'Alessandro Magno* (Venice, 1558).
6 Petrarch, *Le vite de gli huomini illustri* (Venice, 1527).
7 'Sum Comedies and Tragedies in Ital.' Though some were 'gottin', far more were not restored.
8 Seneca. L. A., *Thyeste*, trans. Lodovico Dolci (Venice, 1543).
9 Piccolomini, A., *Della philosophia naturale* (Rome, 1551).
10 Trissino, G. G., *La Sophonisba* (Venice, 1553).
11 Montemayor, J. de, *La Diana: Los siete libros* (Milan, 1561).
12 Torres Naharro, B. de, *Propalladia* (Naples, 1517).
13 Giovio, P., *Dialogo de las Empreses militares y amorosos* (Lyons, 1562).
14 'Sum bukes of Amadis in Spanish'.
15 'Dictionaire, Latin and Spanish' (?MS).
16 Herberay, N. de, *Le premier livre de Dom Flores de Grèce* (Paris, 1552).
17 Bandello, M., *Histoires tragiques,* trans. P. Boaistuau (Paris, 1559).
18 'L'institution du prince escrite à la main, fol.' (MS in vellum).
19 'Ane orison in latin and frenche handvret'.
20 Ronsard, P. de, *Oeuvres* (Paris, 1560).
21 Espence, C. d', *Oraison funèbre de Marie Royne douairière d'Escoce* (Paris, 1561).
22 Rovere, J. de, *Les deux sermons funèbre du feu Roy Henri* (Paris, 1559).
23 *L'entrée faicte au Roy Charles neufiesme a Rouen* (Rouen, 1563).
24 Paradin, C., *La cronique de Savoye* (Lyons, 1552).
25 Sauvage, D., *Chronique de Flandre* (Lyons, 1561–2).
26 Paradin, C., *Alliances généalogiques des rois et princes de Gaule* (Lyons, 1561).
27 Lemaire des Belges, J., *Les illustrations de Gaule* (Paris, 1548).
28 Turnèbe, A., *Epithalamium Francisci Valesii et Mariae Stuartae* (Paris, 1558).
29 Virgil, *Deux livres d'Enéide* (Paris, 1561).
30 Plato, *Le premier et second et dixième livre de justice ou de la Republique*, trans. L. Le Roy (Paris, 1555).
31 Plutarch, *Les vies des hommes illustres*, trans. J. Amyot (Paris, 1559).
32 Zonaras, J., *Les histories et chroniques du monde*, trans. J. de Maumont (Paris, 1561).
33 Anacreon, *Les Odes,* trans. R. Belleau (Paris, 1556).
34 Vico, E., *Omnium Caesarum verissimae imagines* (Venice, 1553).

35 Strada, J. de, *Imperatorum iconum* (Lyons, 1553).
36 'Titius Livius in blak veluet'.
37 Rouille, G., *Icones insignium virorum* (Lyons, 1559).
38 Virgil, *Bucolica*. In eight (various) editions.
39 Murmellius, J., *Tabulae in artis componendorum versuum rudimenta* (Paris, 1550).
40 Giraldi, L. G., *Pinax iconicus antiquorum et variorum in sepulturis rituum* (Lyons, 1556).
41 Coccius Sabellicus, M. A. (unspecified).
42 Dorstenius, T., *Botanicon* (Frankfurt, 1544).
43 Tiraqueau, A., *Commentarii de nobilitate et jure primogeniorum* (Paris, 1549).
44 Jerome, St, *Octavus tomus Operum* (in psalmos) (Basle, 1526).
45 *Canones et decreta concilii Tridentini* (Rome, 1564).
46 Staphylus, F., *The Apologie* (Antwerp, 1565).
47 Hall, E., *The Union of the Two Famelies of Lancaster and Yorke* (London, 1548).
48 'Chronicle of Scotland, wrettin with hand.'
49 Strada, J. de, *Epitome du thrésor des antiquitez* (Lyons, 1553).

Appendix II

Some books said to have belonged to Queen Mary

1 Horae, French, 15th c., W. Murray Threipland, 1889 (*Exhibition of the Royal House of Stuart, London* no. 310.).
2 *Heures à l'usaige de Romme* (Paris, 1498). Chantilly, Musée Condé.
3 Livre d'heures. No details. Douai, Bibl. Municipale (*Notes and Queries*, ser. l, iv, 418).
4 Liber precum. No details. Cheltenham, Private owner 1831 (ibid., ser. 8, vi, 223−4).
5 Horae *BVM*, Flemish, 15th c., J. Rylands Library, Manchester University, MS Lat. 21 (Formerly earl of Crawford).
6 Horae. No details. Private owner (London, *Royal House of Stuart Exhibition Catalogue*, no. 316).
7 Liber precum, 15th c. Leningrad, State Hermitage Museum (doubtfully genuine).
8 Liber precum, 15th c. Paris, BN, MS Lat. 1405 (formerly in Avignon).
9 Horae (Sarum), French-Italian, c. 1544. Arundel, Duke of Norfolk (formerly Lord Herries).
10 Horae BVM, vellum, French, BL, Add, MS 25696.
11 Horae BVM (Roman), vellum (*Cat. des livres de L. Potier*, l^e partie, lot 119, Paris, 1856). (Formerly in Niort and Poitiers.)
12 *Horae in laudem Mariae ad usum Romanum* (Paris, 1549). Rheims, Bibl. Municipale.

13 *Officium BVM*, Pius V revision (Paris, 1574). (P. Lacombe, *Livres d'heures au XVIe siècle*, Paris, 1907, no. 467.)
14 Homer, *Odyssey,* Greek−Latin. No details. Private owner (Pererborough, 1889, no. 311).
15 Bible. No details. HM the Queen (Peterborough, no. 156).
16 Jammetius Textor, F., *De diversis regulis juris antiqui*, 1523. (G. Smith and F. Benger, *A Collection of Armorial Binding*. London, 1927.)
17 Leslie, J., Tranquillitatis animi preservatio, 1573. BL, Add. MS 4818.
18 Munster, S., *Cosmographia*, 1556. (Sharman, p. 13.) (Rejected.)

5

The Roman Connection: Prospects for Counter-Reformation during the Personal Reign of Mary, Queen of Scots

IAN B. COWAN

The relationship between Scotland and the papacy in the years following the Indult of 1487 and before the Reformation of 1559—60 was complex. Administratively the pope retained the privilege of providing royal nominees to elective benefices and retained in consequence his right to papal taxation in form of the common services. In terms of non–elective benefices, the rules of reservation, which occasioned multiple petitions for each vacancy, continued to be applied, and if promises to pay annates were not always fulfilled, the allegiance of the Scottish church to Rome seemed in these terms unshakeable, if in others political and religious unrest already threatened the stability of that relationship.[1]

In terms of diplomatic communication this appeared to be equally true, for if there had been times when contact was casual and infrequent, attempts to promote liaison between Scotland and the papacy were intensified in the period immediately before 1560. On the financial side, the initiative came from the crown which made several requests for authority to tax the church. If such petitions were made in the name of Mary, queen of Scots, her mother, Mary of Guise, as regent, was their more likely instigator. Nevertheless, the welfare of her kingdom depended upon the maintenance of papal subsidies on whatever pretext they were sought which, in terms of a plea on 2 October 1555, were ostensibly to repair the ravages of war. On that occasion the request for an annual tax of two-tenths was accepted by Pope Paul IV, but a further request on 27 December for an annual pension of 30,000 *livres*, avowedly to help reform the church was not so readily accepted as the pope may have had some understandable doubts as to the true destination of such taxation.[2] Instead he acceded to one-quarter of the tax previously requested; a grant which was subsequently, but reluctantly renewed. Such requests, to which the pope could accede without diminishing his own resources, continued to be honoured and the appointment of Cardinal Trivulzio as legate to Paris charged to work for the pacification of Europe, was utilized not only as a means of delivering the dispensation for the marriage of the Dauphin François and Mary, but also for authorizing the prolongation for yet another year of a taxation of one-twentieth on church property.[3]

In ecclesiastical terms, Cardinal Sermoneta, described by the queen as 'protector of our suits with your holiness', was charged as cardinal protector by Paul IV to visit Scotland in 1556 and report on the state of the churches there.[4] His recommended reforms, if not entirely feasible, contain interesting proposals which if followed might have significantly changed the course of Scottish ecclesiastical history.[5] Little was done to follow this initiative, however, and although Cardinal Trivulzio, who dealt with Scottish business as papal legate to Paris in 1557–8, requested leave to appoint an apostolic visitor with widespread powers of enquiry, nothing more was heard of the idea.[6] Likewise, the plea made by Henri II, king of France on 29 June 1559, that the pope should appoint Nicholas de Pellevé, bishop of Amiens, as a legate to Scotland, was ignored by Paul IV who claimed that the new sovereigns, François and Mary, had not asked for it; more realistically he may have perceived that a foreign bishop would not have been acceptable to Scots of either persuasion.[7] Following the death of Paul IV in 1559, his successor Pius IV, at the instigation of François II, showed less hesitation and on 26 January 1560 appointed Pellevé as legate to Scotland; he arrived with French reinforcements before 17 February.[8] If opinions vary as to his policies, with George Buchanan claiming that he meant to slaughter all those hostile to Rome and France, he clearly had the support of François and Mary who in November 1559 had ordered him to 'compone' differences by means of a national assembly and in April 1560 realistically commanded him to bring back their rebellious subjects 'by all gentle means with amnesty for the past'.[9]

None of these objectives was achieved and in all this the pope was little more than a bystander who was not only kept uninformed as to the danger to the faith in Scotland, but also remained apathetic to Mary's claim to the English throne. Pius, however, honoured her with a golden rose, ironically presented on 17 August 1560, the very day on which the Reformation parliament ratified the Scots Confession of Faith, but he nevertheless regarded her as 'a woman and absent' from her country.[10] The death of François II on 5 December was to rectify at least one part of that dismissive remark and thereafter successive popes began to show not only more concern for her welfare, but also some interest in her religious constancy. As to Mary herself, the end of her marriage and the hostility of Catherine de Médicis left her little choice but to follow the advice given by a conference convoked by the cardinal of Lorraine at Joinville, which was attended by two veterans of the Scottish campaigns Jacques de la Brosse and the vicomte de Martigues, as well as Pellevé, who had been ambassador to Scotland in 1559, to follow a policy of friendship towards Queen Elizabeth to whom she might well succeed.[11] At a later stage, in the rather different circumstances of 1562, the cardinal even indicated that Mary might embrace the religion of England, but she was unprepared to compromise her Catholic principles that far.[12] But that option, when suggested in 1561 by the English ambassador in France, Throckmorton, was firmly rejected. So was the offer made on behalf of the Catholic magnate, the earl of Huntly, by John Leslie, the future bishop of Ross; he tried to persuade the queen to sail to Aberdeen where she could rely on the earl (who was later to boast that he could have raised three whole shires on her behalf) and his associates to support her against her Protestant subjects.[13] The decision was virtually made for her since the course of action recommended by her advisers at Joinville corresponded closely with that of her half-brother, Lord James Stewart, who headed the Protestant regime governing in her name in Scotland.

In response to this new awareness of her situation, Mary, before her departure from France, assured the pope, in whose personal favour she at that time basked, of her religious constancy and thereafter confirmed that she would rather die 'than swerve from obedience to his Holiness and to the Apostolic See'.[14] Faced with such intransigence, it is hardly surprising that the queen's return to Scotland on 19 August 1561 aroused the personal suspicions of John Knox who was convinced that Mary had tricked Lord James into complying with her deep-laid schemes to restore papacy in Scotland; a view which was reinforced by his belief that 'sche has plainlie purposed to wrak the religioun within this Realme; to the Roman Antichrist sche hath made her promeise; and from him sche hath taken money to uphold his pompe'.[15] So far as Mary's actual position was concerned the key to her attitude was predetermined by the national situation, for, after landing at Leith, she aligned herself, not with the unreliable earl of Huntly, but instead with Lord James and William Maitland of Lethington, both of whom were politically committed to the Protestant party.[16]

Nevertheless, if Mary did not actively seek to promote Catholicism, she remained the only figure to whom Catholics could turn, for the door was always open to a change of policy as long as she refused to countenance officially the reformed church or ratify the Treaty of Edinburgh and the acts of the Reformation parliament. In fact, however, this failure sprang from political considerations outwith the realm, and internally Mary, in accordance with her own fluctuating authority, was to act on more than one occasion as though statutes which she had refused to confirm had the force of law. Thus while the act forbidding the saying of mass remained unratified, a proclamation of the privy council, with similar intent, issued within days of her return, was to be acted upon when political necessity dictated.[17]

This dual policy can also be discerned in the financial sphere for while here, too, Mary resolutely refused officially to countenance the Protestant settlement, she accepted in 1562 some measure of financial compromise by which the reformed church should be maintained from a general taxation of the benefices of the old church. Two-thirds of the former revenues were to be retained by their possessors for their lifetime but the remaining one-third was to be collected by the government for allocation between itself and the ministry.[18] Politically, this scheme can be viewed in various ways. In one respect, it left the structure of the church intact and theoretically made it possible to envisage a successful Counter-Reformation — a policy which Knox always considered feasible. On the other hand, it allowed the reformed church some financial provision and was consequently statesmanlike in its attempt to reconcile varying interests. In actuality Mary's primary interest appears to have been neither to hold out hope to the old church, nor to give unofficial recognition to the new, but rather to ensure adequate finance, not only for her own administration, but also to maintain her position on the international scene. Thirds of benefices were remitted by Mary, quite irrespective of religious persuasion, but progressively became less available to the reformed church as 'the gaird, and the effaires of the kytcheing' became more demanding. Increasingly Mary's position was dictated by political and financial considerations and religious motivation played little effective part in her decisions.[19]

In a more positive fashion, the downfall of the principal Catholic magnate in the realm, the earl of Huntly, was effected by Mary, and not at the instigation of James Stewart, by then earl of Moray, who certainly had a vested interest in destroying his political rival, who by chance also happened to be a Catholic. On this occasion, a deliberate effort was made to play on Mary's Catholic sympathies by the countess of Huntly who showed Mary's emissary the private chapel at Strathbogie Castle in which candles, ornaments and altar books had been left along with rich vestments from Aberdeen cathedral in anticipation of a royal visit.[20] The appeal was in vain and after the defeat and death of the earl at Corrichie in October 1562 the vestments were removed to Holyrood and turned to secular uses including a bed for Darnley and a doublet for Bothwell.[21] To Mary, who had demonstrated true statesmanship in her refusal to risk restarting civil war, it was a task well accomplished, but she also knew that her Catholic friends in France, Spain and elsewhere in Europe might see matters in a different light. In writing to her uncle, the cardinal of Lorraine, in January 1563 she asked him 'to make my excuses if I have failed in any part of my duty towards religion', but rather than signifying repentance, the tone of the letter, it has been suggested, shows 'no regret that circumstances had compelled her to lay low her greatest Catholic subject'.[22] In adopting this attitude, political realities and the maintenance of royal authority were more to Mary than any phantom of religion.

The exact nature of the situation in Scotland was incomprehensible to the papacy and in order to elicit information the pope dispatched a Jesuit father, Nicholas de Gouda, as his special envoy to Scotland. The brief authorizing his commission was issued on 3 December 1561, but not validated until thirteen days later.[23] Not until 18 June 1562 was de Gouda to arrive at Leith to a bitterly hostile reception. Forced to seek refuge at the family home at Megginch in Perthshire, of Edmund Hay, later provincial of the Jesuit order in France, he found it extremely difficult in Scotland. After some delay, Mary reluctantly met him in a furtive interview on 24 July when her Protestant courtiers were at sermon.[24] If de Gouda declared himself impressed by Mary's goodness and defencelessness, her answers to the papal brief which he read to her must have given him some cause for concern, for she not only declared herself to be helpless, but also refused a safe-conduct to the emissary in order that he might communicate to the Scottish bishops a second papal summons to the Council of Trent.[25] The means of preserving Scottish Catholicism was never seriously discussed, while the envoy's suggestion that a Catholic seminary might be founded was rightly dismissed as impracticable.[26]

Mary's attitude in this matter was followed by the Scottish bishops who still remained nominally true to the catholic cause; only one, the bishop of Dunkeld, agreed to see de Gouda, while of the others, only the archbishop of St Andrews deigned to reply to his overtures.[27] Henry Sinclair, bishop of Ross, but resident in Edinburgh as president of the Court of Session and fearful of his position, resolutely refused to meet the envoy, even when personally requested to do so by the queen.[28] In the face of such unwillingness to his challenge, it is hardly surprising that de Gouda left Scotland on 3 September 1562.[29]

By this juncture the pope, prompted by an initiative taken by the cardinal of Lorraine, was anxious to promote a Catholic marriage between the Archduke Charles of Austria and the Scottish queen. Mary's unrealistic setting of her her heart on the Infante Don Carlos of Spain, had already had the effect of sowing doubts in the mind of the papacy as to the sincerity of her promises; by December 1562 the pope was pointedly suggesting that she should take Mary Tudor as her model 'who surely did not defend the cause of God timidly'.[30] Despite this injunction, the relationship between Mary and the holy see continued to deteriorate. Pleas to send representatives to the Council of Trent, an issue from which Mary deliberately distanced herself, fell on deaf ears, although in a letter read at a public session of 10 May 1563, she announced her adhesion to its decrees, notwithstanding her inability to send envoys; a declaration which was not entirely truthful for while she informed the pope that she was now doing her best 'to make a number of our prelates go to the council', her real intention, as she needed her few loyal bishops beside her, was quite the opposite.[31]

Despite official reluctance to promote Catholicism at a national level, the presence of Mary at Holyrood undoubtedly encouraged and strengthened Catholic allegiance in Edinburgh and its neighbouring burgh of the Canongate, both of which became a haven for recusants. There were attempts to remove Catholics such as proclamations by the town council of Edinburgh on 2 October 1561 'chargeing all monks, freris, priestis, nonnys, adulteraris, fornicatouris, and all sic filthy personis, to remove thameselfiss out of this town and boundis thairof within xxiiii houris, under the pane of carting throch the toun, byrning on the cheik, and banessing the samin for evir', but this was countermanded by the queen and the town's magistrates were summarily dismissed.[32] Likewise a proclamation of 1562 restricting the holding of public office to professed Protestants had to be withdrawn 'for eschewing of hir anger'.[33]

The queen's private chapel at Holyrood became the centre of Catholic activity for the capital and could be described as 'nothing less than a Catholic parish kirk'.[34] After an incident at her first mass when a mob who attacked a servant carrying altar candles tried to force their way in until denied entry by Lord James Stewart, the queen's command that no one should molest any of her domestic servants, and those who had come out of France with her in the practice of her religion, was respected. This privilege which was interpreted by the Protestant lords as a request for private worship within her own household was quickly granted, despite Knox's warning that their liberty in allowing the queen's mass would be their thraldom before long.[35] In time, however, this concession came to be interpreted more widely and on 8 August 1563, while Mary was in Stirling, several Edinburgh Catholics attended mass at Holyrood, but when on the following Sunday this was repeated two of the pickets who had come to take note of those who attended mass, broke into the chapel, only to be evicted by the palace guard.[36] Nevertheless, twenty-two Catholic worshippers, men and women, were 'delatit for arte and parte of the cuming to the chapell of our soueran ladeis Palice of Halyrudehouse...And swa, becumyng commoune manifest transgressouris, violatouris and brakaris of our souerane ladeis Proclamationis...aught to be adiugit and punesit to the deid'.[37] The actual punishment was not to be quite so drastic, for Mary on her return to Edinburgh counter-attacked by demanding the trial of the Protestants who had broken into her chapel. A compromise was evidently reached; the trial of the accused was adjourned and the charges against the Catholics quietly forgotten.[38] Use of the chapel, however, remained uncurtailed. Within it children were baptized, sometimes from the conviction of the parents, as in the case of an Edinburgh merchant, John Graham, who openly defended the doctrine of the mass, but on other occasions to escape the censures of the kirk when the children in question were illegitimate.[39] Marriages were frequently celebrated there, but while the queen's influence in her political ascendancy could secure the release of David Hoppringle of Edinburgh whom the magistrates had imprisoned for a Catholic marriage, the plight of Paul Wallace, accused of fornication in September 1566 (because his marriage in the queen's chapel was not recognized by the Canongate kirk session), was much more perilous as the queen's political influence declined.[40] The queen's presence encouraged many who would have agreed with the parishioner who claimed 'my hart gevis me to the mes and thairfor I can nocht come to this commonion'.[41] The Catholic schoolteachers of the burgh and neighbouring Leith also remained active; one, William Roberton, defied all the efforts of the magistrates to dislodge him and another, the priest John Scott, claimed exemption from the authority of the Canongate kirk session 'because he was of the Queen's religioun' and also had royal permission to teach in the burgh.[42] The protection of the queen was an important element in all this, for a Leith schoolmaster was less fortunate in 1572 when albeit the capital offence was treason, he was 'accusit for saying of mess qua was condemnit be an assyse and theireftir hangit'.[43] Before the deposition of the queen in 1567 active Catholicism was very evident among the Edinburgh populace: and in March 1565 as many inhabitants of that burgh were reported to have been present at a mass as those who attended the Protestant service.[44] The apprehension of the priest Sir James Tarbot, who had officiated at a private mass on Palm Sunday and was thereafter tied to the market cross in his vestments and subjected to egg-throwing, did not act as a deterrent and indeed occasioned a riot when Catholic supporters took it upon themselves to intervene on his behalf.[45] Faced with such intransigence, the General Assembly had appealed on 25 June 1565 that 'the word of God and his true religioun now presentlie receivit might be established, approved and ratified, throughout the whole realm, alsweill in the Queen's Majesties awin person as in the subjects'.[46] Nevertheless, in the remaining two years of her reign it has been estimated, no doubt with some exaggeration, that some 9,000 and 12,000 Catholics received communion in her chapel.[47]

Outwith Edinburgh such privileges were not so easily accorded and efforts to maintain Catholicism were left to the initiative of local families who could expect little or no assistance from the queen, except in isolated instances as on 6 March 1564 when James Young, vicar of Fishwick was place 'under our soverane leideis speciall protectioun'.[48] Financial concessions were readily available, sometimes on humanitarian grounds as the remission of thirds to John Stevenson, parson of Furvie, 'ane auld blynd man', but more often as personal concessions such as those accorded to the prior of the Charterhouse and a monk of Lindores, which had both been sacked by Protestant mobs in 1559.[49] If, however, the queen could protect her co-religionists she was not only forced in 1562 to order the bishop of Dunkeld to desist from administering the sacraments according to the Catholic rite, but was equally unable to protect several eminent Catholics, including the archbishop of St Andrews and the prior of Whithorn who defied the law and celebrated mass at Easter 1563.[50] Mary and her privy council took no official action against the offenders, but when the lairds of Ayrshire arrested some of the offending priests, including two monks of Crossraguel who had officiated at Maybole and Kirkoswald, and wrote to Quintin Kennedy and other leading Catholics in the west that they would in future seize offenders and put them to death, Mary had no defence against these threats.[51] Her attempt to persuade Knox, who was summoned to Lochleven and confronted with a demand that the persecution of Catholics, especially in the west of Scotland, should cease was immediately met with the observation that it was she who should observe the laws of Scotland which had made Catholicism illegal.[52] However, confrontation was avoided when on the following morning, Mary assured Knox, presumably on the advice of Lord James, that she would enforce justice against all Catholics who had attended mass.[53] After trial the defendants, including Archbishop Hamilton, were sentenced to be imprisoned during the queen's pleasure.[54] Their sentence was brief, but Mary was not always able to intervene as when Father John Black, a Dominican friar, was killed, shortly after the murder of Riccio.[55]

In truth, hopes of any meaningful concessions to Catholicism disappeared with the murder of Darnley and Mary's continued protestations that she 'would die in the Catholic faith' could at best only refer to her own personal intent and as her affair with Bothwell prospered even this was increasingly to become a matter of doubt.[56] Whatever her motives, the possibility of further Catholic concessions never reappeared and as her political position grew more perilous, Mary revealed the extent to which her religious attachment was immersed in political reality when, faced with the complete collapse of her policies, she began in October 1566 to make concessions to the reformed church whereby succession to lesser benefices was assured to Protestants, thereby conferring a degree of official recognition upon the new faith.[57]

Increasingly Mary's policies had become motivated by financial rather than religious considerations. From April 1565 Mary was apparently not reluctant to arrogate papal authority to herself and began to grant in considerable numbers confirmation of feu-ferme of kirklands which were in her eyes 'as lauchfull and of als greit strenth and avale, as gif the samin had bene obtenit and purchast fra the Pape or sate of Rome'. By this date such remunerative transactions augmented by papal subsidies appeared to be the only means of financing and implementing her political and personal policies, although she was still able to run her household on the revenues from the estates in France which formed her jointure.[58] Unfortunately for her ambitions, successive popes after Paul IV were interested more, even if intermittently so, in furthering Counter-Reformation and for this reason, if no other, Mary had to reassure the papacy of her anxiety to restore the true faith. It was, nevertheless, difficult to convince the popes that she had the cause of Scottish Catholicism at heart when she was clearly not mistress of her own destiny, and it was only when the earl of Moray opposed her marriage to Darnley that the opportunity to utilize her beliefs as a bargaining weapon arose. Moray's opposition may have been personal and political, but it could be disguised as a means of safeguarding Protestantism against a Catholic match designed to revive that faith, even if he and Maitland had been involved throughout much of 1564 in negotiations for a marriage with Don Carlos.[59] The General Assembly, in apparent contradiction to Mary's policy to date, was certainly sufficiently alarmed to declare on 25 December 1565 that the realm was again in danger of being polluted by the mass. The queen, they declared, 'hath given answer in plaine words that the religion in which she hath bene nourished (and that is meare abomination) she will mainteane and defend'.[60] In a sense they were right: within the space of two months Mary was trying to persuade a number of magnates, Protestant as well as Catholic, to attend the mass again. And there were also rumours of the restoration of the mass outside the confines of her private chapel — in the parish church of the capital.[61]

The Chaseabout raid had given Mary an opportunity to pose as the champion of a Catholic faction, but her ability to measure up to the challenge was doubtful. Nevertheless, the commissioning of William Chisholm, bishop of Dunblane, to seek a dispensation in Rome for her marriage to Darnley was also used as the occasion to ask the papacy for a subsidy to assist her in the conflict ahead. According to the bishop in his audience with the pope, 'the pious queen cannot not make use of what is her own'. If, however, she could raise 10,000 to 12,000 men for four or five months she would renew the rights of the crown and would restore 'religion to splendour'.[62] All that was required to achieve this was 300,000 ducats. Pius IV was not convinced and while the bishop received 'fair words' little more was forthcoming until he could be convinced that Mary had abandoned her policy of religious compromise.[63] Philip of Spain who had also been informed of her desire to follow a Catholic policy was equally unimpressed.[64] His caution was well advised for following their marriage Mary and Darnley reissued a proclamation which the queen had promulgated in August 1561 in which they declared their intention of preserving the faith and privileges of the Protestant church prohibiting anyone on pain of death from altering the state of religion that existed in Scotland at the time when the queen returned from France.[65] Unaware of this declaration the pope, having heard in late winter of Mary's marriage to Darnley, died on 9 December 1565 hoping that a brighter day would dawn.[66]

The new pope, Pius V, in pursuance of the policy of his predecessor, and apparently unperturbed by their irregular marriage, congratulated Mary and Darnley, who at the Candlemas following his wedding was to flaunt his somewhat lukewarm faith by proceeding through the streets of Edinburgh with lighted tapers, as having, as he had heard, 'restored the due worship of God throughout the while realm'.[67] They were exhorted to complete the good work by showing severity to heretics.[68] This appeal prompted Mary to send Chisholm back to Rome whence he arrived from Paris on 25/26 April 1566. Ostensibly he travelled to make the customary profession of obedience to a new pope, but in reality to renew the appeal for a subsidy. His arrival, which followed the news of Riccio's murder and the threat to Mary's life, proved to be an occasion which found the pope more than sympathetic to her cause.[69]

By 15 May the pope in consistory, while speaking 'of aid for the queen of Scotland, praised her for her manly courage, and said that she shamed many Catholics of Germany who had not the boldness to confess their faith openly'.[70] Even then Pius was not prepared to provide an open-ended undertaking to finance Mary's schemes. Instead, despite the archbishop of Glasgow's advice that a foreigner was not likely to be well received, he chose as legate to Scotland Vincenzo Laureo, who had succeeded him as bishop of Mondovi.[71] Yet doubts still persisted as to Mary's sincerity and Laureo was detained in Paris until the queen could be persuaded to execute leading Protestants, a plan which, following the death of Riccio, seemed more feasible. Even Knox in writing the preface to his History in May 1566 thought that Catholic worship would spread in Scotland. 'Although messes be multiplied in all quarteris of the realm', he wrote 'who can stop the Queen's subjects to lyve of the Queen's religioun'.[72] He need not have worried, Mary was per-suaded by Moray and Sir James Melville of Halhill to pardon Riccio's assassins and Laureo's demands not only went unheeded, but demon-strated a marked lack of papal understanding of the true situation in Scotland.[73]

Laureo was placed in an impossible position. The pope was reluctant to authorize payment, but pressure to pay was mounting. In the event he compromised, or tried to buy time, by authorizing one instalment of 4,000 *scudi*, to be followed by four similar payments, in all 20,000 *scudi*, but letters despatched from Rome on 16 September and received on 5 October ensured that no further payments could be made until the nuncio reached Scotland.[74] Even then he was not 'to disburse anything at all if on your arrival you should see the money already paid has borne no fruit for religion'.[75] Despite the pope's suspicions, Laureo continued in his futile attempt to accomplish his mission by trying to persuade the cardinal of Lorraine to despatch two messengers, Bishop William Chisholm and Father Edmund Hay, to urge Mary to punish some of her seditious subjects. The wisdom of Laureo's persistence in the face of his orders to return to Rome is questionable, but there can be little doubt of his belief that Catholicism in Scotland 'would go to manifest ruin' with her death.[76]

Even before the envoys left France on 3 December, however, Mary's attitude had become established in letters received about 20 December which, although urging Laureo to visit her, stated that she wished to receive him 'under some other colour than that of religion'.[77] Yet even then hopes of some progress remained in view of her protestation that delay in summoning the nuncio had been caused ' because we behuiffit to mak ane conventione of the nobilitie' in order to seek approval for his visit.[78] The birth of her son and his impending baptism into the Catholic faith also raised expectations for a return to Catholic obser-vances. Even the pope was convinced of progress and allowed Laureo to remain in Paris until further reports were received from Scotland. Mary, however, was in no hurry to satisfy their curiosity, delaying meeting the envoys for almost a month after the prince's baptism. Despite reports that the Catholic stalwart, Lord Seton, might be sent with three ships to collect the nuncio the queen's attitude remained unchanged; 'she could not stain her hands with her subjects' blood'.[79] Laureo had no alternative but to set out for Italy on 10 April 1567 with the bulk of the proposed subsidy of 20,000 *scudi* still unspent. Attempts to persuade the pope to pay the balance met with cold replies from a pope who asserted that he would redeem the outstanding balance from his Parisian bankers.[80] From 1565 onwards Mary had made valiant efforts to gain financial support from the papacy. In that sense, Mary had expected as much as much of Rome as it did of her. Their disappointment was mutual and, to some extent, justifiable.

To impugn Mary's Catholicism in this way is not, however, a sufficient answer to those who would stress the queen's personal devotion to her religious faith. Both to the pope and his personal emissary, de Gouda, Mary asserted that she would 'rather die at once than abandon her faith'.[81] She unswervingly refused to desist from attending mass and although a political construction can be place on this resolution, her own words, as reported in 1565, have a ring of truth when she said to Sir Thomas Randolph, 'What wolde you that I sholde mayke marchandize of my religion, or force myself to your menestors willes? Yt cane not be so.'[82] Mary's personal belief was undoubtedly sincere, but in spite of the case which can be mounted in favour of her personal devotion even this has been challenged in terms of her marriage to Darnley and her affair with Bothwell certainly raises questions about it.

The issue with the Darnley marriage revolve around the question of her dispensation for their union. As first cousins, Mary and Darnley were related within the second degree of consanguinity, while more distant relationships may have placed them in a blood relationship within the fourth degree. If the latter was inconsequential the closeness of their relationship undoubtedly demanded a papal dispensation, for while delegation of authority in matrimonial cases was granted to archbishops, bishops and legates, this was invariably restricted to relationships of the third and fourth degrees — as is exemplified by the privileges enjoyed by John Hamilton, archbishop of St Andrews from 6 March 1555 onwards.[83] Even if the archbishop had been entrusted with wider powers, he would have been unable to dispense in this particular case as all dispensations for princes were reserved for the pope's personal disposal.[84] Recourse to the pope was therefore essential and to this end William Chisholm, bishop of Dunblane, was commissioned to seek a dispensation on Mary's behalf.

The bishop's introduction to Cardinal Borromeo is dated 24 May 1565, but he did not leave Scotland until after 28 June on which day a letter requesting safe-conduct through England was dispatched by Mary to Elizabeth.[85] The bishop must have left shortly after that date, for having visited the cardinal of Lorraine en route, he arrived in Rome on 14 August.[86] By that date a courier who had arrived on 20 July had already requested a dispensation at the behest of the cardinal. In these circumstances rumours that approval had been granted, according to some reports as early as 17 July, appear to be totally unfounded. All the evidence points to a dispensation granted no earlier than 14 August and probably not before 1 September, when the pope declared that he had ordered the dispensation and an accompanying brief to be drafted and expedited without delay. On 2 October 1565, Chisholm left Rome bearing the dispensation and five accompanying briefs.[87]

If the pope ultimately felt some urgency in this matter, his concern was misplaced for Mary had anticipated his concession by several months. On 22 July 1565 the banns of her forthcoming marriage had been 'proclamit in the paroche kirk of Sanctgeill, in Halyrudhous, and in the chepell royall' and one week later she and Darnley were married by the bishop of Brechin.[88] It has been suggested that unrestrained passion led the queen to ignore the necessity of a papal dispensation, but this judgement is of doubtful validity.[89] Alternatively it has been argued that she acted on the presumption that permission to marry had already been granted in Rome, but this assertion savours of special pleading.[90] The only possible reason for speed was political. If some of her advisers supported the match, the forces of opposition to the marriage were amassing under the leadership of Moray and it was deemed politically expedient to marry in order to crush the incipient revolt.

Expediency does not necessarily free Mary from the charge of defying canon law which as a devout Catholic she might have been expected to follow. Catholic historians have tended to be defensive on this issue while those hostile to Mary have exploited it to the full. But was her action heinous in the eyes of her contemporaries? An examination of similar matrimonial dispensations shows that the great majority were sought retrospectively, sometimes many years after the event and even after the birth of several children.[91] Given that there was no other impediment such 'marriages' were recognized in canon and Scots law as valid unions and any offspring regarded as legitimate.[92] Mary in this respect chose the path which the great majority of her subjects had similarly followed. It in no way impugned her Catholicism, although public announcement of the date of the dispensation might have caused some embarrassment.

The same cannot be said of her affair and subsequent marriage to the earl of Bothwell. In terms of the former there is little doubt, whether it is seen in terms of infatuation or practical politics that Mary had conceived an affection for Bothwell even before Darnley's death, but it must be seriously doubted as to whether she was carrying the earl's child at that time.[93] More likely than not Bothwell first came to Mary's notice as a reliable servant, a politician whose uses to the crown, as an uncommitted Protestant who was not markedly pro-English, were inestimable not only to herself, but arguably to her co-religionists, as more and more of the magnates began to disapprove of Mary's policies. The search for a strong man to replace the ineffectual Darnley was not simply an emotional attachment, but one to which Mary was politically committed if her failing policies were to be revived. The replacement of Darnley might also have been considered a political necessity, although whether this commitment went as far as plotting his assassination is questionable. Whatever her participation in that deed, her actions subsequent to the murder stemmed not only from a desire to hide her moral shortcomings, but also from a growing sense of political isolation and hostility to her policies from among the magnates, most of whom at court were Protestants anyway.

If Mary's relationship with Bothwell before the murder of Darnley must occasion some doubt, there is no less room for conjecture following that event. By mid-April 1567, the earl had become her only means of political survival, and her collusive abduction by Bothwell on 24 April appears to have been an acknowledgement of that fact.[94] The case for forcible abduction is not strong and Mary was to stress thereafter that she had not married under duress. Before marriage could take place, however, the arrangements for Bothwell's divorce from his wife, Lady Jane Gordon, had to be expedited. On 3 May Lady Bothwell was given judgement against her husband in the Protestant commissary court, but more significantly their marriage was formally annulled on 7 May be the Catholic archbishop of St Andrews, whose consistorial jurisdiction had been restored by Mary, on the basis that they had allegedly not received a dispensation for their marriage, which was within the fourth degree of consanguinity.[95] Mary's part in this deception, for Archbishop Hamilton had himself granted such a dispensation, taxes the ingenuity of her most devoted admirers.[96] The occasion of her marriage to Bothwell on 15 May 1567 presents her supporters with their greatest problem, however, as the subsequent ceremony of marriage to a man, at best, a nominal Protestant was unpredictably conducted according to the Protestant form by Adam Bothwell, the reformed bishop of Orkney.[97] Mary's attachment to her faith had reached its lowest ebb. In consequence, it is hardly surprising that six weeks after this event the pope declared that it was not his intention to have any further dealings with Mary 'unless, indeed in times to come he should see some better sign of her life and religion that he has witnessed in the past'.[98] Mary at this stage, it was believed, was apparently willing to embrace Protestantism in order to salvage her political career. Her co-religionists were understandably shocked by her apparent religious insincerity. They believed that she was apostasizing for the basest of motives, and not until after her deposition and imprisonment in England did interest in her religious constancy become alive again. By 1568 Archbishop Beaton of Glasgow could report that Mary had begun to serve God again with more devotion than she had shown for some time previously, but the pope as yet was not quite so certain.[99] Only as her years of imprisonment dragged on did her reputation as a sufferer for religious constancy increase, and by then interest was activated by the political motivation of those whose real concern for her faith was no greater than that which Mary herself had displayed at an earlier period in her career.

Notes

[1] I. B. Cowan, *The Scottish Reformation* (1982), 49—53, 65—7, 89—114.

[2] *Papal Negs.*, xix, 22, 522—5.

[3] ibid., xxiv, 3—4.

[4] ibid., 524—5.

[5] ibid., 525—30.

[6] ibid., xxvi, 4—9.

[7] ibid., xxxv—xxxvii, 21—5.

[8] ibid., xliii.

[9] George Buchanan, *The History of Scotland*, ed. J. Aikman (1827—9), ii, 358—9; *CSP Scot.*, i, 263—4, 344.

[10] Donaldson, *Scotland*, 102; C. Burns, 'Papal gifts to Scottish monarchs: the golden rose and the blessed sword', *IR*, xx (1959), 183—5.

[11] *Papal Negs.*, 61—3, 435—44; J. de la Brosse, *Histoire d'un capitaine bourbonnais au XVIe siècle: Jacques de la Brosse 1485 (?)—1562* (1929), 279.

[12] *CSP Scot.*, i, 597, 603; *CSPF 1561—2*, 512, 523.

[13] *CSP Scot.*, i, 555. See White, ch. 3 above, for Huntly's standing.

[14] *Papal Negs.*, 83, 87.

[15] Knox, *History*, i, 354—5; ii, 6.

[16] ibid., ii, 7—8; Hay Fleming, *Mary*, 285—6; Melville, *Memoirs*, 91; *CSPF 1561—2*, 278.

[17] *RPC*, i, 266—8.

[18] ibid., i, 201—3.

[19] Knox, *History*, ii, 103.

[20] *CSPF 1562*, 329. See White, ch. 3 above, for Mary's reaction to Huntly's mass.

[21] J. Robertson (ed.), *Inventaires de la royne d'Escosse douairiere de France: Catalogues of the jewels, furnitures, books and paintings of Mary Queen of Scots, 1556—1569* (1863), 49—54.

[22] *Papal Negs.*, 163; Fraser, *Mary*, 203.

[23] *Papal Negs.*, 73—81.

[24] ibid., 113—39.

[25] ibid., 132.

[26] ibid., 138.

[27] ibid., 122, 135.

[28] ibid., 120—1, 134.

[29] ibid., 139.

[30] ibid., 73, 75.

[31] ibid., 162—3, 169.

[32] *Extracts from the Records of the Burgh of Edinburgh* [*Edin. Recs.*] (Scottish Burgh Records Society, 1869—92), iii, 125.

[33] ibid., iii, 140—1.

[34] M. H. B. Sanderson, 'Catholic recusancy in Scotland in the sixteenth century', *IR*, xxi (1970), 88. See Hay Fleming, *Mary*, 257n, and J. G. Dunbar, 'The palace of Holyroodhouse', *Arch. J.*, cxx (1964), 242—54, for descriptions of the various chapels at Holyrood.

[35] Knox, *History*, ii, 8—9; Knox, *Works*, vi, 131.

[36] Knox, *History*, ii, 87.

[37] Pitcairn, *Trials*, i, 433—5. See Lynch, *Edinburgh*, 287ff, for their identities. No further notice of the case exists, although a date had been set for trial.

[38] Pitcairn, *Trials*, i, 435n; Lynch, *Edinburgh*, 122n.

[39] *Edin. Recs.*, iii, 152—3, 162; Sanderson, 'Catholic recusancy,' 102—3.

[40] *Buik of the Kirk of the Canagait, 1564—1567*, ed. A. Calderwood (SRS, 1961), 55—6.

[41] ibid., 38.

[42] *Edin. Recs.*, iii, 131, 135, 139, 141—51, 190, 193—7, 215; *Buik of the Canagait*, 8, 11.

[43] *Diurnal*, 301.

[44] Keith, *History*, ii, 268.

[45] Knox, *History*, ii, 141—2; cf. *Edin. Recs.*, iii, 195—6; *CSP Scot.*, ii, 144—5, 148—9.

[46] *BUK*, i, 59.

[47] *Papal Negs.*, 496, 520—1.

[48] *RSS*, v, 1619.

[49] *Thirds of Benefices*, 89; *RSS*, v, 2561, 2947, 3435, 3572.

[50] Knox, *History*, ii, 70.

[51] ibid., ii, 70—1.

[52] ibid., ii, 71—4.

[53] ibid., ii, 74.

[54] ibid., ii, 76; Pitcairn, *Trials*, i, 427; *Diurnal*, 75.

[55] Knox, *Works*, ii, 592—5.

[56] *Papal Negs.*, 386n.

[57] *RPC*, i, 487—8, 494. Cf. Lynch, ch. 1 above, for an alternative interpretation of this point.

[58] *APS*, ii, 545. See Greengrass, ch. 8 above, for the jointure.

[59] See Adams, ch. 6 below.

[60] *BUK*, i, 68—76; Knox, *History*, ii, 174, 175—7.

[61] *CSP Scot,* ii, 254. See also Lynch, ch. 1 above, and Goodare, ch. 7 below, for Candlemas 1566.

[62] *Papal Negs.*, 205—6, 208—9.

[63] ibid., 200, 211—13.

[64] ibid., 211—15.

[65] *RPC*, i, 266—8.

[66] *Papal Negs.*, c.

[67] *CSP Scot.*, ii, 254; *Papal Negs.*, 232—3. Cf. Lynch, ch. 1 above, for Darnley's Candlemas investiture.

[68] *Papal Negs.*, 233.

[69] ibid., 234, 452—5.

[70] ibid., 238.

[71] ibid., cvii—cviii, 263.

[72] Knox, *History*, ii, 5.

[73] Melville, *Memoirs*, 152—4.

[74] *Papal Negs.*, 269—70, 276—7, 284—5.

[75] ibid., 284—5.

[76] ibid., 285—8, 297—9, 302—3.

[77] ibid., 320—4.

[78] ibid., 327.

[79] ibid., cxviii, 367—8, 370—1.

[80] ibid., cxxvii, 380—6.

[81] ibid., 118, 132.

[82] J. Stevenson (ed.), *Selections from unpublished Manuscripts in the College of Arms and the British Museum illustrating the Reign of Mary Queen of Scotland, 1543—68* (1837), 124.

[83] *Papal Negs.*, xcii and n; *Liber Officialis S. Andree* (1845), pp. xl, 164.

[84] *Papal Negs.*, xciii and n.

[85] ibid., lxxviii, 201—3.

[86] ibid., 196, 199, 203.

[87] ibid., lxxix—lxxxvii, 197, 200, 210—11, 215—27; the location of the original brief has long been a matter of dispute (ibid., 217—18 and n), and although its source has been identified (ibid., 218n) as Armario XIII no. 38, this too appears to be inaccurate. The present location of the volume entitled 'Dispense matrimoniali per re, principi, nobili 1531—97', which contains the brief, is Armario XII, vol. 211 which is now accessioned in the Vatican Library as Cod. Vat. Lat., 12398, fos 12—12v (I owe this reference to Mr J. J. Robertson).

[88] *Diurnal*, 79—80; *Facsimilies of the National Manuscripts of Scotland*, 3 vols (London 1867—71), iii, no. xlviii.

[89] Fraser, *Mary*, 230.

[90] *Papal Negs.*, xciv—xcv.

[91] This is clearly revealed by a study of such dispensations contained in Acta Sacra Paenitentiariae Apostolicae held in the Vatican archives and which with special permission of the regent of the Penitentiary have been examined and analysed for Scotland by scholars from the universities of Dundee and Glasgow.

[92] J. C. Barry (ed.) *William Hay's Lectures on Marriage* (Stair Society, 1967), xlv, 317.

[93] Fraser, *Mary,* 342−4; cf. Donaldson, *Scotland,* 125.

[94] Fraser, *Mary,* 314−17.

[95] *Diurnal,* 110; Claude Nau, *Memorials of Mary Stewart* (1883), clxiii−clxvi.

[96] W. Fraser (ed.), *The Sutherland Book* (1892), iii, 131−2. A papal dispensation also appears to have been obtained; Vatican Library: Cod. Vat. Lat., 12398, fos 14−15v.

[97] Melville, *Memoirs,* 178−9; *Diurnal,* 111−12.

[98] *Papal Negs.,* 396−8.

[99] ibid., cxxxiii n.

6

The Release of Lord Darnley and the Failure of the Amity

SIMON ADAMS

You have heard how the queen did give my lord of Lennox and his son leave to go into Scotland to take possession of their inheritance, but now news is brought to the queen that he is married to the queen of Scots.

Elizabeth Hilgate[1]

There are many grounds on which the conduct of Elizabethan foreign policy can be criticized. Rashness and carelessness, however, are not among them. Laborious weighing of alternatives, prolonged debate and frequent prevarication were the norm. Exceptions to the rule attract attention precisely because they were so much out of character. The leading example is the appropriation in December 1568 of the bullion being dispatched from Spain to the duke of Alva. No less controversial was the permission to visit Scotland granted to Henry Stewart, Lord Darnley, in January 1565. If the results were dramatic, the episode itself remains obscure. It has been described as 'not the least of the riddles of the period' and 'an interesting enigma'.[2] The origins of the controversy are clear enough: had Darnley not been in Scotland, his marriage to Mary would not have taken place, or if it did, it would have been under very different circumstances. Was his visit arranged deliberately? The debate began at the time of the marriage and has been carried on in most studies of Mary's reign. Yet the background to the visit itself has never been examined in detail. Even the most recent account of the Darnley marriage has concentrated on the events after his arrival rather than those that preceded it.[3]

The partisan nature of so much Marian literature has inspired a number of conspiratorial interpretations of both the visit and the marriage. These have involved not only Mary and Elizabeth, but also the

123

Lennox Stewarts, Sir William Cecil, and Robert Dudley, earl of Leicester. Only Sir William Maitland of Lethington and James Stewart, earl of Moray, have been exempted, though Mary did accuse Moray in one of her more hysterical outbursts of arranging the Darnley marriage as part of an intrigue against the house of Hamilton.[4] Nor are the theories mutually exclusive; the perennial fascination with the duel between the queens has inspired speculation that Mary and Elizabeth were engaged in rival plots over Darnley.[5] A reconstruction of the circumstances of Darnley's release must begin, therefore, by surveying the major conspiracy theories and assessing the evidence on which they are based. The ostensible reasons for Darnley's visit and the problems created by the exile of the Lennox Stewarts will then be examined. Lastly, the episode must be set in its true context: the novel politics of 'the amity', the central issue of Anglo-Scots relations between 1561 and 1565.

Lacunae in the sources are responsible for much of the controversy, though the reasons for them may not in themselves be sinister. The work so regularly employed to provide a running commentary on Anglo-Scots affairs, the *Calendar of State Papers relating to Scotland and Mary, Queen of Scots,* comprises in the main the dispatches of the English agent in Edinburgh, Thomas Randolph.[6] His own papers have disappeared, and by no means all the outgoing English correspondence survives. If we possessed the letter to Randolph of 5 February 1565 in which Cecil outlined the reasons for releasing Darnley, much speculation would be unnecessary.[7] Three key letters from Elizabeth to Mary, those of 5 March 1564, 5 July 1564 and 5 March 1565, are also missing. Mary's own correspondence is notoriously sparse, whether or not she is accurately reported in the instructions for Sir James Melville of Halhill as stating that 'we vse not to reserve any copie of our famylier lettres wreten with our awen hand'.[8]

Of the other figures, few Lennox papers survive, and only in the case of Maitland of Lethington and Leicester can significant fragments of their relevant correspondence be traced.[9] Randolph was the only resident diplomatic agent in Scotland, and the surviving dispatches of the French and Spanish envoys in London (Paul de Foix and Diego Guzman de Silva) are both incomplete and unreliable.[10] A heavier weight has therefore been placed on contemporary and near-contemporary narratives. In the autumn of 1565 Cecil drew up two surveys of the decline in relations between Elizabeth and Mary, but these skate over the events of January.[11] More controversial, however, are two accounts of Scottish provenance: the famous description by Melville of his embassy to London in September 1564, and Mary's own later memoir 'Contre la legereté du mariasge'.[12]

The 'Marian conspiracy' is first encountered in English State Papers in the autumn of 1565. In a memorandum he composed at the time of the Chaseabout Raid, Cecil included among the 'principal matters to be objected' against Mary the charge of 'practising to have the Lord Darnley into Scotland to be her husband, whilst she bore the queen's majesty in hand'. Elizabeth rehearsed the same theme, that Darnley 'was secretly enticed to pass into Scotland upon other pretences, for private suits for lands and such like', in a defence of her conduct towards Mary sent to France in 1570.[13] In the work of Froude, Philippson, Henderson and Sir John Neale, the Marian conspiracy has figured prominently.[14] It is based on the argument that Mary sought only two candidates for a second husband. Her first choice was the Infante Don Carlos; her second, after Philip II had vetoed Don Carlos, was Lord Darnley. The alternatives, the Archduke Charles of Styria or the earl of Leicester, were never taken seriously, and any willingness to co-operate with Elizabeth was simply a diplomatic manoeuvre.

The central difficulty for this theory is establishing the date when Mary discovered that the Don Carlos marriage was impossible. Serious negotiations began in the summer of 1563, and were conducted with Cardinal Granvelle and the duchess of Aerschot through her French secretary, Pierre Raulet.[15] A flurry of appeals to Granvelle in the early months of 1564 revealed Mary's impatience.[16] Philip II, on the other hand, had serious reservations about the match. He took careful soundings among his senior councillors during the autumn of 1563, and at the beginning of 1564 decided that Don Carlos's doubtful mental stability made it unwise. Yet, possibly to avoid embarrassing questions, his decision was not made public immediately. Much to Granvelle's annoyance, the instructions (19 January 1564) for the newly appointed ambassador to London, Diego Guzman de Silva, contained no reference to the marriage.[17] The king's preference for the Archduke Charles was finally announced in dispatches to Granvelle and Guzman on 6 August 1564.[18] When these new instructions reached their destinations is not clear, however. Guzman's earliest surviving reference to them is found in his dispatch of 27 November. A cryptic postscript to that of 4 September, that he would do all in his power to advance the Austrian match with Mary, but was ready if the king decided to revive the marriage to Don Carlos, suggests that he had not received Philip's letter by then, or if he had, did not regard it as final.[19]

Those who have argued that Mary agreed to the restoration of Matthew Stewart, earl of Lennox, in April 1564 so that Elizabeth would permit Darnley to visit Scotland have therefore been forced to claim that Mary 'must have' deduced Philip's decision from the Spanish silence.[20] But of this there is no proof. A variant theory has associated Mary's change of policy with the famous embassy of Melville to London in September 1564. This episode, however, presents its own difficulties. The first is a further problem of chronology. In his *Memoirs* Melville claims he spent nine days at the English court, but provides only two dates: the creation of Lord Robert Dudley as earl of Leicester (Michaelmas) at which he says he was present; and that of his instructions, which is given as 28 September. The latter is clearly a copyist's error for the 18th, the date of a letter he carried from Maitland to Cecil. Since he also brought letters from Moray and William Kirkcaldy of Grange of the 19th, it can be assumed he left Edinburgh on either the 19th or 20th.[21] He implies that he arrived at the English court several days before Dudley's creation, but Cecil records him as arriving on the 29th.[22] He probably left London with Thomas Randolph on or about 7 October.[23]

Melville's instructions also deserve scrutiny. His *Memoirs* include his 'general instructions', drafted by Maitland and signed by Mary. These were to smooth over any bad feeling caused by an angry letter Mary had written when Elizabeth attempted to delay the earl of Lennox's departure; to propose a meeting at Berwick between 'men of credit' to resolve the proposed Dudley marriage; and to see that the English parliament, due to be recalled, did not threaten Mary's claim to the English succession.[24] Neither Darnley nor the Spanish match are mentioned. These instructions appear to have been genuine for Mary described the embassy in the same terms in a dispatch to Archbishop Beaton on 2 November. Moreover, a letter from Dudley to Maitland complaining about Mary's sharpness, referred to in the instructions, survives.[25] Melville also claims to have had verbal orders 'to deall with the queen of England, with the Spanish ambassadour, and with my lady Margaret Douglas [the countess of Lennox]'. Apart from his discussions with Elizabeth (which will be discussed later), it is doubtful whether these amounted to much, for Guzman's dispatch of 9 October refers to him only in passing.[26]

Lastly, there is the question of the relationship between Melville's embassy and the earl of Lennox's return to Scotland. Lennox finally left the English court shortly after 1 September, reaching Berwick some time after the 19th, and Edinburgh on the 22nd.[27] Although it seems probable that their paths crossed, whether his departure was known before Melville himself left Edinburgh is not clear. It may, indeed, have been the case that a request for Lennox's release had been one of Melville's verbal instructions, which was thereby rendered redundant. What cannot be maintained is that Melville's embassy marked a new departure in Mary's policy towards Spain or the Lennox Stewarts.[28]

The Spanish negotiations were being conducted elsewhere. In November Maitland informed Beaton that 'I fynd her mynd only applyit to Spaine. ...some mocion was langsyne maid thairin by the bishop of Aquila. ...bot of late we have hard little or nothing in it'. Beaton was to 'enter as off yourself in franck communication with the kyng of Spaine's embassadour in that court touching the said kyngs sone'.[29] These instructions were never rescinded and as late as March 1565, much to the embarrassment of Don Francesco de Alava, Beaton continued to press for a decision over Don Carlos.[30]

The 'Elizabethan conspiracy' has figured prominently in defences of Mary. On one level it is simply a mirror image of the Marian. Mary is portrayed as wishing to reach an equitable compromise with Elizabeth when the latter allowed Darnley to visit Scotland, precisely to confuse the issue. He was 'the English snare' (Andrew Lang), or a 'trojan horse' (Antonia Fraser).[31] The basic problem for this theory is reconciling Elizabeth's permission to Darnley with her vehement opposition to the match when she learnt of it. The suspicion that Elizabeth may have released Darnley deliberately and that her opposition to the marriage was insincere was reported by Randolph as current in Scottish circles in the summer of 1565.[32] But if Darnley was used in this way, why was Elizabeth prepared to run the risk of a match? The explanation has been found in her fear that Mary would in fact accept the Leicester marriage. Her earlier proposal of Leicester was, therefore, equally insincere: Elizabeth sought simply to keep Mary unmarried indefinitely, using whatever device came to hand.

If Mary was playing fair, she would still need firm evidence of Elizabeth's insincerity before turning to Darnley. Two episodes in March 1565 has been advanced in this connection. The first is the arrival on the 16th of Elizabeth's now-missing letter of 5 March, in which she stated that she would not allow Mary to be declared heir apparent by parliament until she had herself decided whether or not to marry.[33] Tytler, Philippson, Henderson and, most recently, Dawson have seen this letter as decisive.[34] Andrew Lang, however, placed the turning-point a week or so later, basing his opinion on Randolph's report that Mary was still willing to negotiate with Elizabeth after reading the letter of the 5th. This was the circulation in Scotland of gossip about a dispute during a tennis match between Leicester and the duke of Norfolk, in which Leicester used (in Lang's words) 'indecent familiarity' towards Elizabeth by employing her napkin as a towel. Lang considered it a deliberate insult to Mary by an Elizabeth who hoped thereby to obtain 'what she desired — a disunited Scotland as a field for intrigue'.[35]

The 'Tennis Court incident' has become so embedded in the history of Elizabethan politics that it is easy to forget that the only source for it is Randolph's warning to Sir Nicholas Throckmorton on 31 March that such stories were being spread maliciously by Lennox's ally John Stewart, earl of Atholl.[36] He mentions it in none of his other letters of that day, nor do either of the ambassadors at the English court report it.[37] This does not necessarily mean that the story is a complete fabrication, but since Mary's reaction to it is unknown, assessments of its impact must remain speculation. We are on firmer ground with the letter of the 5th, for Randolph reports Mary's angry response that she had been 'abused' by Elizabeth in some detail.[38] Dr Dawson concludes that the letter 'represented a complete departure from previous English policy. . . . Mary had been led to believe that an acceptable marriage on her part was the essential precondition to recognition; hence her willingness to consider Leicester's suit'.[39] If Elizabeth was not intriguing, she was at the least careless.

The question of Elizabeth's motives in proposing the Leicester marriage remains. Most comment has been scathing: it was either bathetic ('worthy of a lending-library romance' in Maurice Lee's words), eccentric, a deliberate insult, or a tactic to block a foreign match for Mary that Elizabeth had no intention of following through.[40] There have, however, been dissenters. Randolph certainly took the marriage seriously, although he has been considered a dupe for doing so.[41] More recently, Wallace MacCaffrey has argued that it possessed 'a certain political logic', the main barrier being the emotional relationship between Leicester and Elizabeth which made it impossible for contemporaries to believe that she would let him marry another woman. Such reservations are countered by Elizabeth's frequent statements that she loved Leicester as a brother. The implication that she did not regard their relations as carnal is clear. Quixotically, perhaps, she may have seen herself as offering Mary her most valued subject, not a discarded lover.[42]

The tortuous arguments demanded by the theory of an Elizabethan conspiracy are further complicated by what has been described as Elizabeth's 'passive' role in Darnley's departure.[43] The focus, as a result, has tended to shift to Cecil and Leicester. It is clear that they jointly advised Elizabeth to release Darnley.[44] The Cecil plot, first described by Melville, is similar to the Elizabethan. Worried by the success of the Dudley marriage, he used the release of Darnley, whom he believed he could control, as a means of confusing the issue.[45] More recently, and particularly in the work of Conyers Read and Jane Dawson, who has argued that Darnley went to Scotland as his 'proxy', Leicester has received more attention. He at least had an obvious motive, for his lack of enthusiasm for the match with Mary is undeniable. Moreover, he gave Darnley every assistance in his visit.[46] A number of contemporary accounts refer to his secret efforts to block the marriage. Melville relates a conversation with Leicester in which the latter claimed it was a plot 'of Mester Cecil his secret enemy', and gave him letters to Moray 'till excuse him at the Queenis hands'. In her memoir, Mary claimed that Leicester warned her through Randolph. Camden, who argues that Leicester still hoped to marry Elizabeth and therefore supported Darnley to avoid being shunted off to Edinburgh, states that he did so by the earl of Bedford at Berwick.[47] Two further pieces of evidence have also been advanced: the letter of thanks Darnley wrote to Leicester soon after he arrived in Scotland, and the fact that Leicester did not sign the privy council's protest to Mary against the match on 1 May.[48]

Despite his apparent motive, the evidence for a Leicester intrigue is not as clear as has been made out. Such has been the established picture of factionalism between Leicester and Cecil that their co-operation over Darnley's visit has been discounted.[49] The tension between them can be exaggerated. Randolph's reports were read by both men; Cecil was fully aware of Leicester's lack of interest in the match to Mary; and there is no suggestion that he suspected an intrigue. Nor was Randolph used as Leicester's secret intermediary. The evidence for Leicester acting independently concerns, as will be seen, Mary's claim to the succession, not the marriage. Darnley's letter is a fairly bland expression of thanks for Leicester's good offices in general. One may equally well have been sent to Cecil.[50] Leicester's absence from the council meeting on 1 May was caused by a riding accident on 27 April that left him bedridden for some days.[51] Sir Nicholas Bacon, the marquess of Northampton and the earls of Arundel and Bedford also failed to sign the protest: only Arundel is said to have refused deliberately.[52]

Of all the participants in the affair, the Lennox Stewarts have received least attention.[53] This neglect has its ironical side, for whatever conclusions the various conspiracy theories lead to, they share the assumption that the Lennoxes were scheming unceasingly for a marriage between Mary and Darnley. Thus (with the main exceptions of Hume Brown and Dawson) it has been taken for granted that once Darnley was able to visit Scotland the marriage was only a matter of time, and moreover that this was common knowledge.[54] The ostensible reason for Darnley's visit, the restoration of the earldom of Lennox, has been considered either a matter of course or a pretext. Such an oversimplification of the Lennox restoration, which had been an important issue in Anglo-Scots diplomacy for over a decade, obscures its significance to the broader relationship between Elizabeth and Mary.

Matthew Stewart had been left an outlawed exile in England by the peace of 1551. His position remained an intransigent one: Henry VIII had promised that he would be restored and Henry's successors were therefore morally obliged to see that he was.[55] The countess of Lennox's demand for recognition as heir to her father, Archibald Douglas, earl of Angus (died *c*.1556) further complicated matters. The Edwardian government had not known what to do with them.[56] After 1553 their position improved, for the countess and Queen Mary had been friends as girls, and Mary regarded the family benevolently. However, her efforts to support their claims in Scotland were brought to a halt by the war of 1557.[57] Elizabeth's accession saw their hopes decline. Not only did she dislike Mary's favourites (whatever the truth of the charges that the countess had tried to turn Mary against her), but more importantly her new policy in Scotland involved an alliance with their leading enemies: the duke of Châtelherault and James Douglas, earl of Morton, 'tutor' to his infant nephew, who also laid claim to the earldom of Augus.[58] Like the peace of 1551, the Anglo-Scots alliance of 1559–60 was made at the expense of the house of Lennox. At the end of 1559 the English council came to suspect that Lennox was negotiating with the French. When challenged, he agreed not to sabotage Elizabeth's policy, but protested that the English were reneging on the promise of Henry VIII and refused to recognize the appointment of Châtelherault as governor of Scotland by the Lords of the Congregation.[59]

The Lennox fortunes revived after the death of François II, for they now had an opportunity to appeal directly to Mary over the heads of both Elizabeth and the Congregation. If Mary turned against Châtelherault and the Lords on her return to Scotland, so much the better. Both the threat Lennox posed and his family's open discontent were fully appreciated. When the son of John Lockhart of Bar was arrested carrying messages for them across the border in January 1562, they in turn were imprisoned. By this time rumours of the countess's hopes for her son were part of the diplomatic gossip of Europe.[60] During the spring and summer of 1562 the English council investigated their activities in detail. From the interrogation of their servants a number of charges were drawn up. Apart from plotting the marriage of Darnley and Mary, they included correspondence with Mary and the Spanish and French ambassadors, hearing mass, and mocking Elizabeth and Dudley. While it is clear that the Lennoxes did not confess everything, the investigation, none the less, was inconclusive. All that could be proved was that Darnley's tutor, Arthur Lallart, had been sent to Mary in the autumn of 1561 to appeal for Lennox's restoration.[61]

This episode had important consequences. Having admitted to the

Lallart mission, Lennox made his 'submission' to Elizabeth in August 1562.[62] The following November, following a barrage of appeals by the countess, he was released from the Tower to join her in house arrest at Sheen. In February 1563 their release was made unconditional.[63] Four months later Elizabeth took up their cause for the first time. At their request she supported their appeals for restoration, both in a letter to Mary and verbally to Maitland and Randolph.[64] During the following year they were increasingly prominent at court: the countess was joint godmother with the queen to Cecil's infant daughter Elizabeth in July 1564.[65] Yet, despite Elizabeth's support, little further is heard of their restoration until April 1564 when a servant of Lennox's (apparently Thomas Fowler) arrived at the Scottish court to obtain Mary's approval.

The silence was due in large part to Randolph (widely believed to be partial to the Hamiltons), who opposed Lennox's restoration and obeyed his instructions with little enthusiasm.[66] Moreover, he was absent from Scotland for much of the period April to October 1564, and learnt of Fowler's errand only at second hand.[67] Mary's agreement to Lennox's restoration therefore presents a mystery, for she had remained scrupulously neutral on the subject in 1562 and 1563.[68] The restoration had the support of other Stewarts, especially Atholl, the protector of the Lennox interest, but it could only be obtained at the expense of the Hamiltons. The agreement of Moray and Maitland has for that reason been attributed to a desire to weaken the position of Châtelherault.[69] The Lennox restoration thus initiated a reshaping of Mary's court that the Darnley marriage concluded ten months later. At this stage it involved an important series of compromises. Moray was appointed lieutenant-general of the kingdom in September; in October Mary herself reconciled Châtelherault and Lennox.[70] The key, however, appears to have been the surrender of the countess's claims to the earldom of Angus. A formal concession was made in November, though it was not ratified until May 1565.[71]

The only known opposition came from Knox and Kirkcaldy of Grange, who were already suspicious of the queen. Randolph quickly relayed their doubts to London.[72] At the beginning of July 1564 Elizabeth herself became concerned and wrote to Mary on the 5th to cancel Lennox's departure that summer.[73] According to Guzman de Silva she had changed her mind because she discovered that Lennox would be accompanied by the countess and Darnley, and feared that a marriage was being plotted.[74] There is some evidence that Mary gave permission to both the earl and the countess to return to Scotland, but the crucial influence appears to have been Randolph who had returned to London at the end of June, having already made it clear that he wished to halt

Lennox's departure.[75] His emphasis on the threat to the Hamiltons and her other friends caused Elizabeth to request via Cecil and Dudley that Moray and Maitland also support the cancellation of Lennox's permission. As Dudley wrote to Maitland 'no man wished more his [Lennox's] going than I or furthered at her majesty's hands after your good likings there was known', but now his 'coming thither' was held to be dangerous.[76]

Elizabeth's intervention backfired badly. It provoked not only Mary, but also Moray and Maitland, to respond that 'factions are not so easily to be suscitat in this country as some perhaps do persuade themselves', a clear hint that Randolph was seen as responsible.[77] Lennox finally departed at the beginning of September, but his wife and son were left as hostages for his good behaviour. He was quickly integrated into the Scottish court; his restoration to the earldom of Lennox was proclaimed on 16 October and ratified by parliament on 13 December. He was, however, careful to assure both Elizabeth and Cecil of his continued loyalty and gratitude. Mary was equally sensitive to Elizabeth's unease and on several occasions stated that she was only restoring Lennox at Elizabeth's request and as a favour to her, though the disarming of domestic opposition may also have inspired her caution.[78]

It was at this point that the question of Darnley joining his father arose. Lennox wished for the two to be enfeoffed together to ensure that the new entail should be unchallenged, and sent a legal opinion to this effect to England.[79] A request appears to have been made to Elizabeth in November (though not, as stated in several places, by Mary), possibly in order to have Darnley present at the parliamentary ratification in December.[80] Elizabeth's refusal revived gossip about a Lennox plot, but the decisive influence may once again have been Randolph, who still wished to limit the Lennox restoration. Not only did he oppose any visit by Darnley, but he also relayed every suspicious rumour.[81] When Elizabeth finally granted her permission at the end of January 1565, no reason was given. What we may suspect, however, is that Randolph had cried wolf once too often. Mary appears to have maintained her neutrality and no formal approaches were made for a Darnley match. At the Berwick conference in November Randolph had 'looked here to have my Lord Darnley mentioned', but 'of whom for all that there was not one word spoken'.[82]

Viewed from this perspective, the release of Lord Darnley loses the appearance of rashness. Indeed, both it and the Lennox restoration as a whole take on the classic characteristics of Elizabethan decision-making: delay, second thoughts and prevarication. More importantly, however, the events of 1564 and early 1565 were themselves very much an aftermath. The central decision had already been taken during the winter of 1562–3, when the Lennoxes were restored to favour and Elizabeth agreed to support their Scottish claims.[83] Her generosity is striking, for she was not usually charitable to persons possessing the blood royal, as her simultaneous treatment of Lady Catherine Grey reveals. Her change of heart towards the Lennoxes has been attributed to an intention to play them off against Mary, should she proceed with the Austrian match.[84] The chronology suggests a different explanation. Whatever suspicions she may have entertained of the Lennoxes at the beginning of 1562, the council's investigations had failed to produce any serious evidence against them, and Mary had remained completely neutral. Lennox made his submission in August, but his release did not come until November, after Elizabeth had recovered from her smallpox attack. He and his wife were not fully restored to favour until the parliament of 1563 had opened. At this point the English succession had become a public issue. The 'Hales Book' ('A Declaration of the Succession to the Imperial Crown of England'), which may reflect speeches made in the Commons, argued that not only were the Lennoxes barred, like Mary, by the will of Henry VIII, but the Lennox claim was further weakened by the bigamous marriage of the earl of Angus and the consequent bastardy of his daughter.[85] It is possible that Lennox and his wife protested to the privy council, for in March depositions were taken from surviving Henrician diplomats (William Barlow and Lord William Howard) about the Angus divorce and Maitland was consulted about the countess's legitimacy and Lennox's claims against Châtelherault.[86]

Elizabeth's change of heart toward the Lennoxes may therefore have involved a tacit compromise: she would support their legitimate claims, if they would abstain from more dangerous intrigues. Such an explanation fits Elizabeth's peculiarly legalistic sensitivity both to obligations left by Henry VIII and to the Stewart claim to the English succession. It also reflects her frequently expressed desire to curb public speculation and debate on the subject.[87] A similar agreement appears to have been struck with Lady Catherine Grey when she was released from the Tower into the custody of her uncle Lord John Grey of Pirgo in August 1563.

If there is a non-controversial explanation for Darnley's visit to Scotland, Elizabeth's decision to let him go can still be criticized as myopic. Whether justified or not, rumours of a possible Mary–Darnley match were rife. Indeed, Elizabeth herself stated later in 1565 that she had released Darnley owing to appeals, made by his parents and friends pleading the only cause expressly to be for the furtherance of his father in Scotland though we lacked not information and reports of sinister and unfriendly meanings towards us in the departing from hence both of the father the earl of Lennox and of his son, yet would we not give place or credit thereto.[88]

Moreover, if Dr Dawson is correct, Elizabeth's reversal of a previous commitment to recognize Mary's position as heir apparent while Darnley was in Scotland was tempting fate to a major degree. An answer to these questions demands an examination of Elizabeth's attitude towards Mary and its relationship to the new amity between England and Scotland.

Much confusion has been caused by the failure to see 'the amity' for what it was. Although there was a unionist element to it, it was not a 'euphemism' for the subordination of Scotland to England.[89] Rather, as Moray, one of its architects, described it, it was a work of God that:

these twa nations joinit in one yland and separated from the rest of the world, quha being sturred oup in times past by the craft of Sathan to shed one ane otheris blood, God haith wonderfully I say bestowed his blessing upon us, overthrowing the work of the adversary quhill he hes convertit the unquenchable inimity to the judgement of man in ane mutual reciproque luif and benevolence betwix the twa nations.[90]

It was thus a symbol for the alliance of 1560, an alliance both Protestant and reciprocal. After Mary's return in August 1561 it took on a more specific significance, for the death of François II brought to the fore the issue that was hereafter to dominate relations between the queens: Mary's refusal to ratify the Treaty of Edinburgh.[91] Although Mary's resumption of direct rule in Scotland made much of the treaty redundant, the clause in which she repudiated her rival claim to the English throne had been a major prize of Elizabeth's diplomacy.[92] The question had already soured relations between the two before Mary's return and had caused Elizabeth to refuse her permission to travel through England.

The antagonism between the queens meant that by the summer of 1561 'the amity' represented the efforts of their leading ministers to prevent their personal enmity jeopardizing the peace. From the start the central figures were Cecil and Maitland, Lord James Stewart and Lord Robert Dudley (as Moray and Leicester then were). As was to be typical of many future Protestant alliances, political interest was reinforced by personal friendship.[93] The groundwork appears to have been laid by Lord James during a visit to the English court on his return from France in the spring of 1561.[94] It was completed by Maitland at a meeting with Cecil and Dudley at Hertford Castle during his embassy to Elizabeth in September.[95] The formal purpose of the embassy was the proposing of Maitland's famous compromise that Mary should renounce her claim to the English throne during Elizabeth's lifetime in exchange for recognition as heir apparent. If accepted, the compromise would supersede the Edinburgh treaty and save the amity. Maitland later claimed that he first devised it at the beginning of 1561. Lord James seems to have known about it in the spring, and suggested it to the English during the summer.[96] However, Elizabeth insisted on the ratification of the treaty (as she was to do consistently hereafter) and refused the compromise on the ground that princes 'could not love their winding sheet'.[97]

Central to Maitland's compromise was the argument that Mary had to be 'allured'.[98] This meant not only to accept the status quo, but even (he hinted) her possible conversion.[99] Implicit was the fear that if the policy failed Mary would turn to 'other councils'. Maitland does not appear to have seen Elizabeth's rejection as definitive, but merely a continuation of the existing tension between the queens. He continued to argue that the compromise was (in Lord James's words) 'the readiest, yea and only moyen' to safeguard the amity.[100] The Hertford Castle agreement was thus an understanding that the four ministers would co-operate in improving relations between their sovereigns. The reception given by the English court to Mary's escort on their return to France in October (in which Dudley appears to have been instrumental) thus became the first example of the new policy at work.[101]

Such minor gestures of good will were, however, overshadowed by the major question of the interview between the two queens. In origin this was an English proposal, offered by Elizabeth in the summer of 1561 as a concession if Mary would ratify the treaty.[102] Maitland later claimed it was promised at Hertford Castle, and when raised again by Randolph later in October, it was taken up by Mary with alacrity.[103] When it was postponed in July 1562 it provoked the amity's first major crisis. The English reason for postponement — the need to keep a watch on the deteriorating situation in France — was not an excuse. Rather Mary's studied neutrality towards the French civil war and the English intervention suggested that, when it came to the point, the amity was not truly reciprocal.[104] It revived the suspicion that, whatever Maitland might say, Mary would still be governed by her uncles and the interests of the house of Guise.[105] Maitland did not help his case when he argued in November 1562 that only the compromise would prevent Mary from taking their part actively.[106]

Mary's neutrality led to both a distinct cooling towards the amity in the English court, and the emergence of an increasingly vocal anti-Marian party, whose spokesman on the council was the lord keeper, Sir Nicholas Bacon.[107] Central to their suspicion of Mary was the Guise connection; from it stemmed a major miscalculation, which underlay the errors over Mary's marriage. Henceforward the English council viewed Scottish politics as a struggle between Guise influence on the one hand, and that of Maitland and Moray on the other. The possibilities that Mary might act independently, or that an anglophobe but independent Scottish faction might emerge after the death in 1562 of the earl of Huntly, its potential rallying point, were discounted. The failure was to some extent a diplomatic one, for Randolph was unable, for all his experience of the Scottish court, to provide an accurate assessment of Mary's intentions, and indeed openly admitted his perplexity. In 1562 and 1563 he was generally suspicious of the Guise connection.[108] In the autumn of 1564 he had swung round to seeing Mary as willing to co-operate fully with Elizabeth.

The revived doubts about Mary fuelled the debate over the English succession precipitated by Elizabeth's smallpox attack in October 1562. The Grey party that emerged in the parliament of 1563 gained much of its importance from the fears that Mary had aroused in 1562. Thereafter the politics of the amity became much more difficult. Elizabeth's own attitude may have been idiosyncratic, but it was at least open and consistent. She would neither see Mary's rights challenged, nor have the succession debated publicly. Yet so long as she remained unmarried herself, the succession question would emerge in every parliamentary session. Her ability to concede to Mary was therefore severely restricted In this respect her willingness to advise Mary about her marriage in 1563 was as much a gesture of conciliation as those she made to the Lennoxes and the Greys.

The Grey party's stand had much in common with that of Knox. His denunciations of Mary's religious policy and claims that she intended a Spanish marriage also became more vocal in 1563. He had accused Maitland, shortly after Mary's return, of being 'too pollitique' and 'courtly'; Maitland had responded by labelling him as seditious. By 1564 the hostility between them threatened to divide the kirk.[109] Likewise the discovery of the 'Hales Book' in the spring of 1564 and the accusation in November that Bacon had encouraged it, created considerable embarrassment for Cecil and Dudley, for those involved (like Lord John Grey) were old friends.[110] Given Elizabeth's intention of protecting Mary's interests, punishment of the Greys was a necessary concession to the amity, yet this was not an issue the English council wanted brought into the open. Precisely how the various charges against the Greys were brought to the queen's attention is still a mystery. There is sufficient evidence to discount the older stories that it was a plot by Dudley to remove Bacon and embarrass Cecil.[111] The coincidence of the two revelations of Grey intrigues with the key points of the Lennox restoration (April and November 1564) encourages speculation that behind them was the countess of Lennox, who had her own reasons for attacking the 'Hales Book'.[112]

The squabble over Lennox's departure further revealed the strains in the amity. By 1564 the four ministers had become more hesitant and prone to take Maitland's line that 'the less meddling, the less danger'.[113] He at least remained consistent in maintaining that his compromise was the only means to achieve a stable settlement between the queens; so much so that Elizabeth complained to Melville that 'he did ring always her knell in her ears, talking of nothing but of her succession.'[114] His closest ally was Dudley, who at about this time seems to have reached the conclusion that Mary's claim to the English throne was unstoppable and that therefore a compromise had to be reached with her beforehand if the status quo was to be maintained. Not only did this search for a compromise inspire his indirect dealings with Mary at the beginning of 1565, but he pursued it more or less consistently until the discovery of the Ridolfi plot in 1571. It has been argued that Dudley was converted to this policy by Sir Nicholas Throckmorton in 1564.[115] However, a somewhat cryptic letter to Maitland on 27 October 1562 suggests that he was already attempting to protect Mary's position in the interests of the amity during the first succession debates.[116] The recent suggestion that Dudley supported the Grey claim at the beginning of 1562 can be questioned. The alternative, that of his brother-in-law Huntingdon, was a weak one, if for no other reason than Huntingdon's own lack of interest in the succession.[117]

While the continued need to come to terms with Mary united Maitland and Dudley, Cecil and Moray became more reticent. Cecil clearly was much influenced by the anti-Marian case, but it is doubtful that he expected he could keep her claim to the succession in suspension indefinitely. His preferred solution was for Elizabeth herself to marry and thus secure a Protestant succession.[118] Indeed the question of Elizabeth's willingness to marry may have been the real area of disagreement between him and Dudley.[119] Cecil's caution provoked Maitland's irritation and accusations of fence-sitting and covert opposition to the amity. Moray appears to have remained loyal to the original aims of the alliance. He was perhaps the most committed unionist of the four, and the most open supporter of the Dudley marriage. Yet his influence on Mary's policy in 1564 is by no means clear.[120]

The tensions in the amity were brought to a head by Mary's marriage negotiations. Whatever dealings she had had with Philip II in 1561, and whatever rumours had circulated about her plans for a Spanish marriage in 1562, only in the spring of 1563 did her marriage become a major issue.[121] Early in March there were widespread reports of a meeting between the cardinal of Lorraine and the Emperor Ferdinand at Innsbruck where the cardinal proposed a marriage between Mary and the Archduke Charles of Styria.[122] This was undertaken without Mary's knowledge; indeed formal notification did not reach her until May.[123] The news coincided with the dispatch of Maitland to London to ensure that the English parliament did not interfere with Mary's claim to the succession, and to offer both England and France Mary's services as a mediator in the war.[124] At the beginning of March he met the then Spanish ambassador in London, Alvaro de La Quadra, bishop of Aquila; during the course of their discussions the question of a marriage between Mary and the Infante Don Carlos was broached. Both participants have left accounts of their conversations, but they conflict on practically every major point.[125] Both state that they had no instructions to commence negotiations, and that the other brought up the subject. La Quadra related that Maitland was prepared to allow a certain revival of Catholicism in Scotland. Maitland reported La Quadra as saying that Philip II was not a 'soldado del papa', but a 'wyse politique prince', who would permit diversity of religion.

If La Quadra is to be believed, Maitland had been sent from Scotland deliberately to initiate negotiations with Spain, whatever he may have told the English. According to Maitland, La Quadra proposed the Spanish match as an alternative to the Austrian. La Quadra has generally been given greater credence.[126] However, there is evidence to suggest Maitland may be the more accurate.[127] La Quadra was definitely exceeding his instructions (and would therefore wish to argue that Maitland initiated the subject), while if Maitland had verbal instructions to that effect, he had no reason to deny them. Soon afterwards he went on to France where Lorraine told him formally of the archducal match. His advice to Mary at this point was very cautious. He warned her that Elizabeth would regard a Habsburg marriage with concern. She was to sound Scottish opinion carefully; but 'alsa to seme to require the quene of England's conseile and advice'. He referred in passing to the archduke, Don Carlos and Darnley as potential consorts, but did not recommend any of them. Mary was to tell no one but Moray.[128] The next month Moray himself informed Dudley that he doubted whether Mary could proceed in the Austrian marriage without taking Elizabeth's advice.[129]

This reappraisal of Maitland's embassy not only clears him of deliberate double dealing, but also relegates the Spanish marriage to the secondary position it initially occupied.[130] Attention was focused on the Austrian marriage, primarily because it came from Lorraine. If La Quadra was moved to offer Mary an alternative, so was Elizabeth, whose choice had been the earl of Arran until his madness had eliminated him. It was at this point that Elizabeth first offered Dudley, though she confused the issue by mentioning his recently widowed brother Warwick as well. There is no evidence that Maitland took her proposal seriously enough to have informed Mary.[131] However, the concern with which the English regarded Lorraine's proposition encouraged him to revive his own compromise on his return to London from France in June, this time as a quid pro quo for Mary's willingness to obtain Elizabeth's consent in her marriage. He found Elizabeth 'slow in promising', and to Dudley at least 'did not dissemble how little cause I had to be satisfied, seeing a good mater lyke to quail in the mid-course'.[132]

In August 1563, however, Randolph was sent north with a partial compromise. Elizabeth's basic request was that Mary's husband should not threaten the amity; the Archduke Charles and any other candidate of the cardinal of Lorraine must be excluded. The hint was also dropped that such a choice would endanger Mary's hopes for the English succession, for 'we well perceive if we do not interpose our authority, it will not be long before it shall appear that as much as wit can engineer will be used to impeach her intention for the furtherance of her title.' Elizabeth would prefer that Mary have 'regard to this nation' and would be willing to offer her 'one as she would hardly think we would agree unto', but a foreigner who posed no challenge to the amity would also be acceptable. On such a marriage, Elizabeth would then proceed to 'the inquisition of her right and title to be our next cousin'.[133] Randolph also carried an impassioned plea from Cecil to Maitland not to follow 'the devises and determinations of the cardinal of Lorraine conceived in a congregation of antichrist's soldiers'.[134]

Mary accepted this proposition as a promise that Elizabeth 'meant to set furth [her title] be all gude meanes to our contentment as ane loving sister', but required to be informed precisely 'quhom she will allow and quhom she will not like'.[135] On 17 November Randolph (who had returned to London in the meantime) was instructed to tell her that both the Habsburgs and the Valois were regarded as hostile, but other choices were not limited to Britain, although he was not to name anyone in particular. If Mary would then

in the choice of her marriage show herself conformable to this. ...we will thereupon further proceed to the inquisition of her right. ...and shall be content to give ear to anything that shall be thought meet by her and her council to be declared on her behalf. And if we shall find the matter to fall out on her behalf, then upon plain knowledge had with whom she shall match in marriage, we will proceed to the declaration of her right as we ought to do for our natural sister or daughter. And if this answer shall not seem to content our sister, you may say that the proceeding herein dependeth so upon her proceeding in the marriage.

If Mary disliked the offer then further discussions would be left to a conference of councillors.[136] At this stage Randolph knew that Dudley was the queen's choice, but he also knew that Dudley was dubious of the whole scheme.[137] He himself told only a few, who by February, if not before, included Moray and Maitland. By the end of January, however, the French had circulated Dudley's name, though most Scots, Randolph reported, did not believe Elizabeth would let him go and thought that either Warwick or Darnley were intended. It was probably this information that finally persuaded Elizabeth to nominate Dudley directly in her letter of 5 March 1564.[138]

Randolph's discussions with Mary were delayed first by her illness, and then (as he complained) by her secretiveness. We can attribute the latter to the Spanish negotiations, about which even Maitland may have known little. That Randolph could detect no interest in the Austrian match was accurate enough.[139] By the eve of the nomination of Dudley only two points had been established: Mary accepted the idea of a conference of councillors to be held at Berwick, but also demanded, for the first time, that her title be declared by act of parliament. Since parliamentary ratification does not appear in Randolph's written instructions, nor is there any evidence he was given verbal orders on the subject, it must be concluded that the proposal was Scottish in origin.[140] When Mary received Elizabeth's recommendation of Dudley, she too expressed doubts as to whether Elizabeth would actually release him; she requested time to consider the proposal, and required to know under what precise terms he was to be offered.[141]

Randolph's departure from Edinbrugh at the end of March 1564 meant that until Melville arrived in London in September there was no regular diplomatic contact between the two courts, except for the brief period between mid-May and mid-June. The Scots still pressed for the Berwick conference, but Mary's decision on Dudley remained in abeyance. French reports claimed that she mocked the idea, and letters from Scotland suggested that his lack of royal ancestry and tainted blood were a barrier.[142] The fate of the request for the parliamentary declaration of Mary's title is mysterious, for a note in Cecil's diary states that Mary on 4 June postponed an interview with Elizabeth until such a declaration was made, although this cannot be confirmed.[143] The 'Hales Book' caused the English embarrassment, but also served to remind Mary of Elizabeth's warnings about the hostility to her claim, and to demonstrate her intention of safeguarding her interest.[144] On the other hand the clash over the release of Lennox had exacerbated the situation. It is clear that by the end of September Elizabeth, worried by the long silence from Edinburgh, was unsure what to do next.[145]

Melville's embassy was signally successful in repairing relations between the queens, whatever impression he gives in his *Memoirs*. He brought an apology from Maitland for the 'intermission of my familiar tooting'; a denial that Randolph's earlier proposals had been regarded lightly; and a request that the proposed Berwick conference be held soon, 'whereupon the matter might draw to a conclusion'.[146] To this Elizabeth consented, and Randolph returned with Melville bearing instructions to make a formal offer of Leicester at the conference.[147] He would be the best marriage to maintain the amity; his blood was of the highest of the nobility; Elizabeth was willing to increase his estate; and she would even fund a joint household with Mary. These responses to ostensible Scottish objections did not disguise a significant rephrasing of the terms for the succession. Leicester himself now became the assurance of Elizabeth's commitment: 'no way in our power more likely than this'. If Mary demanded 'present surety', she was being insincere in her offers of friendship. If this offer was not satisfactory, then other grounds would have to be found for the amity.[148]

Although Mary continued to express doubts whether Elizabeth would in the end release Leicester, Randolph was more optimistic about her attitude.[149] Otherwise, the prelude to the Berwick conference (which met on 18 November) was not auspicious. Moray and Maitland warned him that Elizabeth's proposal on the succession was too vague; only a parliamentary declaration would serve. Maitland later claimed that he believed Randolph was saving something for the conference itself, and that this was not the full extent of the English offer.[150] At Berwick, however, the impasse was revealed. Randolph made it clear that there would be no further concessions on the succession as part of a Leicester marriage: 'If they think by firmness, policy or practice or any other means to wring anything out of your majesty's hands, they were but abused and did deceive themselves.' Maitland in turn restated what he considered as essential for the marriage: a yearly revenue out of England, 'and by parliament [to] establish the crown unto her if God of your majesty do his will and leave you without children'.[151]

The stalemate reached at Berwick in November 1564 should have brought the negotiations to an end. Yet Randolph's optimism about

Mary, however misplaced it appears in retrospect, combined with the general desire to maintain the amity kept them going.[152] He himself sought (at some Scottish prompting) to capitalize on Mary's apparent interest in the marriage by persuading Leicester to become a more active suitor.[153] According to Throckmorton, the pressure Elizabeth put on Leicester at this time was considerable.[154] Although Leicester's refusal to take part was unaltered, Randolph continued to believe as late as March 1565 that if he made the effort Mary would be his.[155] Simultaneously, further efforts were made to persuade Elizabeth to budge on the succession. Early in December Moray and Maitland asked Cecil for more concrete proposals than those of Berwick. He answered on the 16th that the offer of Leicester was as far as Elizabeth would go; there would be no ratification of Mary's title, though rivals would be suppressed.[156] They in turn replied that for marriage to an Englishman, ratification was essential. Leicester himself, through Throckmorton and Henry Killigrew, was helping Maitland to orchestrate pressure on Elizabeth to concede to Mary's demands.[157] It was this campaign, and not a wilful decision to reverse her policy, that inspired Elizabeth's letter of 5 March 1565. Her Berwick offer was reaffirmed: Leicester himself would be enough to maintain the amity, parliamentary ratification would not follow automatically. The letter did not mark a change in an established policy, but a refusal to shift from a position adopted several months before.[158]

In the light of the impasse over the declaration of Mary's title, Leicester's refusal to play the suitor diminishes in importance. Had Mary displayed more interest it might have been a different story. The impasse also helps to explain the apparent English myopia over Darnley. Satisfying Lennox and his countess at least served to curb their ceaseless agitation in the English court. Neither Mary, Moray nor Maitland had displayed any formal interest in Darnley. Mary's leading concern at this point was in obtaining Elizabeth's consent to the declaration of her title; intriguing over Darnley would only jeopardize her position. Thus while both Foix and Guzman deduced from Darnley's departure that Elizabeth had given up on Leicester, their conclusions were no more accurate than they had been in the past.[159] Even Randolph, so vehement about the Lennoxes in general, was worried more by the alienation of the Hamiltons than a marriage.[160] Moreover, as Cecil was reported as saying on 24 March, the countess was still a hostage in England.[161]

Darnley's arrival in February 1565 had little immediate impact in Scotland. His reception was simply that due to the heir of a leading peer.[162] Yet the English had miscalculated on his longer-term effect. The amity had been based on the assumption that Maitland and Moray would remain Mary's leading councillors. But Lennox's return five months earlier had already triggered a shift in the Scottish court. Randolph had warned of this possibility, and his letters of the summer of 1565 have a distinct 'I told you so' ring to them.[163] Yet even he did not take Moray and Maitland seriously when they warned at Berwick that their position would be endangered without an English compromise.[164] Nor did the continued discussions in December suggest any weakening of their position. The arrival of the 5 March letter worried Randolph, but he initially suspected a revival of Guise influence and a return to France.[165] However, by mid-March the reshaping of the court around Darnley had begun. Atholl, who had long been a guardian of the Lennox interest, appears to have been the central figure.[166] He was now joined by the earl of Caithness, Lords Ruthven and Home, and Lord Robert Stewart, whom Randolph regarded with great suspicion.[167] David Riccio, who had replaced Raulet as Mary's French secretary in December, may have appeared more important in hindsight.[168] It was against this restructuring of the court in late March and April 1565 that the Darnley marriage must be understood. Melville's story that it was Darnley who first proposed marriage may have some truth in it.[169] Mary herself later referred to pressure from the Stewarts 'and others of her surname'.[170] Both Lennox and Darnley claimed that the countess was innocent of their actions.[171]

We shall probably never know whether the countess of Lennox deserved her fearsome reputation for intrigue. The key point, however, is that Elizabeth chose, albeit after some hesitation, to disregard it. Darnley was allowed to visit Scotland because Elizabeth was obliged to live up to her word to the Lennoxes, upon which the compromise over the succession debate depended. She could further discount any danger owing to Mary's apparently co-operative mood. The obsession with Guise influence led to a complete failure to appreciate that Mary might choose an independent course. A similar obsession with the duke of Alva underlay the seizure of the treasure ships three years later. By seeing Mary as confined to a static choice between the party of the amity or the Guise, both of which involved a foreign marriage, the English overlooked the possibility of a third option that did not – the Lennox Stewarts.[172]

The relationship between the release of Darnley and Elizabeth's letter of 5 March was thus an accidental one. Elizabeth's offer of the Leicester marriage was a sincere, if quixotic, attempt to maintain the amity, not unlike her equally quixotic efforts to find a compromise solution to the Netherlands rebellion later in the century. Regardless of Leicester's willingness to co-operate, the marriage, and with it the amity, foundered on the Scottish demand for parliamentary ratification of Mary's title. The importance assigned to the English parliament's possible involvement in the establishment of the succession is striking. The dispatch of Maitland in 1563, Melville in 1564 (and Robert Melville in 1566) to safeguard her interests should parliament meet was as much an 'interference' in English politics as Elizabeth's advice on her marriage was in Scottish affairs. Mary's intransigence on this score cannot be underrated. Essential to the amity was compromise and reciprocity; when it came to the English succession, Mary demanded all and conceded nothing.

Notes

I should like to thank the British Academy, the Carnegie Trust for the Universities of Scotland and the History Department of the University of Strathclyde for their financial support of the research that made this essay possible. Quotations in English have been modernized, but not those in Scots.

[1] BL, Sloane MS 3199, fo. 258, Elizabeth Hilgate to Philip Hilgate, 23 Apr. 1565.

[2] Donaldson, *Scotland*, 117; Fraser, *Mary*, 218; K. P. Frescoln, 'Thomas Randolph: An Elizabethan in Scotland' (West Virginia Univ PhD., 1971), 198, observes that historians are 'perplexed' by the decision.

[3] J. E. A. Dawson, 'Mary, queen of Scots, Lord Darnley and Anglo-Scots relations in 1565', *International History Rev.* viii (1986), 1–24.

[4] See her letter appointing Châtelherault lieutenant-general in 1568, Sir W. Fraser, *The Lennox* (1874), ii, 437. There are hints in PRO, SP 52/11/180v, on which see below n. 12.

[5] M. Philippson, *Histoire du règne de Marie Stuart* (1891), ii, 268; T. F. Henderson, *Mary, Queen of Scots: Her Environment and Tragedy* (1905), i, 310. Cf. M. Lee, *James Stewart, Earl of Moray* (1953), 130.

[6] Vol. i (1547–63) includes documents located elsewhere, but only a few are found in vol. ii (1563–9).

[7] Referred to in PRO, SP 52/10/15, Randolph to Cecil, 12 Feb. 1565.

[8] Melville, *Memoirs*, 112. Enough fragments survive, however, to suggest that this was not completely true. Mary apparently burnt Elizabeth's letter of 5 July 1564 at her request, see PRO, SP 52/9/92v.

[9] The Leicester and Maitland papers are discussed in S. Adams, 'The Lauderdale papers, 1561–1570: the Maitland of Lethington state papers and the Leicester correspondence', *SHR,* lxvii (1988). Some Lennox manuscripts are printed in vol. ii of Fraser, *The Lennox.*

[10] Foix's diplomatic papers are now to be found in BN, fonds français 6621. They are transcribed in PRO 31, 3/25, and most of those of Scottish interest are printed in Teulet, *Relations,* and *Papiers.* For Guzman de Silva see *Correspondencia de Felipe II con sus embajadores en la córte de Inglaterra* (Codoin,

lxxxix, 1887), ii; these dispatches together with a few further documents are translated and summarized in *CSP Spain 1558–67* (1892). Some of his correspondence with the duchess of Parma is printed in J. M. B. C. Kervyn de Lettenhove, *Relations politiques des Pays-Bas et de l'Angleterre sous le règne de Philippe II* (Brussels, 1882–1900).

[11] BL Cott. MS Caligula B X. fos 354–7, 'Principal points to be remembered and considered in the matter of Scotland' was drafted on 24 Sept. 1565. It or a summary was read to the council meeting held to debate the Chaseabout Raid on 26 Sept. (see Caligula B X, fo. 358). A slightly later review 'A collection of such matters from 4 June 1564 to October 1565' was included in Cecil's 'diary', printed in W. Murdin (ed.), *Collection of State Papers left by William Cecil, Lord Burghley* (1759), 757–8; a copy can be found in Cottonian MS Caligula B IX, fos 216–18v. The 'diary' itself (Murdin, *Burghley Papers*, 755–6) gives a slightly different account of the course of events.

[12] PRO, SP 52/11-180. Printed in Labanoff i, 296–8; crudely summarized in *CSP Scot.*, ii, 233. This is not an easy document to assess. It is a holograph draft, but undated and to an unknown correspondent. It has been calendared Oct. 1565, and seen as a defence of the marriage and Mary's policy toward Moray, but its English provenance suggests it may have been written after 1568. Cf. A. Strickland, *Lives of the Queens of Scotland* (1853), iv, 94. For Melville's embassy, see *Memoirs*, 111–27.

[13] BL, Cott. MS Caligula B X, fo. 351, 'A consideration of the whole matter of Scotland', 24 Sept. 1565. [D. Digges], *The Compleat Ambassador* (1655), 13.

[14] J. A. Froude, *The Reign of Elizabeth*, 458–9, 478; J. E. Neale, *Queen Elizabeth I* (1952), 132–3. See also n. 5 above.

[15] See below, 138–9.

[16] Labanoff, i, 197–213 *passim*; E. Poullet (ed.), *Correspondence du Cardinal de Granvelle, 1565–1582* (1877), 586; and PRO, SP 52/11/80.

[17] Poullet, *Correspondence*, i, 584. The draft of Guzman's instructions (corrected by Philip) is found in AGS, Estado 8340, fo. 178; they are printed in Codoin, lxxxix, 3–11. For the debates over Don Carlos in Oct. 1563, see C. Weiss (ed.), *Papiers d'état du Cardinal de Granvelle* (1850), vii, 223, 244–5.

[18] The instruction to Granvelle is printed in Weiss, *Papiers d'état*, viii, 211–2; the draft is AGS, E 8340, fo. 181. The instruction to Guzman is printed in *CSP Spain*, i, 371, but not in Codoin.

[19] *CSP Spain*, i, 378, 396, cf. Codoin, lxxxix, 34, 61.

[20] See e.g. Strickland, *Lives*, iv, 49–50; Philippson, *Histoire*, ii, 230, 244; Lee, *Moray*, 124; Donaldson, *Mary*, 77.

[21] Melville, *Memoirs*, 120. Hay Fleming, *Mary* 325–6. J. P. Lawson, the editor of Keith, *History*, ii, 228, suggested the 20th. The letters are calendared in *CSP Scot.*, ii, 74–5. BL, Egerton MS 1818, fo. 33 is a draft of Maitland's letter. The earl of Bedford reported Melville as en route on the 25th, *CSPF, 1564–5*, 211.

[22] Murdin, *Burleigh Papers*, 757. Leicester's creation involved some preparation, for the French ambassador was invited two days in advance (*CSP Spain*, i, 382). It is also worth noting that it was accompanied only by the grant of the manor of Kenilworth; the lordship of Denbigh and Kenilworth Castle had been given

to him in June 1563. It is doubtful that the creation was a spontaneous response to Melville's embassy. The French offer to elect Dudley to the order of St Michael may have inspired the choice of Michaelmas. See ibid., i, 385.

[23] Melville is referred to in Randolph's instructions of 4 Oct. Randolph's first dispatch from Edinburgh (24 Oct.) included Mary's thanks to Leicester for his courtesy to her ambassador. See *CSP Scot.*, ii, 79, 84. Mary announced Randolph's arrival and Melville's return on 11 Oct. and 2 Nov., Labanoff, i, 241, 247.

[24] Melville, *Memoirs*, 112–15. Lee, *Moray*, 127 n. 55 suggests that the version printed in Labanoff (i, 231–4) is more accurate. This was, however, simply derived from a French translation of the *Memoirs*.

[25] Labanoff, i, 247. Dudley's letter (missing the final page) is now BL, Egerton MS 1818, fos. 20–1 (printed in Philippson, *Historie*, i, 278–81).

[26] Melville, *Memoirs*, 111, 127; Codoin, xxxix, 46.

[27] Fraser, *Lennox*, i, 394; *CSPF 1564–5*, 207.

[28] Henderson and Philippson see the embassy as a response to the breakdown of the Don Carlos marriage (*Mary*, 281; *Histoire*, i, 278–81). Philippson (*Histoire*, i, 292), Strickland (*Lives*, ii, 397), and Andrew Lang (*History of Scotland* (1907), ii, 135) argue that Melville had secret instructions to expedite Darnley's journey north.

[29] BL, Egerton MS 1818, fo. 18 (printed in Philippson, *Historie*, iii, 475–7). This appears to be a list of passages for encyphering. Philippson (*Historie*, i, 294) sees it as a draft of secret instructions for Melville, but a reference to the mission of Juan Baptista assigns it to early Nov. 1564 (cf. *CSP Scot.*, ii, 93), and the context fits Beaton better.

[30] Beaton's conversations with Don Francisco de Alava from Nov. 1564 to Mar. 1565 are found in Teulet, *Relations*, v, 4–9. Cf. Labanoff, i, 248, and *CSP Spain*, i, 399. Only M. A. S. Hume, *The Love Affairs of Mary Queen of Scots: A Political History* (1903), 217–25, Henderson (*Mary*, i, 312–3), and Lee (*Moray*, 115 n. 3) note that Mary was still negotiating over Don Carlos as late as the eve of the marriage with Darnley.

[31] Lang, *History*, ii, 137; Fraser, *Mary*, 220.

[32] PRO, SP 52/10/103, 112, to Leicester, 21 May, 3 June 1565. Cf. Melville, *Memoirs*, 130, and Knox, *History* ii, 140, though Knox cautiously leaves it as 'some write'.

[33] See n. 158 below.

[34] P. F. Tytler, *History of Scotland* (1882), iii, 190–1; Philippson, *Histoire*, i, 322–5; Henderson, *Mary*, i, 310; Dawson, 'Darnley', 8–9.

[35] A. Lang, 'New light on Mary, Queen of Scots', *Blackwood's Magazine*, clxxxii (1907), 26. Cf. F. A. Mumby, *Elizabeth and Mary Stuart* (1914), 344, 357, and Lee, *Moray*, 133.

[36] PRO, SP 52/10/49. Only the last page survives.

[37] Randolph also wrote to Leicester (BL, Egerton MS 1819, fo. 50), Sir Henry Sidney (NLS Adv. MS 1.2.2., art. 24) and Cecil (*CSP Scot.*, ii, 139). His letter to Cecil does refer to gossip emanating from London, but he mentions only that concerning the vestments controversy.

[38] NLS, MS 3657, fos 18–20, to Leicester, 20 Mar., published in part by K.

P. Frescoln, 'A Letter from Thomas Randolph to the earl of Leicester', *Huntington Library Q.*, xxxvii (1973), 83–8.

[39] 'Darnley', 8. Cf. Lee, *Moray*, 132.

[40] *Moray*, 121.

[41] For the debate over Randolph, see Philippson, *Histoire*, i, 306; Henderson, *Mary*, i, 294; and Mumby, *Elizabeth and Mary*, 344.

[42] W. MacCaffrey, *The Shaping of the Elizabethan Regime* (1968), 166. Elizabeth claimed she loved Dudley as a brother most dramatically when near death in Oct. 1562, but see also PRO 31, 3/25/138, Paul de Foix's report on a conversation with Cecil, 18 Feb. 1565, and SP 52/10/60v, instructions for Throckmorton, 24 Apr.

[43] Fraser, *Mary*, 267.

[44] PRO, SP 52/10/15, Randolph to Cecil, 12 Feb. 1565. Cf. *CSP Spain*, i, 391.

[45] Melville, *Memoirs*, 130. Cf. Philippson, *Histoire*, ii, 315, and Lee, *Moray*, 130. For Cecil's claim to control Darnley in Mar. 1565, see Teulet, *Papiers*, ii, 33–5.

[46] C. Read, *Mr. Secretary Cecil and Queen Elizabeth* (1955), 315, 317; Dawson, 'Darnley', 4–7. Dr Dawson does, however, consider the evidence that Darnley was Leicester's proxy to be 'inconclusive'.

[47] Melville, *Memoirs*, 126, 129. PRO, SP 52/11/180v. W. Camden, *Annales* (English edn, 1625), 115. For Leicester's good offices to Darnley, see PRO, SP 52/10/25, Randolph to Leicester, 19 Feb, 1565.

[48] Read, *Cecil*, 317; Dawson, 'Darnley', 7, 14. The letter from Darnley (21 Feb.) is now BL, Add. MS 19401, fo. 101.

[49] Read, *Cecil*, 315. The subject of relations between Leicester and Cecil at this point is too large to be discussed here, but Cecil was quick to play down rumours of antagonism in Aug. and Sept. 1564 (see BL, Lansdowne MS 102, fo. 98, to Sir Thomas Smith, 12 Sept. 1564).

[50] On his joint correspondence to Leicester and Cecil, see BL, Cott. MS Caligula B X, fo. 286, Randolph to Cecil, 20 Mar. 1565.

[51] See PRO 31, 3/25/188, and *CSP Spain*, i, 428–9. Leicester did, however, have at least one meeting with Cecil and Maitland in his chamber.

[52] BL. Cott. MS Caligula B X, fo. 290v, a copy of the protest, includes the signatures of 13 councillors. Bedford was at Berwick. Read (*Cecil*, 317) states erroneously that Bacon was still in disfavour. *Acts of the Privy Council of England, 1558–70* (1893), vii, 208–13, reveal him sitting regularly during Apr. Given his strong hostility to Mary, his absence suggests that failure to sign the protest may not have had the significance attributed to it. For Arundel's refusal, see *CSP Spain*, i, 431.

[53] The only biographies are those of Strickland, *Lives*, ii, for the countess, and Fraser, *Lennox*, i, for the earl. See Goodare, ch. 7 below, for the Lennox Stewart restoration in Scotland.

[54] P. Hume Brown, *History of Scotland* (1911), ii, 78–9; Dawson, 'Darnley', 7–8.

[55] *CSP Scot.*, i, 496–7, 528. PRO, SP 12/23/106, Lennox to council, 20 June 1562.

[56] See PRO, SP 10/15/144, duke of Northumberland to Cecil, 11 Dec. 1552.

[57] The countess had been a member of Mary's household at Beaulieu in the early 1530s; see Strickland, *Lives*, ii, 285, 307. For Mary's assistance, *CSP Scot.*, i, 197—8.

[58] For the rumours that the countess had tried to turn Mary against Elizabeth, see Strickland, *Lives*, ii, 347, and PRO, SP 12/22/77—8, 12/23/17—18. She denied them with her usual vehemence, see Ellis, *Original Letters*, ii, 335.

[59] See *CSP Scot.*, i, 278—311 *passim*, and PRO, SP 12/11/48, Lennox to Cecil, 28 Feb. 1560. Also Lynch, ch. 1 above, for the Hamiltons' dynastic aims.

[60] *CSP Scot.*, i, 545, 597—8; *CSP Spain*, i, 227; PRO, SP 12/21/105; H. Robinson (ed.), *The Zurich Letters* (1846), 125.

[61] PRO, SP 12/22/75, 77—8, 23/10—12, 31. The story that Darnley himself had been sent to Mary in early 1561 (Strickland, *Lives*, iv, 370) appears to be a myth. See *CSP Scot.*, i, 527—8.

[62] PRO, SP 12/24/2, 9. The submission itself, assuming it was written, has disappeared. See also *CSP Spain*, i, 251, the countess of Lennox's defence of her conduct, written to the Spanish ambassador in July 1562.

[63] PRO, SP 12/25/42,94,193; 27/12, 249.

[64] PRO, SP 52/8/82, Elizabeth to Mary, 16 June 1563. Cf. SP 52/9/92, Maitland to Cecil, 13 July 1564, and Knox, *History*, ii, 64.

[65] Murdin, *Burghley Papers*, 756. *CSP Spain*, i, 264.

[66] On his general opposition to the Lennoxes, see BL, Cott. MS Caligula B X, fo. 287v, to Cecil, 20 Mar. 1565. For his Hamilton bias, Melville, *Memoirs*, 228, and Philippson, *Histoire*, ii, 317. On his speaking for Lennox, see PRO, SP 52/9/92, 170, Maitland to Cecil, 13 July 1564, and Randolph to Cecil, 2 Dec. 1564.

[67] Randolph's movements can be traced from his correspondence in SP 52/9; he was in Edinburgh only between mid-May and mid-June. For Fowler's errand, see Knox, *History*, ii, 64, and *CSP Scot.*, ii, 59, 61.

[68] *CSP Scot.*, i, 589, 592.

[69] Thus Knox (*History*, ii, 64), but his bias against Maitland is clear.

[70] Philippson, *Histoire*, ii, 283, 285.

[71] See Fraser, *Lennox*, ii, 262, and BL, Cott. MS Caligula B X, fo. 284. Also Goodare, ch. 7 below.

[72] Lang, *History of Scotland*, ii, 134. PRO, SP 52/9/63, 65.

[73] Murdin, *Burghley Papers*, 757. Melville, *Memoirs*, 107—8, claims Elizabeth's letter urged Mary not alienate the Hamiltons.

[74] *CSP Spain*, i, 374. Kervyn de Lettenhove, *Relations politiques*, iv, 67, 78.

[75] PRO, SP 52/9/92, Maitland to Cecil, 13 July, refers to 'they'. For Randolph, see SP 52/9/77v, to Cecil, 22 May 1564.

[76] BL, Egerton MS 1818, fo. 31, n.d. (*c*.July—Aug.), last page missing.

[77] PRO, SP 52/9/92v, Maitland to Cecil, 13 July 1564.

[78] Labanoff, i, 235. PRO, SP 52/9/119, 121, Lennox to Elizabeth and Cecil, 30 Sept. 1564. Cf. Maitland's speech to parliament, printed in *Warrender Papers*, i, 41—4.

[79] BL, Egerton MS 1818, fo. 32. The provenance and the English endorsement, 'A device for the earl of Lennox and his son touching their possessions in Scotland', suggests it was sent to Leicester. Cf. *CSP Spain*, i, 391.

[80] For the appeals for Darnley, see BL, Cott. MS Caligula B X, fos 276−7, Randolph to Elizabeth, 7 Nov., and Cecil's diary, Murdin, *Burghley Papers,* 756−7. The two versions of the diary give different dates, 12 and 27 Nov. There is no evidence, as stated in *CSP Spain*, i, 399, and repeated by Strickland (*Lives*, ii, 397) and Fraser (*Mary*, 219) that Mary wrote to Elizabeth for Darnley's release.

[81] Murdin, *Burghley Papers*, 757. BL, Cott. MS Caligula B X, fo. 284, Randolph to Cecil, 3 Dec. 1564; Landsdowne MS 102, fos 107−9, Cecil to Sir Thomas Smith, 30 Dec. 1564. However, see Mary on pressure from the countess of Lennox, PRO, SP 52/11/180−v.

[82] BL, Cott. MS Caligula B X. 282, Randolph and Bedford to Elizabeth, 23 Nov. 1564. Cf. PRO, SP 52/9/153, Randolph to Cecil, 3 Nov.

[83] Read, *Cecil*, 307.

[84] Philippson, *Histoire*, ii, 203; Lee, *Moray*, 123−4.

[85] See the MS version, said to have been a speech in the Commons, PRO, SP 12/27/89ff.

[86] PRO, SP 12/28/39, 41; *CSP Scot.*, i, 690−4, reveals that Maitland was consulted during the council's discussions. Randolph had been instructed to obtain similar evidence in Scotland when Lennox was imprisoned in 1562, see ibid i, 602, 605, 612, 614.

[87] See e.g. her interview with Maitland in Oct. 1561, n. 97 below, and her answer to the Commons petition on 28 Jan. 1563, PRO, SP 12/27/143−4.

[88] BL, Cott. MS Caligula B X, fo. 368, instructions for Mildmay (?) for a cancelled embassy to Mary, Nov. 1565.

[89] As described by Frescoln, 'Randolph', vi.

[90] BL, Egerton MS 1818, fo. 21, to Dudley, 25 May 1562. See Lynch, ch. 1 above, for the implications in the loosening of the amity in 1565.

[91] The initial decision against ratification had been taken by the government of François II in the autumn of 1560. L. Paris (ed.), *Négociations, lettres et piéces diverses relatives an règne de François II* (1841), 475−7, 608−9.

[92] For the dispute over the *deinceps* clause, see Lee, *Moray*, 82−3.

[93] The central role of the four is noted by Melville, *Memoirs*, 127. The only modern authority to observe this is Donaldson, *Mary*, 74.

[94] BL, Egerton MS 1818, fo. 13, to Dudley, 7 Oct. 1561, and *CSP Scot.*, i, 558. Cf. his attempt in the summer of 1561 to allay Mary's suspicions of Elizabeth, BL, Add. MS 32091, fos 189−91, to Mary 10 July 1561.

[95] For references to this meeting see BL, Add. MS 35125, fo. 8, and PRO, SP 52/5/59−60, Maitland to Dudley, 14 Nov. and 26 Dec. 1561. Although Hertford Castle is specifically referred to in the latter, the chronology is not clear. Maitland left Scotland on 1 Sept. and returned in early Oct. Cecil was at Hertford Castle on 3 Sept.; the meeting may have preceded Maitland's interview with Elizabeth.

[96] *CSP Spain*, i, 306; *CSP Scot.*, i, 541, 558; BL, Egerton MS 1818, fo. 13, Lord James to Dudley, 7 Oct.

[97] Maitland's well-known account of his interview with Elizabeth is printed in J. H. Pollen (ed.), *A Letter from Mary, Queen of Scots to the Duke of Guise, January 1562* (SHS, 1904), 38−45.

[98] Donaldson, *Mary*, 73.

[99] *CSP Scot.*, i, 558, 575, 577.

[100] BL, Egerton MS 1818, fo. 13, to Dudley, 7 Oct. 1561.

[101] BL, Add. MS 35125, fo. 8, Maitland to Dudley, 14 Nov. 1561, and Egerton MS 1818, fo. 15, Lord James to Dudley, 26 Dec. 1561.

[102] *CSP Scot.*, i, 540.

[103] ibid., i, 562; *CSP Spain*, i, 306. Cf. Frescoln, 'Randolph', 110; BL, Add. MS 35125, fo. 8, and PRO, SP 52/5/59−60, Maitland to Dudley, 14 Nov. and 26 Dec. 1561.

[104] The Guise in fact supported the interview, see BL, Add. MS 19401, fo. 84, bishop of Amiens to Mary, 21 Apr. 1562. For Mary's taking of their side in the war, see ibid., fo. 92, to Elizabeth, n.d. 1562. Cf. White, ch. 3 above, for Mary's attempt to allay English suspicions by her abruptly arranged progress to the north-east and treatment of Huntly.

[105] For the English response, see PRO, SP 70/39/106−v, Cecil's memorandum on the war in France of 20 July, and BL, Cott. MS Caligula B X, fo. 209, his memorandum on the meeting of 30 July. Cf. BL, Egerton 1818, fo. 25, Maitland to Mary, 2 June 1562, and Elizabeth's letter to Mary, 15 Oct., printed in Pollen, *Letter to Guise*, 75.

[106] *CSP Scot.*, i, 666−7.

[107] See his speech to the council opposing the interview, July 1562. There are many copies; I have used Henry E. Huntington Library, MS HM 1340, fos 22−5v. There is an interesting reference to the earlier reception of Mary's French train on fo. 25.

[108] BL, Cott. MS B IX, fo. 181−v, to Dudley, 18 Nov. 1562; *CSP Scot.*, i, 683−4, 688; PRO, SP 52/9/7, to Elizabeth, 21 Jan. 1564. See White, ch. 3 above, for the position of Huntly in an anti-English faction in 1561−2; also Holmes, ch. 9 below for continuing suspicions of Guise aims.

[109] Knox, *History*, ii, 81−5, 93−134 *passim*; Hume Brown, *History of Scotland*, 77; *CSP Scot.*, i, 556; ii, 24.

[110] For Dudley's relationship to Lord John Grey, see BL, Harleian MS 6990, fo. 60, to Cecil, 26 Apr. (1564), and Add. MS 34079, fo. 7, from Lady Mary Grey, 25 Nov. 1564.

[111] For Leicester's plot to remove Bacon in Nov. 1564, see Camden, *Annales*, 110. Bacon's letters to Cecil of 26 Nov. and Leicester of 28 Dec, (Huntington Lib., MS HM 1340, fos 85v, 86−7), however, show that he saw Leicester as an ally at this point, not an enemy.

[112] It is not irrelevant to note that Randolph clearly suspected the countess of Lennox as being responsible for the spreading of the hostile gossip about the English court in Mar. 1565. PRO, SP 52/10/49, to Throckmorton, 31 Mar.

[113] NLS, MS 3657, fo. 5, to Dudley, 1 Oct. 1563.

[114] *CSP Scot.*, ii, 100−1.

[115] Dawson, 'Darnley', 5.

[116] BL, Egerton MS 1819, fo. 35.

[117] BL, Harleian MS 787, fo. 16, Huntingdon to Dudley, Apr. 1563. Marie Axton, 'Lord Robert Dudley and the Inner Temple revels', *Historical J.*, xiii (1970), 365−7 has argued that Dudley's patronage of *Gorboduc* revealed his support for the Grey claim. A contemporary narrative (BL, Add. MS 48023, fo.

359v) states that the play publicized a marriage with him rather than Eric XIV of Sweden.

[118] See PRO, SP 52/10/118v, for the advice of the council of 4 June 1565, and BL, Cott. MS Caligula B X, fo. 350v, 'A consideration of the whole matter of Scotland', 24 Sept. 1565, both drafted by Cecil.

[119] In Aug. 1566 Leicester told a French envoy that his knowledge of Elizabeth from childhood had led him to believe she would never marry. BN, fonds français 15970, fo. 15v, Jacob de Vulcob to Jacques Bochetel de la Fôret, 6 Aug. 1566. Whether he was so sure earlier can, of course, be debated.

[120] See Lee, *Moray*, 126–7.

[121] Cecil claimed that a marriage with Don Carlos was being arranged by the Guise in July 1562 (PRO, SP 70/39/106). Paul de Foix also assumed that Lethington was then negotiating for a Spanish marriage; Teulet, *Papiers*, ii, 28–9. The Spanish documents contain no reference to any such negotiations.

[122] See the report of Huguenot agent in London, BUPG, Archives Tronchin MS 146, fo. 131, Robert de La Haye to Coligny, 11 Mar. 1563.

[123] Lorraine's letter to Mary was delayed in transit, BL, Add. MS 19401, fo. 98, P. Raulet to ?, 21 May 1563. Cf. *CSP Scot.*, ii, 8. In her memoir (PRO, SP 52/11/180) Mary claimed the negotiations had been undertaken without her knowedge or consent, and Maitland said the same to Guzman de Silva in Apr. 1565 (*CSP Spain*, i, 421–2). Maitland learnt of the marriage directly from Lorraine in Apr. (NLS, Adv. MS 6.1.13, fo. 15, to Mary, 16 Apr.).

[124] Labanoff, i, 161, 166, prints his instructions. See also Frescoln, 'Randolph', 135, and *CSP Spain*, i, 683–4.

[125] Compare BL Add. MS 32091, fos 195–7, Maitland to Mary, 9 Mar. 1563 (printed in Philippson, *Histoire*, iii, 458–65), with Codoin, lxxvii, 491–3 (*CSP Spain*, i, 309–10, and Kervyn de Lettenhove, *Relations, politiques*, iii, 267–8).

[126] Both Henderson, *Mary*, i, 260, and Philippson, *Histoire*, 186–7, observed the discrepancy. Philippson regarded La Quadra as the more accurate, but on purely circumstantial grounds.

[127] In his letter to Mary of 19 Apr. 1563, Maitland refers to Don Carlos only as one of several choices, NLS, Adv. MS 6.1.13, fos 15–16. In the instructions for Beaton in Nov. 1564, he refers to the motion 'maid thairin by the bishop of Aquila', BL, Egerton MS 1818, fo. 18.

[128] NLS, Adv. MS 6.1.13, fos 15–16, to Mary, from Chenonceaux, 19 Apr. 1563. This was formerly Phillipps MS 4899, its earlier provenance is unclear.

[129] Bodleian Library, Ashmole MS 1729, fo. 230, 20 May 1563.

[130] The relationship between the two has caused no little confusion. Fraser, *Mary*, 212, misreads the Austrian match as a response to Maitland's negotiations. Donaldson, *Mary*, 77, sees Elizabeth offering Dudley in response to the Don Carlos match, when it was the Austrian that worried her.

[131] Frescoln, 'Randolph', 158. It is worth noting that the only source for Elizabeth's offer of the Dudleys in Mar. 1563 is La Quadra's report of his conversations with Maitland. *CSP Spain*, i, 313.

[132] NLS, MS 3657, fo. 5, to Dudley, 1 Oct. 1563. Cf. *CSP Scot.*, ii, 20, and BL, Cott. MS Caligula B X, fo. 218, Instructions for Randolph, 20 Aug.

[133] BL, Cott. MS Caligula B X, fos 218–28, 228–9, Instructions for Randolph,

20 and 24 Aug. If Maitland was not being flattering, this compromise may have been inspired by Dudley. See Maitland's letter of 1 Oct., NLS, MS 3657, fo. 5.
[134] BL, Add. MS 32091, fo. 199v, 20 Aug. 1563.
[135] BL, Egerton MS 1818, fo. 23.
[136] BL, Cott. MS Caligula B X, fos 261–2v.
[137] Magdalene College, Cambridge, Pepys MS i, 91–3, Randolph to Dudley, 15 Jan. 1564.
[138] PRO, SP 52/9/7, 28, to Elizabeth, 21 Jan., to Cecil, 21 Feb. Cf. *CSP Scot.*, ii, 33.
[139] *CSP Scot.*, ii, 33; BL, Egerton MS 1818, fo. 27, to Dudley, 13 Dec. 1563. Randolph commented that 'her heart' was in Spain, but could tell little else. PRO, SP 52/9/7, to Elizabeth, 21 Jan.
[140] PRO, SP 52/9/41–3, to Cecil, 8 Mar. Cf. 52/9/53, to Cecil, 30 Mar., and BL, Cott. MS Caligula B X, fo. 265. Randolph did comment in a hypothetical manner about parliamentary ratification in Feb., PRO, SP 52/9/29.
[141] PRO, SP 2/9/49, 51, to Cecil, 18 Mar., to Elizabeth, 30 Mar.
[142] Labanoff, i, 242–3. Cf. PRO, SP 52/9/88–9, Maitland to Cecil, 23 June 1564, Kirkcaldy to Randolph, 19 Sept. English sensitivity on this score owed something to the memory of Mary's joke that Elizabeth was going to marry her 'horsekeeper' in the autumn of 1560. See BL, Add. MS 35830, fo. 66, Robert Jones to Throckmorton, 30 Nov. 1560.
[143] Murdin, *Burghley Papers*, 755.
[144] See PRO, SP 52/7/77, 132, 144–v, and BL, Egerton MS 1818, fo. 41v. Cf. M. Levine, *The Early Elizabethan Succession Question* (1966), 69.
[145] PRO, SP 52/9/113, to Cecil, 23 Sept.
[146] BL, Egerton MS 1818, fo. 33, to Cecil, 18 Sept.
[147] BL, Cott. MS Caligula B X, fos 270–2v, 4 Oct.
[148] PRO, SP 52/9/131v–2, Instructions for Randolph and Bedford, 7 Nov. Cf. BL, Lansdowne MS 102, fo. 102, Cecil to Smith, 4 Oct. 1564, on Dudley's preferment being 'earnestly intended'.
[149] BL, Cott. MS Caligula B X, fo. 275, to Elizabeth, 7 Nov.
[150] *CSP Scot.*, ii, 92.
[151] BL, Cott. MS Caligula B X, fo. 282, Bedford and Randolph to Elizabeth, 23 Nov. Randolph and Bedford also wrote to Leicester, but this letter, which might shed considerable light on the whole episode, has not been seen since 1824 (Adams, 'Lauderdale papers', appendix 1).
[152] For Mary's lack of interest in the Dudley offer at this point, see Labanoff, i, 243–4. For Randolph's optimism, PRO, SP 52/9/170, to Cecil, 2 Dec.
[153] BL, Egerton MS 1818, fos 25–6v, 29, Randolph to Leicester, n.d. (Dec.–Jan.), 6 Feb. 1565. PRO, SP 52/10/6,9, to Cecil, 13, 18 Jan. 1565.
[154] Magdalene College, Cambridge, Pepys MS, i, 395, to Leicester, 21 May 1565. Throckmorton included himself among the supporters of the match.
[155] NLS, Adv. MS 1.2.2., art. 24, to Sir Henry Sidney, 31 Mar.
[156] *CSP Scot.*, ii, 96–7, 102. Cf. BL, Lansdowne MS 102, fos 107–9, Cecil to Smith, 30 Dec. 1564, 'when it cometh to the conditions demanded I see her then remiss of her earnestness'.

[157] BL, Egerton MS 1818, fo. 29, Killigrew to Maitland, 18 Dec. [1564], NLS MS 3657, fo. 8, Throckmorton to Maitland, 18 Jan. 1565. On the closeness of Killigrew, Throckmorton and Leicester, see PRO 31, 3/25/188, Foix's report of 10 May 1565.

[158] The later descriptions of the letter make it clear that the parliamentary declaration was the central issue, BL, Cott. MS Caligula B X, fos 354, 358 (Cecil's summaries in Sept.), and PRO, SP 52/10/60v, instructions for Throckmorton, 24 Apr. The reference to the possibility of her marrying is a novelty, but may reflect a certain touchiness, encountered elsewhere, over the implication in the Scottish demands that she would be childless. Compare, for example, the passage in the instructions for the Berwick conference (SP 52/9/132), 'or as though God would change our determination in not desiring to marry, we should not by likelihood have children'.

[159] PRO 31, 3/25/133 (Teulet, *Relations*, ii, 189–90), Foix's report of 14 Jan. 1565. Guzman apparently informed Granvelle similarly, Weiss, *Papiers d'état*, ix, 63.

[160] PRO, SP 52/10/15, to Cecil, 12 Feb. 1565. NLS, MS 3657, fo. 20, to Leicester, 20 Mar.

[161] Teulet, *Relations*, ii, 190.

[162] BL, Cott. MS Caligula B X, fo. 354v. PRO, SP 52/10/25, Randolph to Leicester, 19 Feb. NLS, Adv. MS 1.2.2, art. 24, Randolph to Sidney, 31 Mar.

[163] See PRO, SP 52/10/102, 112–v, to Leicester, 21 May, 3 June 1565.

[164] BL, Cott. MS Caligula B X, fos 281v 283, Randolph and Bedford to Eilzabeth, 23 Nov. 1564. The warning was repeated in Dec., *CSP Scot.*, ii, 96–7.

[165] PRO, SP 52/10/44–v, to Leicester, 27 Mar. He had no idea of the state of Mary's negotiations with Spain, BL, Cott. MS Caligula B X, fo. 287, to Cecil, 20 Mar.

[166] *CSP Scot.*, ii, 85.

[167] BL. Cott. MS Caligula B X, fo. 287v, to Cecil, 20 Mar. Cf. fo. 354, Cecil's summary. Donaldson, *Queen's Men*, 72, sees Lennox's party largely as a figment of Randolph's imagination on the grounds he was too 'anglicized' to attract support in Scotland. Cf. Lynch, ch. 1 above, on this point, and Goodare, ch. 7 below, on Lord Robert.

[168] Melville, *Memoirs*, 132–3; Knox, *History*, ii, 106. Randolph took Riccio seriously in the summer of 1565, PRO, SP 52/10/112, to Leicester, 3 June.

[169] *Memoirs*, 134.

[170] BL, Egerton MS 1819, fo. 50, Randolph to Leicester, 31 Mar. refers to her surname, as does Mary in her memoir, PRO, SP 52/11/180v. Maitland told Guzman in Apr. that pressure from her subjects was responsible for the marriage, *CSP Spain*, i, 421.

[171] Fraser, *Lennox*, i, 446. She did, however, discuss the possibility with Guzman in Mar., *CSP Spain*, i, 413.

[172] See Lynch, ch. 1 above, for the stance of an independent monarchy adopted in 1565–6.

7

Queen Mary's Catholic Interlude

JULIAN GOODARE

Queen Mary's marriage to Henry Stewart, Lord Darnley, and the subsequent murder of David Riccio in Holyrood Palace, are among the most widely known episodes of Scottish history. Yet how well are they really understood? They are usually seen as somehow connected: the Darnley marriage marked a new direction for Mary's policy, which led to a build-up of opposition which burst out in the slaughter of the queen's secretary. Was the queen initiating a Catholic reaction, which provoked a violent Protestant response? Or was she making a bid to free the crown from the political tutelage of her advisers, the earl of Moray and William Maitland? Probably she intended neither; but the restoration of the Lennox Stewarts, the marriage itself, and still more the rebellion of Moray and the Hamiltons, produced a major shake-up in Scottish politics which had led to intricate complications by early 1566. That was the moment when Mary, briefly, tried to cut through the elaborate web of policy and patronage, at once cautious and ambiguous, which she and her chief advisers had woven since her return to Scotland in 1561. It forms an illuminating contrast in an otherwise tolerant and conciliatory reign.

Mary had to marry for dynastic reasons; Darnley was a congenial choice, but she had been courted by more dynastically attractive foreign princes. In many ways he was elevated *faute de mieux*; by early 1565 he was virtually the only remaining candidate for her hand apart from the earl of Leicester.[1] Unlike a foreign prince, his irruption into domestic politics inevitably threatened the dominant noble faction. Moray was 'the sorrowefulleste man that may be' when the English failed to deflect Darnley's rise. Meanwhile Châtelherault feared the ruin of the house of Hamilton.[2]

Moray's precipitate withdrawal from court, and later rebellion, threw the political scene into confusion; but this brought Mary new opport-

154

unities in the summer and autumn of 1565. Did she have a broad coalition of support, drawn together for a variety of motives on a short-term basis, or did she create a party prepared to move in a definite direction, whether royalist or Catholic?[3] Most nobles had some preference for either sermon or mass, sometimes strongly expressed. But only in a few individuals — such as Glencairn on the one side, or Seton on the other — was there an evident willingness to put their faith above self-interest, the traditional ties of kin and marriage, or traditional enmities of feuds. Still, the revolution of 1559—60 had been carried out by nobles with largely traditional motives; a counter-revolution might spring from the same roots.

The Marian courtier, Lord Herries, saw that traditional aristocrat, Châtelherault, as the most militant of the rebels in 1565, but even he had, in 1562, been willing to consider an alliance with Catholic magnates to protect his own interests;[4] and the parvenu Moray hoped for an agreement, Herries considered, with the queen.[5] The rebels of 1565 had mixed motives and each had his own bargaining price. Moray was the most prominent individual, but his importance has been exaggerated, partly by the reports of the English ambassador Thomas Randolph (who obtained much of his information from Moray's associates) and partly by Mary's personal bitterness at her half-brother's betrayal. In any case he was contending for formal recognition of his special position in the state and certainly not just for the Protestant faith. The inadequacy of the appeal to religion is illustrated by Glencairn's failure to bring out his Cunninghams in 1565 compared with 1559—60. By contrast, the Hamiltons were out in force: they knew that they were defending their dynastic position against their hereditary Lennox foes; they were the real nucleus of the rebellion of 1565. Religion played only a subordinate role in it.[6]

In Mary's party, we search in vain for a nucleus of committed Catholics. She certainly had Catholic supporters in numbers, though they did not act as a party. Most of them were hardly conspicuous in maintaining the mass, which was perhaps just as well, since Mary still expected them to acquiesce in the religious status quo. What she sought from her supporters was not allegiance to Rome, but opposition to the Moray—Campbell—Hamilton rebel alliance.

The French ambassador, de Foix, touched on this without realizing it, when he observed that Mary's supporters put their private quarrels above her service.[7] She herself would have been well aware that she was turning noble rivalries to advantage in building a coalition. Thus Atholl, a known Catholic sympathizer, was also interested in his own advancement at Argyll's expense: Mary made him lieutenant of the north. By contrast, Caithness though a Catholic was inconspicuous in the queen's party: he had a feud with Marischal.[8] Protestants could be royalists for similar reasons: Lindsay 'schamfullye lefte' Moray through a dispute with the rebel Rothes over the sheriffship of Fife.[9]

Loyalty to the crown and to 'the authority' was a potent political principle: an active principle, as for the maverick Bothwell, or a passive one, as for Marischal who just wanted a quiet life. Mar had a conservative dislike of rebellion; Home disliked the thought of losing his job as a Border warden. Many must have glowed with patriotism as they lined up against the English-backed rebels: after all, there were no Frenchmen in the royal army, unlike in 1559–60. 'Catholic' sympathies often had less to do with the mass than with general conservatism and dislike of England; but plenty of Protestants shared these feelings. These were the foundations on which Mary clearly proposed in the summer and autumn of 1565 to build a broad coalition which involved at least as many Protestants as Catholics. As well as promoting Erskine to the earldom of Mar, she restored the forfeited Huntly, and recalled the exiled Sutherland and Bothwell. Huntly and Bothwell soon developed a close alliance. The rehabilitation of the Gordons and Hepburns, with wide influence in the north-east, Lothian and Borders, is a reminder that support for the previous regime had been less than universal.

Was the queen fundamentally dissatisfied with that regime, which had served her for four years? If so, here was her chance to purge its supporters. But the government was slow to put the rebels to the horn and quick to pardon deserters; Moray himself received a charter as late as June.[10] A tougher line, taken more decisively, would have been quite possible, given the rebels' weakness; but for Mary this would have risked committing the crown to the hands of a single faction. Should Moray be overthrown without the support of conservative Protestants, a dominant faction might emerge to imperil the crown's freedom of action. The sixteenth-century Stewart monarchy was prone to such faction crises, in one of which Mary would lose her throne. That it did not happen in 1565 must be due at least in part to her skill in conciliating the various elements of a broad-based coalition.

Mary's greatest single success in 1565 was to secure the adherence of the earl of Morton and his Douglases. He was 'knowen to be a favorer of the Confederat Lords', and in September Randolph claimed that he had actually joined them; but this turned to be just wishful thinking. It had been the earl of Lennox who recruited him for the queen.[11] Morton's motive was clear, for the deal involved Lady Lennox's renunciation of her claim to the Angus estates which he was administering, but the negotiations had been protracted and were concluded only in May, the same month as Moray left the privy council.[12] The earl of Lennox was a curious but important figure in all this alliance-building. On the face of it, his forfeiture and twenty-year absence from Scotland must have made it difficult for him to call on the Scottish magnate's traditional network of local support. He was also alleged to be ineffective as a politician; Randolph scoffed at his 'smale conduct'.[13] But the fact was that since his return to Scotland in September 1564, many had been courting his favour, and he made energetic efforts to build up a party of supporters. Considering that it was Mary's marriage to his son which was causing all the fuss, it is high time that Lennox was rescued from historians' neglect.

The reshuffle of political loyalties, according to an English report of February 1565, turned on attitudes to Lennox.[14] The author clearly exaggerated the hostility to him, another piece of wishful thinking; most of those listed ended up as his colleagues. But for this very reason we can take the report to be more reliable on Lennox's adherents. Committed Protestants, such as Home, Bothwell and Ruthven, were listed along with Catholics, like Atholl, Seton and Caithness. Lennox himself was a master of the religious quick-change act: having supported both sides in turn in the 1540s, he had been exiled for leading the Protestant opposition (the 'allyantes' of Cardinal Beaton had not forgiven him for this). But his wife, a girlhood friend of Mary Tudor, was a prominent figure amongst English Catholics, and he himself could easily pose as a Catholic when it suited him.[15] What was it that united such diverse elements in his support? The simple answer is ambition. The Moray–Maitland regime had become static and frustrating; to Lennox's backers, the direction of his bandwagon was less important than the fact that it was rolling. Erskine, Home, Fleming and Lord Robert wanted earldoms, while Ruthven was after the treasurership.[16] This was hardly a stable basis for a faction, which is why we find these fairweather friends of Lennox on opposite sides later.

Evidence for Lennox's efforts to build his own party comes from a list of fourteen lairds knighted at the time of Darnley's own elevation to the earldom of Ross in May 1565. Randolph sneered that they 'never showde anye greate token of their vasellage', but this was the whole point: Lennox, not the queen, drew up the list, providing us with a unique snapshot of his position in Scottish politics. The fourteen were: William Douglas of Hawick (son of James Douglas of Drumlanrig); Robert Drummond of Carnock; James Home of Synlaws; Patrick Houston of Craigton (or of that Ilk); William Livingston of Kilsyth; John Maxwell of Nether Pollok; John Mure of Caldwell; William Murray of

Tullibardine; William Ruthven of Ballindean; Alexander Stewart of Dalswynton (son of Alexander Stewart of Garlies); James Stewart of Doune; Robert Stewart of Strathdoun; Robert Stewart of Lairgs; and James Stirling of Keir.[17]

Lennox's most important task was to curry favour with the other nobles. Knighting one of their kinsmen or henchmen might elicit a helping hand from them in his assault on the summits of power. Thus, Ruthven of Ballindean was Lord Ruthven's uncle. Home of Synlaws was Lord Home's successor as warden of the east march. Drummond of Carnock had an Erskine connection traceable over thirty years. Livingston of Kilsyth was a kinsman of Lord Livingston; however, he was among the murderers of Riccio when the head of his house remained loyal to the queen, so there may have been a stronger Lennox connection than is apparent. Maxwell of Nether Pollok was connected with Herries, and Mure of Caldwell was a dependant of Eglinton.[18] These were all crucial connections. Ruthven, Home and Erskine were early Lennox supporters. Livingston, as a close friend of Mary, was one of those whose favour Lennox needed to win to press the marriage. Eglinton is interesting as being the only Catholic noble who benefited from Lennox's honours list. The equivocal Herries was generally regarded as a crafty politician, and might easily have persuaded Lennox of his goodwill.

As for Douglas of Hawick, he was Herries's cousin. However, as a descendant of the earls of Douglas he was clearly if not closely related to Lady Lennox. His father had been associated with Lennox's father, and later was one of the 'assured Scots' in Lennox's party in the 1540s; but he changed sides and was even in action against Lennox. Douglas of Hawick and his father both joined Moray's rebellion briefly in September, alone among Darnley's knights; no doubt the connection with Herries proved stronger than that with the Douglases.[19]

Lennox himself happened to have few relatives, but his household was not neglected. Two of the knights were Lennox's kin: Stewart of Doune, commendator of Inchcolm, and Stewart of Dalswynton. The latter's father had fought for Lennox in the 1540s, while he himself was killed fighting alongside Lennox at Stirling in 1571. That famous and controversial document, the Second Casket Letter, has 'Caldwellis sone' and Houston of Craigton as Lennox's retainers. Houston had been a Protestant since the 1540s, and was singled out as a 'doer' for Lennox in the English report of February 1565. Another Protestant of the 1540s, with a different Lennox connection, was Stirling of Keir: we meet a servant of Lennox's in England, working as a spy for Keir.[20]

Two others were prominent enough to be worth cultivating in their own right. Tullibardine, a powerful Perthshire laird, became comptroller in August 1565. Although connected to the Erskines by marriage, he never nailed his colours permanently to the mast of any faction; he held his post through every government upheaval until his retirement in 1583. He was listed as a strong Lennox supporter in February and his father had been a Protestant activist in the 1540s. Stewart of Strathdoun was better known as Lord Robert, Mary's half-brother and the future earl of Orkney. Lennox lodged with him and his wife, sister of the erratic earl of Cassillis,[21] on his return to Scotland; ambition seems to have drawn them together, and they were often mentioned as associates thereafter.[22] A knighthood for him was an obvious move for Lennox, for it would both please the queen and bolster his own party. Stewart of Lairgs was probably the younger Lord Robert, most obscure of Mary's half-brothers: he was granted this estate among the forfeited Sutherland lands in 1563. Although inactive, he was not entirely unimportant: when Moray granted him the priory of Whithorn in 1568, he missed a chance to recruit Fleming for the king's party. Lord Robert then set the priory in tack to Stewart of Garlies, father of the knight most closely connected with Lennox.[23]

The knights also tell us much about Lennox's religious tastes at that time. Five of them had connections with the Protestant party of the 1540s. Six—Douglas of Drumlanrig, Houston of Craigton, Murray of Tullibardine, Stewart of Garlies, Stewart of Doune and Stirling of Keir—were at the Reformation parliament, while Lord Robert the elder would have been there but for enmity to the Hamiltons.[24] Only the insignificant Mure of Caldwell had any identifiable Catholic connections. No wonder Moray found it hard to convince people that Lennox planned to overthrow Protestantism.

This, of course, was not the only accusation hurled by the rebels. Their manifesto of September 1565 charged Mary with favouring 'strangers . . . being men of base degrie'.[25] In an age of hierarchy and xenophobia, Riccio paid the ultimate penalty for being a low-born foreigner. What was the nature of the new regime? There was no wholesale shake-up of the administration in the summer of 1565. Only one office-bearer was dismissed: John Wishart of Pittarrow, the comptroller, who had joined the rebels. Those who kept a low profile, from Maitland downwards, were not troubled. James MacGill, the clerk register, John Bellenden, the justice clerk, and Robert Richardson, the treasurer, also continued to attend the privy council regularly. All three were committed Protestants; MacGill and Bellenden even received the accolade of inclusion on an assassination 'hit list' of six drawn up by the papal nuncio, Vincenzo Laureo, bishop of Mondovi.[26]

There were some new faces at the council table. One of them was

John Leslie, who played down any change of direction: 'the queen, thus deprived of her usual councillors, was compelled to choose new ones.'[27] Leslie was a Catholic; so was Simon Preston of Craigmillar, the new provost of Edinburgh, though Knox thought him 'most willing to set forward Religion'.[28] But there had never been any rigid exclusion of Catholics; and the newcomers were more than balanced by an influx of Protestants. Richard Maitland of Lethington (father of the secretary) and Robert Carnegie of Kinnaird ('frende to the Duke')[29] had served Mary of Guise. Alexander Gordon, the reforming bishop of Galloway, had 'laboured much' for the restoration of his nephew Huntly.[30] We have met William Murray of Tullibardine, the new comptroller, as one of Darnley's knights. Finally James Balfour of Pittendreich, an able lawyer, was ambitious in politics and devious in religion.[31] When he became clerk register in 1566, he was closely involved with the publication of Scotland's parliamentary statutes. Was it entirely coincidence that the first edition had to be hurriedly suppressed because it included all the old anti-Protestant legislation?[32] Yet as a group, these men seem better fitted to bring stability and efficiency to the administration than to carry out a religious counter-revolution.

The queen's household, however, was different. Mary had more scope here to favour those she pleased; naturally these would include Catholics. David Riccio was clearly a key figure, but he was not alone: according to Knox, Mary relied on 'the council of David and Francisco, the Italians, with Fowler the Englishman, and Master James Balfour'.[33] John Francisco de Busso was master of the household, Thomas Fowler a Catholic servant of Lennox. Other Catholics were employed as ambassadors to Catholic courts. Mary does seem to have been surrounding herself with more Catholics than before, but they remained outside the major offices of state, and even, with one or two exceptions, outside the council. The nature of their influence is unclear.[34] It would have had its greatest potential in areas where direct royal patronage was important; but there is no clear evidence that patronage was being diverted in the interests of a Catholic policy.

Household government may well have been more congenial to Mary: she could transact important business informally, and did not have to sit demurely knitting while the men deliberated round the council table. But the council remained important, as the drafting in of so many able and independent Protestants shows. Bolstering the administration with Protestants, while confining the Catholics to the household, may have been a deliberate choice on Mary's part, just as she relied on both Protestant and Catholic nobles to rule in the localities of a highly decentralized, feudal kingdom. All in all, her major error was probably not her favour shown to Catholics, but her reliance at court and in the royal administration on lesser men, at the expense of what the rebels called the 'wholsome advice and counsell of her Majestie's ancient nobilitie and barons'.[35] This was soon seen to be fraught with danger.

To Philip of Spain, Mary wrote that she would 'spare neither life nor goods' to maintain 'the crown, and the liberty of the [Catholic] Church for ever'. But at home, she promised her subjects that 'as nane of thame hes hiddertillis bene molestit in the quiet using of thair religioun and conscience, sa sall thai not be inquietit in that behalf in ony tyme to cum'.[36] In both cases, she was presenting the most persuasive argument to the audience concerned. Her words alone have been the source of endless futile controversy; we need to concentrate on her deeds.

Protestant restiveness led to growing tension in early 1565. There was, for instance, an organized hunt for Catholic Easter services in Edinburgh, which resulted in bloodshed.[37] Mary reacted as she often had before: to protect Catholics from attack within the framework of the religious status quo. In June, the General Assembly for the first time demanded the abolition of the mass 'not only in the subjects, but also in the Queens Majesties awin person'; she mildly asked them not to 'prease her to offend her awin conscience'.[38] But she was making Protestant gestures. Despite her 'ungodlye cerimonies' at Easter, Randolph noted that she was eating meat in Lent for the first time and not attending mass often; he hoped it would lead to her conversion, and in May there was a rumour that she had actually been converted.[39] She was willing to hear Protestant preaching — if not from Knox — and at Livingston's house in June she attended her first Protestant service, which was 'reckoned a great matter'.[40]

Was Mary after a final, statutory settlement of religion? It seems that she had in mind a recipe for a settlement — a recipe including at least a spoonful of toleration. Religion was legally based merely on a royal proclamation of 1561 in favour of the (Protestant) status quo. In September 1565, a new proclamation set out 'thair Majesteis sinceir meaning towart the establishing of religioun' by parliament, in which none were to be 'preissit in the fre use of thair conscience' — a phrase Mary often used. She had suggested something similar at a convention in May.[41] According to Randolph, it was not just Mary's 'will to continue papistry' but 'her desire to have all men live as they list' which 'offendeth the godly men's consciences'.[42] Toleration proposals upset the hard-line Protestants scarcely less than full-blooded Catholicism; but support might well have been found for a project which offered official recognition for the reformed church in return. France and Poland provided precedents. Mary that summer was careful to assure Catherine de Médicis that the rebels had 'the liberty of their conscience...I have changed nothing in the order to which they themselves consented'.[43] It was not just to Protestants that Mary disclaimed Counter-Reformation fervour.

Although Mary continued to correspond extensively with both Spain and France, her Catholic diplomatic activity bears no marks of a systematic anti-Protestant programme. She approached Catholic courts for aid against the rebels, but then her efforts ceased entirely. Evidently she aimed merely to win through the crisis, not to build long-term alliances. As for the toleration project, it was probably shelved on the rapid collapse of the rebellion, but it cannot be dismissed as merely an empty promise. The queen envisaged the possibility of the rebels holding out until the following spring, when she would have had to carry the policy through.[44] Since she did give official backing to the reformed church eighteen months later, it is not surprising to find that it was also a policy option in 1565. But there were no negotiations on such a settlement during the crisis of 1565; negotiations are never easy once armies have taken the field.

If Mary had really intended to set forward the old religion, she would have had to revitalize the old church structure. She had neglected it completely, and reform would have been a daunting task. She did indeed appoint three committed Catholics to bishoprics in 1565–6: William Chisholm to Dunblane, John Sinclair to Brechin and John Leslie to Ross. But she then employed them elsewhere as crown servants: Chisholm as a diplomat, Sinclair as president of the Court of Session, and Leslie on the privy council. Leslie never visited his diocese, and Chisholm spent little time even in Scotland. This was hardly likely to advance reform, and financial stringency made things worse. Church revenues were alienated, such as those of the diocese of Ross which were signed away to Darnley in May 1565, and a stream of parish benefices went to non-clergy.[45] With a fine impartiality, Mary also raided the Protestant ministers' thirds of benefices, prompting Knox to complain that 'the ministry was like to decay and fail'.[46] But it does seem that if she sought a Counter-Reformation, it was a remarkably secular one.[47]

By the end of 1565, it must have seemed as though the crisis was past. 'Things were in quiet all this winter', said Herries.[48] Hopes grew for the Chaseabout exiles' return and the restoration of harmony. Early in December the Hamiltons were pardoned; Châtelherault was exiled for five years, but meanwhile Archbishop Hamilton was 'well made of'.[49] This was a highly significant move, which would have been seen as the prelude to further pardons. It is true that all the other rebels were at the same time summoned to a parliament set for the following February.[50] But this was probably just a manoeuvre to put pressure on the English, who were then dragging their feet over negotiations to restore normal relations, without the prospect of an arranged marriage for Mary. Randolph does not seem to have been unduly worried by it. He did mention the parliament on 25 December, saying that it was rumoured that liberty of conscience would be granted; but it was not definite, and a month later it was 'still uncertain whether [it] will hold or not; her husband presseth so earnestly for the Crown Matrimonial'.[51]

For Mary and Darnley had fallen out. There had been 'jarres' between them in October, and Lennox later wrote that Mary 'suddenly altered' her affection for Darnley 'about November'.[52] Their relations became more frosty after Mary pardoned the Hamiltons, hereditary foes of the Lennox Stewarts. In December it was Darnley, not Mary, who was opposed to further pardons. Lennox was beginning to search for a stance from which to put pressure on the queen; and significantly he chose the Catholic ground which Mary seemed to have ignored. Darnley at Christmas 'never gave greter token of his religion then that thys laste nyghte, he was at mattynes and masse in the morninge before daye ... thoughe she her self the moste parte of the nyghte sat up at cardes'.[53]

The card-playing queen was taking a greater gamble than she knew; her position was by the winter of 1565/6 becoming dangerously insecure. England and the exiles were as yet far from being placated; some of the nobles who remained with the queen, such as Morton, were more and more restive at this. Meanwhile Lennox, who should have been her strongest supporter, was manoeuvring against her. Her most consistent course would have been to pardon one or two more exiles, to rely a little more on the Anglophile nobles, and to return to the policy of pursuit of *détente* with England more vigorously. There were, however, contradictions developing in her policy: the new regime lacked singleness of purpose. The English were upset when Thomas Fowler was sent to England in disguise at Christmas. Was he 'to secretly ascertain the feelings of certain people ... towards his queen', or 'seeking the advancement of his master' (Lennox), as Mary claimed when he was arrested?[54] Then Argyll (who though a rebel was not in exile but lurking in the Highlands) was deprived of Bute; this was surely due to pressure from the man to whom the island was granted — Lennox.[55] If Lennox interests continued to complicate royal policy, so already did those of Bothwell. The appointment of this notoriously anti-English earl as head of the Scottish delegation for negotiations with England on Border problems, if justifiable in terms of his prominence in local politics, was hardly a conciliatory gesture towards Elizabeth. Bothwell, like Lennox, was also still profiting at the rebels' expense: in December he had been granted a pension formerly belonging to another of the rebels, Glencairn, 'be ressoun of eschete'.[56] But despite all this, Randolph was able to report that 'some parte of her extremitie is asswaged' towards Moray.[57] Glencairn thought it safe enough to creep back from Berwick 'to his own country' (Ayrshire) at this time.[58]

January's policy was confused, but still generally conciliatory. However, February saw a dramatic new departure. The curtain-raiser was at Candlemas, 2 February, when Mary urged a number of her leading nobles to attend mass. Lennox, Atholl, Cassillis, Eglinton, Seton and Caithness, all Catholics, did so; Fleming (though normally considered a Catholic sympathizer) refused, as did the known, if varied Protestants, Lindsay, Huntly and Bothwell. Mary seems to have hoped that a record of support for the crown could somehow be transformed into support for Catholicism. There was even a suggestion to restore the mass at St Giles'.[59]

What caused this *démarche*? Contemporaries had no doubt that it was the separate but near-simultaneous arrival of no less than three envoys from France: Clernault de Villemont from the cardinal of Lorraine, John Thornton from Archbishop Beaton, both around 27 January, and Jacques d'Angennes, from Charles IX, a week later. Clernault brought a brief from the new pope, Pius V, congratulating Mary and Darnley, somewhat prematurely, on 'lately . . . restoring the due worship of God throughout your whole realm' and professing himself 'ready to satisfy your wishes'. Thornton's despatches have not survived, but Randolph's indignation against him got the better of his syntax. 'There was a bande lately devised, in which the late pope, themperor, the king of Spayne, the duke of Savoy, with divers princes of Italie, and the queen Mother, suspected to be of the same confederacy, to maintaine papistrye throughout Christendome. This bande was sent out of France by Thorneton and is subscribed by this quene.' Bedford, a week later, wrote more soberly that Mary's acceptance of the league was 'not yet confirmed', but added that 'Clerevault with his coming hathe moche altered her disposicion as well towching religion as to the earle of Murray'.[60] D'Angennes brought no such secrets in his diplomatic bag. His was ostensibly a more innocent mission, bringing the order of St Michael for Darnley; it was conferred at a mass in the chapel royal.[61]

What we have to decide is not whether there was a formal Catholic league, for we know there was not; it is what these various emissaries told Mary. At the time of their departure, Lorraine, Beaton and Chisholm, all militant Catholics, were together in Paris and could concert measures. We cannot now unravel all the threads of this web; but it seems clear that they made promises of some kind to Mary to encourage her to crack down on heresy, and to divert her from her conciliatory course. That was what James Melville thought, and he was deep in Mary's counsels at this time. 'Sche tok a resolution . . . to prolong [i.e. postpone] the Parlement quhilk was set to forfalt the lordis that wer fled. Seigneur David apperit to be also wone to the same effect.' But

ther wes a Frenche gentilman send hame here, callit Monsieur de Villemonte, with a commission to stay the Quen, in nawayes til agre with the lordis protestantis that wer banissit, because that all catholik princes wer bandit to rut them out of all Europe: quhilk was a devyce of the Cardinal of Lorraine, laitly com bak from the concile of Trent. . . . Quhilk unhappy message haisted fordwart divers tragicall accidentis.[62]

So Mary began another round of Catholic diplomacy. Word was sent to Chisholm to go to Rome to take up the pope's offer of aid.[63] By 14 February, Randolph was writing that 'mo practyzes then are nowe in hande ther were never', and he did not mean just the Riccio murder plot which had begun in response. There was 'never . . . more mescheif intended to those whome I am bound to honour and serve'; and mischief was intended to Randolph himself too. On the following day he was ordered out of the country, as his part in supplying money to the rebels the previous August had been discovered.[64]

'Give him only his due': Mary refused Darnley the royal arms when he was invested with the order of St Michael.[65] This was taken as a signal that the forthcoming parliament, now fixed for 7 March, would refuse him the coveted crown matrimonial. The whole question of whether the parliament would be held had turned on this; but by the end of February it was clear that even more drastic measures were imminent. Mary had declared that she would 'have the masse free for all men that wyll here it'; she wrote afterwards that the intention was 'to have done some good anent restoring the auld religion, and to have proceeded against our rebels according to their demerits'. Leslie confirms this, writing that the two measures proposed were 'one allowing the bishops and rectors of churches the full exercise of their ancient religion, and the other punishing the leaders of the conspiracy'.[66]

Up to now, Mary had triumphed: her popularity and success had never been more forcefully demonstrated than during Moray's rebellion. But with the exiles, their friends in Scotland and Lennox all hostile, she was becoming dangerously isolated and could not afford to be overconfident. She dismissed a warning of plots, saying that 'our contre men wer weill wordy'.[67] It seems that she later had some more concrete information — on 6 February she ordered Tullibardine and John Stewart of Traquair into ward.[68] But they were still at liberty when the murder took place. The parliament was approaching fast now, and Mary's opponents knew that it was time for action, not words.

The genesis of the plot, according to Ruthven, was 'about the 10th of February', the day of Darnley's investiture and shortly after the about-turn in Mary's policy.[69] Riccio, long resented, was an obvious sacrificial victim; but it is equally obvious that the plotters acted when they did 'to get the parlement stayed' as well as 'to mak a chenge in court'.[70] Lennox concurred actively in the plot. The master of his household was among the murderers.[71] Darnley has usually been represented merely as the tool of Morton, Ruthven and Lindsay, but his father's influence must be taken into account. Ruthven in his apologia did his best to heap blame on Darnley, but there may be some truth in his description of Darnley's prominent role — particularly his insistence that Riccio should be attacked in the queen's presence. And while Darnley's knights were never all Lennox's toadies, it is worth noting that at least five of them were connected with the plot: Douglas of Hawick, Livingston of Kilsyth, Tullibardine, Stewart of Doune and Stirling of Keir.[72]

Riccio was sacrificed on the altar of politics, not religion; it was the exiles' impending forfeiture that provoked their sympathizers to take up the assassin's dagger. Ruthven, for instance, scarcely mentions religion, though there was no reason why he should not have denounced Mary's plan to restore the mass. Mary seems to have made no secret of this plan; yet even Knox and Buchanan portray the conspirators as angered solely by a hastily devised forfeiture campaign.[73] But the conspirators had not long since been in arms against Moray: 'it was not for his cause, bot for ther awen particulairs.'[74] Such a sweeping attack on a group of nobles, who were far from isolated politically despite their exile, had not been seen since the fall of the Black Douglases: if Mary could get away with this, what else might she not do? It is no wonder that Morton 'fearit a revocation' of lands alienated during Mary's minority.[75] As for Lennox, ostentatiously Catholic since Candlemas, he might have been expected to welcome the queen's new direction; but he was really sulking at his exclusion from power. In the following week he executed an effortless volte-face, joining the Anglophile lords in order to reassert his political influence. It was the nobles' traditional position in the state which was at stake.

The fateful parliament assembled on 7 March 1566, and the Lords of the Articles were elected. Ruthven later accused Mary of packing them: 'you chose them all at Seton' (where she had stayed on 1–2 March). The spiritual lords were Archbishop Hamilton, the bishops of Dunkeld,

Brechin, Orkney and Galloway, and the commendators of Lindores (John Leslie) and Balmerino (John Hay). The temporal lords were Huntly, Bothwell, Morton, Marischal, Crawford, Atholl and Lennox, 'with the commissionaris of burrowes'.[76] It was a fair cross-section of Mary's supporters at the time, equally balanced in religion, with the Catholics Hamilton, Dunkeld, Brechin, Lindores, Crawford, Atholl and Lennox, and the Protestants Orkney, Galloway, Balmerino, Huntly, Bothwell, Morton and Marischal. This was only slightly more Catholic in flavour than the Lords of the April 1567 parliament, when the queen was making concessions to the reformers. But on the question of forfeiting the exiles, the position was much more ominous: only Hamilton, Balmerino and Morton might have had any sympathy for them.

In the event the loyalties of the Lords were not put to the test. Mary had sown the wind, and two days later she reaped the whirlwind. Her supper-chamber was invaded and Riccio butchered, with an implicit threat to her own life. This was probably Darnley's idea, as Ruthven said; only he and his father could have had solid hopes of benefiting from a disputed succession which would have set either Lennox himself, or possibly the exiled Châtelherault, on the throne. But Mary resourcefully escaped from Holyrood and reached Dunbar with Bothwell's help. The lords who hastened to join her there were Huntly, Fleming, Seton and Livingston; in addition, Atholl, Crawford, Marischal, Sutherland, Caithness, Home, Borthwick and the Hamiltons re-entered Edinburgh with her.[77] Mary was holding on to her supporters of the previous summer, with the addition of the reconciled Hamiltons, but with the defection of Lennox, Ruthven, Lindsay and the Douglases.

Darnley had discharged the parliament, and it was not reassembled. Instead Mary pardoned the Chaseabout rebels whom she had intended to forfeit. Power had slipped from the conspirators' grasp, and they had been forced to flee — but they had succeeded in their immediate aims. It had been brought home to Mary how narrow her own power-base had become, and she moved once more to broaden her support and build a new coalition. Moray, Argyll and Glencairn were back on the council by the end of April, having patched up a superficial reconciliation with Huntly, Bothwell and Atholl. After Riccio, there were no more low-born favourites and no more government through the household. So the nobles were firmly back in the saddle.

All this was bad news for the papal legate, Laureo. He was appointed in May 1566, with authority from Pius V to disburse a subsidy, and arrived in Paris in August. Having authorized payment of the first instalment, he waited for a sign that the queen would take some practical steps for the old religion — such as inviting him to Scotland.

Mary, though keen to get the money, hesitated until October about the invitation; by then, disillusioned, Laureo abandoned his mission. Scotland in 1566 offered only a bleak prospect for the papacy.[78]

Mary's tentative efforts to foster Catholicism outside her own household were at an end; instead, she turned to cultivate the Protestant church. In May, the bishopric of Brechin was returned to a Campbell lay titular on Sinclair's death; in October, she granted succession to the lesser benefices to the ministers. In December, the prince received a Catholic baptism, but this hardly signalled a Catholic *démarche*. Only four nobles attended; and three days later, the queen gave the reformed church supplies and £10,000 in cash. From then on there was a series of grants to burghs of local friary lands.[79] The project to revive the mass amongst the nobility had long since disappeared without trace.

Moray's Cassandra-like warnings about the Darnley marriage went unheeded by Protestant Scotland. Outside his immediate circle, the nobles saw no threat to their interests from a Lennox Stewart restoration. Paradoxically, it was Moray's rebellion itself which sowed the seeds of a Catholic policy. Mary crushed him so easily that she became temporarily blinded to the need for restraint in crown action. When, in February 1566, the chimera of a European Catholic revival appeared before her, she fell victim to her own over-confidence. The temptation was irresistible to breathe new life into the mass, to promote toleration, and to strike a final blow at those who had raised the standard of militant Protestantism against her. Her bold but ill-prepared scheme was an aberration in a policy which was otherwise cautious and conciliatory.

In the end it was the threat to the nobility, rather than to the Protestant faith, which roused opposition in a way that the tergiversating Lennox had never done. The reaction when it came was swift, brutal — and successful. Mary, having realized her mistake too late, was nevertheless able to retrieve her position with considerable bravery and astuteness. The long-term damage to her circumstances is open to debate; but for the time being, she was back in control and stepping up her efforts at conciliation. Her Catholic interlude had lasted just five weeks.

Notes

[1] See Adams, ch. 6 above, for the attempted Leicester match in 1564–5.

[2] *CSP Scot.*, ii, 136–7, 144.

[3] Mary's supporters can be seen at a series of extraordinary council meetings: *RPC*, i, 339–41, 346–7, 361–2, 379.

[4] See White, ch. 3 above, for Châtelherault's flirtation with Huntly in 1562.

[5] Herries, *Memoirs*, 71.

[6] Donaldson, *Queen's Men*, chs. 4, 5.

[7] Teulet, *Relations*, ii, 220–1.

[8] *RPC*, i, 357; *SP*, ii, 339; Knox, *History*, ii, 105.

[9] *CSP Scot.*, ii, 173.

[10] *RSS*, v, 2108; *RPC*, i, 349–50, 365; Herries, *Memoirs*, 72–3; *Registrum Honoris de Morton* (1853), i, 12–13.

[11] Herries, *Memoirs*, 73; *CSP Scot.*, ii, 205; G. R. Hewitt, *Scotland under Morton* (1982), 5.

[12] See Adams, ch. 6 above, for details.

[13] *CSP Scot.*, ii, 168.

[14] *CSP Scot.*, ii, 118–19.

[15] See Adams, ch. 6 above.

[16] *CSP Scot.*, ii, 173.

[17] *CSP Scot.*, ii, 161; Ellis, *Original Letters,* I, ii, 204.

[18] *SP*, iv, 101, 472–3; *RPC*, i, 140; *RMS*, iv, 1973; *CSP Scot.*, ii, 257; *RPC*, i, 241; W. Fraser, *Memorials of the Montgomeries, Earls of Eglinton* (1859), ii, 201–4.

[19] Knox, *History*, ii, 163; *SP,* vii, 119; *RSS, v, 2367.*

[20] *APS*, iii, 424; *SP*, iv, 153–4, 158–9; A. Lang, *The Mystery of Mary Stuart* (1901), 395; Donaldson, *Queen's Men*, 39; *CSP Scot.*, ii, 252–3.

[21] See Lynch, ch. 1 above, for Cassillis's two conversions 1564–6.

[22] P. D. Anderson, *Robert Stewart, Earl of Orkney, Lord of Shetland* (1982), 45.

[23] *RSS*, v, 1463, 1704; Donaldson, *Queen's Men*, 88; G. Donaldson, 'The bishops and priors of Whithorn', *Trans. Dumf. and Galloway Nat. Hist. Antiq. Soc.*, 3rd ser., xxvii (1948–9), 147. Lord Robert was also connected with Tullibardine, to whom he granted the foud (or sheriffship) of Shetland in July 1565; Anderson, *Robert Stewart*, 47.

[24] *APS*, ii, 525–6; Anderson, *Robert Stewart*, 11.

[25] Calderwood, *History*, ii, 573.

[26] *Papal Negs.*, 278. The others were Moray, Argyll, Morton and Maitland.

[27] Forbes Leith, *Narratives*, 103.

[28] Knox, *History*, ii, 171; Lynch, *Edinburgh*, 117.

[29] *CSP Scot.*, ii, 174.

[30] Knox, *History*, ii, 189.

[31] See Durkan, ch. 4 above, for Balfour's religion; also Lynch, ch. 1.

[32] See Lynch, ch. 1 above, for the printing of the statutes in 1566.

[33] Knox, *History*, ii, 167.

[34] See Durkan, ch. 4 above, for an explanation of their influence at court.

[35] Calderwood, *History*, ii, 572.

[36] Labanoff, i, 282; proclamation, 12 July 1565, *RPC*, i, 338.

[37] See Cowan, ch. 5 above, for the Tarbot incident; also J. E. A. Dawson, 'Mary, queen of Scots, Lord Darnley and Anglo-Scottish relations in 1565', *International Hist. Rev.,* viii (1986), 11–12.

[38] *BUK*, i, 59, 67.

[39] *CSP Scot.*, ii, 141, 157–8.

[40] Knox, *History*, ii, 147, 153.

[41] *RPC*, i, 372; *CSP Scot.*, ii, 212; see also ibid, ii, 172.

[42] Keith, *History*, ii, 269.

[43] Labanoff, i, 289–90.

[44] Labanoff, i, 289.

[45] *RSS*, v, 2066; *RSS*, v, x.

[46] *Thirds of Benefices*, xxv; Knox, *History*, ii, 175.

[47] Cf. Lynch, ch. 1 above, for a different emphasis in analysing Mary's Counter-Reformation of 1565–6.

[48] Herries, *Memoirs*, 73.

[49] *CSP Scot.*, ii, 242–3.

[50] *RPC*, i, 409.

[51] *CSP Scot.*, ii, 247; E. Russell, *Maitland of Lethington* (1912), 244–5.

[52] *CSP Scot.*, ii, 223; A. Lang, *The Mystery of Mary Stuart* (1901), 59.

[53] *CSP Scot.*, ii, 247; see also Fowler to Lady Lennox, Dec. 1565, *HMC Salisbury*, i, 324. But see Lynch, ch. 1 above, for Mary's card-playing.

[54] *CSP Scot.*, ii, 246; *CSP Spain*, i, 522; Labanoff, i, 313; *HMC Salisbury*, i, 325.

[55] *RSS*, v, 2538.

[56] *RSS*, v, 2512.

[57] *Selections . . . illustrating the reign of Mary, Queen of Scotland* (1837), 150–1.

[58] Knox, *History*, ii, 178.

[59] *CSP Scot.*, ii, 254–5; R. Gore-Browne, *Lord Bothwell* (1937), 224; *Diurnal*, 88.

[60] *Papal Negs.*, 232–4.

[61] Cf. Lynch, ch. 1 above, for the importance of the investiture.

[62] Melville, *Memoirs*, 146–7.

[63] *Papal Negs.*, 232–6.

[64] Randolph to Leicester, 14 Feb. 1566, *SHR*, xxxiv (1955), 137; *CSP Scot.*, ii, 256–7.

[65] Knox, *History*, ii, 178.

[66] Ellis, *Original Letters*, I, ii, 206; Labanoff, i, 343; Forbes Leith, *Narratives*, 108. See also Lynch, ch. 1 for the position of Mary's bishops.

[67] Melville, *Memoirs*, 140.

[68] Signet letter, 6 Feb. 1566, Traquair House MSS.

[69] Lord Ruthven, 'A discourse of the late troubles . . . ', Keith, *History*, iii, app. xi.

[70] Melville, *Memoirs*, 148.

[71] ibid., 150.

[72] *RSS*, v, 2883, 3149; Ellis, *Original Letters*, I, ii, 217; *RPC*, i, 405.

[73] Knox, *History*, ii, 179; George Buchanan, *History of Scotland*, ed. J. Aikman (1829), ii, 423.

[74] Melville, *Memoirs*, 150.

[75] ibid, 148.

[76] *Diurnal*, 89.

[77] Claude Nau, *Memorials of Mary Stewart*, (1883), 17–19; *CSP Scot.*, ii, 269.

[78] *Papal Negs.*, 264–87; see Cowan, ch. 5 above, for Laureo's mission.

[79] *RSS*, v, 2806; Donaldson, *Scotland*, 125.

8

Mary, Dowager Queen of France

M. GREENGRASS

For twenty-seven years, Mary Stewart was a dowager queen of France and the fact that she was absent for all but one of those years can sometimes obscure the continued importance of this French connection to her. Although it surfaced on numerous occasions and in different contexts, its emotional significance was perhaps best captured in her last will when she asked to be buried in Rheims, close by her cardinal uncle, Charles de Lorraine.[1] She remained to the end of her life a French queen.

Dowager queens at the court of France never, of course, commanded the status or real power that queen mothers sometimes acquired in periods of minority and royal tutelage;[2] but they retained an acknowledged position in the royal family, enjoying privileged access to the king for themselves and their servants, rights of evocation (*committimus*) to the royal council for legal cases involving themselves or members of their entourage, and rights to appoint to royal posts in the lands which formed their dowry.[3] That Mary took these duties seriously is clear from her correspondence. The degree to which she obtained up-to-date information about the mercurial politics of France during the civil wars — and her ingenuity in doing so during her captivity in England — is remarkable. Even after she had been transferred to the closer confinement of Tutbury in January 1585, for example, she still was able to follow the first stages of the Catholic League in France.[4] She was probably in a better position to assess the significance of the proclamation of Joinville (March 1585) and the subsequent Treaty of Nemours (July 1585) than most provincial governors in France; though in her circumstances it is not perhaps so surprising that she followed these events as though her life depended on them.

Her long absence from France created, however, its own dilemmas. Status at the later Valois court — and not least for its ladies — required a perennial cultivation of protectors and suitors, substantial resources, a good knowledge of where to lay hands on administrative talent, legal skills and an accurate appreciation of the right moments to advance one's own interests. But the France that Mary had known in her brief honeymoon reign as queen to François II had faded in the civil wars. By 1568 and the beginning of her English captivity, the dukes of Guise and Montmorency and the king of Navarre, all of whom had played a prominent part in her nuptials a decade previously, were dead, either assassinated or in battle.[5] In March 1578, a decade later, the cardinal of Guise, the last of her Lorraine uncles, died. He had been protector of her interests in France after the death of the great cardinal of Lorraine four years previously in December 1574.[6] The protectorship was a position with formal authority; Charles claimed in legal documents that he was 'procureur général et surintendant des affaires de la Reine d'Ecosse'.[7] He had automatic rights of access to, and precedence in, her council as well as powers to dispose of the seals of her chancellor and to dispense the revenues of the dowry as pensions to whom he pleased.[8] Mary was reduced to asking her ambassador to approach the cardinal to let her have some disposal of posts in her duchy: 'car je veux en avoir le principal grand mercy, et les donner à ceulx que bon me semblera pour mon service'.[9] With this in mind, perhaps, no formal protectorship was apparently continued after the death of the cardinal of Guise, although it certainly persisted unofficially.[10] The Lorraine family in France was by then principally composed of her young cousins, the eldest of whom had been only ten at the time of her nuptials to François II in 1558, just old enough to take part in the marriage celebrations by joining a mock procession into the ballroom on a hobby-horse.[11] With him on that occasion was her young brother-in-law, Henri of Valois. When he became king of France in 1574, France's court and politics became dominated by a generation which Mary had only known as young adolescents; they had grown up in a world very different from that which Mary remembered in France.[12] Of those that remained and held influence, only the duke of Nevers and her mother-in-law, Catherine de Médicis, would have been vividly recalled by her.

At the centre of Mary's interests in France lay her jointure, granted her by her marriage contract signed at the Louvre on 19 April 1558.[13] By its terms, if François died as king of France without heirs, she was to receive, as a portion, revenues equivalent to 60,000 *livres tournois* (or £30,000 Scots) annually, to be assigned on the county of Poitou and duchy of Touraine. These were the traditional jointures of the queens of France and the county had been the property of François I's dowager queen, Eleanor of Austria, until her death in the previous year. The clauses relating to the jointure were accepted in their entirety within weeks of François II's death and, by an ordinance of 20 December 1560, arrangements were set in hand for the constitution of the dowry.[14] All the customary features of French royal apanages were approved; the rights pertaining to the estates included the nomination to all church benefices in the duchy within the gift of the king as well as all royal offices, 'ordinaire' and 'extraordinaire', that is, civil and military. The mature trees of the forests were specifically protected from wholesale felling, although such timber needed for the necessary maintenance of the duchy's houses, mills and buildings was permitted to be cut. The ordinance also warned that many portions of the duchy were likely to have been alienated, assigned or otherwise committed since the donation of 1558, something all too likely to have been true in the conditions of undeclared bankruptcy of the Valois monarchy in 1559–60. The duchy therefore had to be evaluated and such assignations as could be revoked or reassigned elsewhere on the royal domain were ordered to be transferred. If the revenues proved insufficient, Mary was to be offered compensation elsewhere to her satisfaction.

The necessary evaluation was carried out in the early months of 1561 by a team of six assessors from the Paris *chambre des comptes* and based on such of the last ten years of accounts of the duchy as its receivers could present to them.[15] From the six points of receipt in the county and the five receipts in the duchy, annual estimated revenues, taking into account all potential repurchases of alienations, only matched about half the necessary annual revenues of the jointure. The assessors therefore proposed, in response to a suggestion from Mary's *conseil des affaires* already constituted in Paris to look after her interests, further assignations in north-east France in the almost dismembered county of Champagne. This was adjacent to much of the Guise's landed patrimony; the archbishopric of Rheims was in the gift of the Lorraine family and the duke of Guise was governor of the province. There was every reason to suppose that the assignations of the receipts of the county at Epernay, St Dizier, St Ménéhould, Chaumont-en-Bassigny, Bar-sur-Aube and Passavant-en-Argonne would be well looked after. Even this gift left a 'supplement' of 15,798 *livres* 13s 4d to make up the portion and this was to be found by a gift of royal tax receipts (see table 1). No *décharge* was in fact assigned before Mary left for Scotland and already the difficulties which would surround the exercise of her dowry rights were beginning to make themselves felt.

The day that Mary took her leave of the French court at St-Germain, the *parlement* of Paris began contesting the grants in Champagne.[16] Apanages were generally created in the heartland of France – Anjou,

Table 1 *Composition of Mary's dowry*

	livres	sols	deniers
County of Poitou			
Recettes ordinaires			
Civray	1,426	11	
St Maixant	1,188	2	
Mese	880	4	7
Chizé	2,436	12	11
Duchy of Touraine			
Recettes ordinaires			
Loches			
Chinon	6,540	12	1
Châtillon-sur-Indre			
Montrichard	1,407	9	6
County of Champagne supplement			
Recettes ordinaires			
Epernay	3,608	5	11
St Dizier	3,834	11	
St Ménéhould	2,235	14	9
Chaumont-en-Bassigny	3,656	18	6
Bar-sur-Aube	411	8	4
Passavent-en-Argonne	147	0	10
Assignation	15,798	13	4
TOTAL	60,000		

Touraine, Bourbonnais, Berry − and not in frontier provinces. The magistrates of Paris contested the granting of rights of nomination of senior royal offices, *baillis* and captains to fortresses in such a sensitive location. The king accepted this but the magistrates returned to create further restrictions on Mary's rights in Champagne in September 1561.[17] By the time the grant had been finally registered by the provincial treasurers in Châlons-sur-Marne on 20 February 1562, the county of Champagne had been shorn of all rights to nominate to posts beyond the ecclesiastical ones. Guise had left court in October 1561 and proved powerless to defend her interests there. Her council further protested that the forests of Epernay and St Ménéhould had been so pillaged by their previous occupants — the duke of Guise and the count of Villars — that only bushes and young trees were left standing.[18] Compensation for this was still being pursued on Mary's instructions by her permanent ambassador in France, James Beaton, archbishop of Glasgow, twenty years later.[19] In addition, not all the alienations of the duchy of Poitou were satisfied by the king and one outstanding alienation resulted in a long lawsuit, the *affaire* Secondigny, which had cost 6,000 *livres* by 1574 and must have cost still more after that since it was still unsettled at the time of Mary's death.[20] More damaging was the failure to secure any assignation of the remaining sums due to her before the beginning of the civil wars. In August 1562, she wrote to M. de Gonnor, the *surintendant des finances* in France protesting that she had received no recompense for the restrictions on her rights in Champagne nor any 'supplement' to her dowry.[21] Although she received an assignation eventually on the *aides* of Poitiers, in the circumstances of French royal finances and despite Guise assistance throughout most of the period up to her English captivity, it was rarely, if at all, honoured. In February 1567, she claimed arrears of 40,000 *livres* and in May 1568, three years' worth of assignation.[22] From Carlisle she complained bitterly to the queen mother on 26 June 1568: 'Le roy me doit quelque argent et je n'ay pas un soul: je n'ay point de honte de vous fayre ma pleinte comme à celle qui m'a nourrie, car je n'ay seulement pas de quoy ascheter une chemise.'[23] Although none of her estate accounts appears to have survived, it is likely, given also the effects of the civil wars on rents in the Touraine and Poitou area,[24] that she never received more than about two-thirds (at the most) of the portion granted to her.

The revenue was, however, more than sufficient to finance a substantial dowager household whilst she was queen in Scotland. From the surviving *état* of salaries and pensions, drawn up in Edinburgh on 13 February 1566, the revenues from the French estates provided her with a substantial retinue.[25] It was not as large as that which she had enjoyed as queen of France,[26] but it still compared favourably with that of the dowager queen of Navarre, Jeanne d'Albret, who enjoyed the huge wealth of the Foix-d'Albret family.[27] It included 174 salaried posts with salaries paid at French rates of remuneration to her Scottish court and council in France as well as a further seventy-eight small pensions to servants in France. The French presence continued to be in a majority even among the salaried officials of her court in Scotland.

This *état* was issued as an instruction for Mary's French advisers to carry out. Mary's council was convened in Paris by the indefatigable archbishop of Glasgow. Beaton's *gages* of 3,060 *livres* were the largest salary by far which Mary dispensed.[28] In addition, he was rewarded with ecclesiastical benefices in her gift and allowed some of the casual revenues of Champagne.[29] But Beaton's expenses at the Valois court over a period of a quarter of a century must have been considerable and his laments of his indebtedness after Mary's death are likely to have been true.[30] There is no evidence of any financial malversation on his part and Mary's confidence in his capacity throughout most of her life – 'il n'y a pas ung plus homme de bien au monde ou plus souffisant' – was justified.[31]

Running estates in France of this size needed legal, financial and managerial skills and time which Beaton could not have been expected to provide. The quality of its senior councillors, the *maître d'hôtel*, chancellor, and legal advisers, was therefore of considerable importance. Mary's council was a distinguished one so long as she was a queen in Scotland, with salaries distributed in 1566 to a total of nineteen individuals, two of whom were officials in the *chambre des comptes* in Paris and three of whom were senior *avocats* in the Paris law courts. A further five were provincial legal figures in the regions where Mary's interests lay. The master of the House (*premier maître d'hôtel*), concerned with purveyance and the dispensation of salaries, was Jean de Beaucaire, sieur de Puyguillon, from a family of royal servants under François I.[32] The chancellor, handling Mary's French seals, was François de l'Aubespine, *président* of the *grand conseil* and a senior figure in the French legal hierarchy who also served on the queen mother's council.[33] The financial affairs of the queen rested in the hands of her treasurer, René Dolu, sieur d'Ivoi in Berry, eventually *secrétaire des finances* and *secrétaire du conseil* of the king.[34] He was well placed in French public life since he had close relatives – probably brothers – as a president in the *chambre des comptes* of Paris and *secrétaire des finances* respectively.

The relationships with the clients of the Lorraine house were naturally strong. François de Beaucaire de Puyguillon, bishop of Metz, and Jean's brother, was also a member of her council. A household servant of the cardinal of Lorraine, he was a 'straw' bishop (*confidentiaire*) to enable the cardinal to extract the temporal revenues from the see of Metz. Among other officials was Pierre Hotman, sieur de Villiers St-Paul, *maître des comptes* in Paris.[35] He was a treasurer for the cardinals of Lorraine and Guise. His son, Charles Hotman, sieur de la Rocheblond, founder member of the Paris urban Catholic League, the *Sixteen*, in 1584, succeeded him as one of her legal advisers and acted on behalf of Thomas Morgan when he was imprisoned. While not all members of the de l'Aubespine family looked to the Lorraine house for protection (François's brother. Claude, *secrétaire du roi*, for example, was not their client), some clearly were more closely attached, particularly Claude's son and, possibly, François himself.[36] Lorraine's protectorship of Mary's interests in France was reinforced by these interrelated connections of service to a degree that it is often difficult at this distance to disentangle the two with any ease.

The only comparable *état* for Mary's French council after 1566 is that for 1573 but from all that we know from her correspondence it is clear that the council's composition altered considerably, many of the changes occurring in or around 1574.[37] It became less a body of skilled administrators with posts in senior French royal service looking after her estates and more a group of Mary's domestic servants enjoying close contacts with the expatriate English and Scottish community in France and engaged in politics. Puyguillon retired in 1574, the same year that his companion d'Esguilly died, and they were not replaced. After an interim, de l'Aubespine was replaced as chancellor by someone of much lesser standing, albeit her own client, Gilles du Verger.[38] He was a president of the *présidial* of Tours (Mary may have appointed him), to whom she had promised the post two years previously. She became godparent to his offspring and secured his compensation when her county of Touraine was sequestered. Du Verger was eventually replaced by a Parisian *avocat* without a royal post, Jean de Champhuan, sieur du Ruisseau, brother-in-law to Mary's secretary in England, Claude Nau de Mauvissière. He became an executor for her last will.[39]

The queen's confidence in her treasurer, René Dolu, also became severely strained in 1574. She accused him of not paying her servants and wrote openly that he acted more in the interests of the French king than hers.[40] It is impossible to determine whether the charges were just, although Dolu certainly attempted to refute them and it is probably significant that they occurred in the context of the negotiations to renew the Treaty of Blois which caused Mary to have the gravest suspicions of the good faith of the French king. She instructed her ambassador in Paris in January 1575 to ask the cardinal of Lorraine to replace Dolu with someone 'qui soit homme de bien et non tant embrouillie' in French royal service. The death of the cardinal presumably prevented the instructions being acted upon and in 1576 Dolu came to England to present his accounts. He was, however, forbidden to go in person to Sheffield and Mary continued to accuse him of negligence.[41] He was finally dismissed in 1581 to be replaced by one of Mary's domestic servants, M. de Chérelles, whose brother would be an agent for the French ambassador in England from September 1585 and in contact with Mary at Tutbury.[42]

Arriving in Paris around 1574 was the notorious Welsh exile, Thomas

Morgan.[43] At what date, if ever, he formally became a member of the council is not clear. He certainly had close relations with it as a receiver of her dowry revenues and, as confidential secretary to the cardinal ambassador, handled much of the secret correspondence between Paris and the captured queen. Through his influence, Charles Paget, close collaborator and fellow conspirator, also joined Mary's Paris servants in 1579. By March 1585, the date of Morgan's arrest by the French king, Morgan was a kind of unofficial secretary of state in exile for Mary, dispensing substantial sums of money and co-ordinating the exile community.

Behind these changes lay some important issues which we can only glimpse on occasions. It seems clear that Mary wanted her council in Paris actively to support the exiles in Paris. Dolu preferred to see Mary's council setting up a fund for the future, rather than dispensing money into the bottomless pockets of the *déracinés*.[44] Mary came to feel that not enough had been done in Paris to secure her release, that her French estates were being diverted to line the pockets of the French king's servants rather than going to the assistance of the exiles and herself. In the conditions of the later captivity, where few administrators of her estates were allowed to visit her, she was compelled to rely on fragmentary and partial information, sufficient only to make her aware that resources and authority were slipping away from her. In the circumstances, it is not surprising that she should reckon that English and Scottish exiles would be more ready to act in her cause. Morgan and Paget encouraged her suspicions and were directly responsible for her unwillingness to trust ambassador Beaton in the last two years of her life.[45]

There is no doubt that Morgan lay at the heart of the last attempts to free Mary from her imprisonment, and his role has often been harshly judged. As Cardinal Allen said, Mary had been 'ruinated' by her servants' 'unfortunate proceedings'. In retrospect, what appears remarkable is Morgan's failure to appreciate Walsingham's penetration of his network of contacts. It is a failure which should, at least in part, be interpreted in the light of the degree of protection which he expected to receive as Mary's servant in France. There is some evidence to suggest that Guise did not entirely trust either Morgan or Paget and they excited the suspicion of at least some of the Jesuit company in France. They were aware that from being a routine administrative organism for a domain, Mary's Paris council had become a focus for the closet world of conspiracy. Queen Elizabeth reflected the fact when she complained to the French ambassador about Mary in 1581: 'Qu'il vault mieulx qu'elle employe son douaire à s'entretenir que faire des menées et praticques en

Espaigne, en Itallye et par tout le monde et en Escosse, pour troubler et atacher une guerre avec l'Angleterre, et praticquer par tout le monde des serviteurs et pensionnaires de sondit douaire . . .'. To which Castelnau added; 'C'est une chose où je me trouve plus empesché, Sire, pour servir ladicte Royne d'Escosse, qu'en nul aultre que ce soit'.[46] The fundamental truth of the accusation had not escaped him.

The material resources of the estates declined considerably in the reign of Henri III. Unusually, the royal domain in France had to support the jointures of two queens and a queen mother, as well as the apanage demands of a prince of the blood who was heir to the throne. It is not entirely surprising, therefore, to find that the county of Touraine was unilaterally sequestered from Mary in 1576 (along with other estates from the French dowager queen Elisabeth) to form an augmented apanage duchy of Anjou for the king's brother, François, duke of Alençon.[47] The pacification at Beaulieu, arrived at in May 1576 with the French Protestants, had indicated the importance of the duke of Alençon to the French throne and the letters patent creating the duchy attempted (rather belatedly) to acknowledge his status. The letters patent creating his duchy were not, therefore, an integral part of the peace process with the Protestants as is sometimes stated.

Mary was unimpressed with the compensation offered by the king and protested impotently that she had lost the best part of her estates.[48] The alternative was the much more scattered county of Vermandois with rights spread over fourteen *bailliages* in Champagne.[49] Since this would not provide complete satisfaction, additional rights had to be found on the royal domain at Senlis and Vitry, to the north of Paris. There was a year's delay before she was able to enjoy the new estates in Champagne and Mary's council instituted legal proceedings in collaboration with the dowager queen Elisabeth before the *parlement* of Paris.[50] The fate of the case is not known, but it may have stimulated the royal council to grant her the additional rights at Senlis and Vitry, foreshadowed in 1576, but only granted formally in 1580.[51] The extent to which Mary was able to enjoy these acquisitions is not clear. The Senlis and Vitry rights were contested by Mary's relative, Madame de Montpensier, and resulted in another lawsuit.[52] That she did not enjoy any of the royal assignations without difficulty may be deduced from the fact that both James VI and even Elizabeth I herself were called on to sue to the French king for a more favourable treatment of her case.[53] Even if we allow that some of her pensions were assigned to James in 1583 to assist him to maintain a court, it is still of significance that Mary's council had to create a substantial *rente* of 30,000 *écus* (*c*.90,000 *livres*) to keep her solvent.[54] In her latter years, Mary was obliged to raise loans in London to pay for her necessities, to borrow from the earl of Arundel and even her secretary, Nau de Mauvissière. The loan from Arundel was only repaid after her death by the king of Spain. Following her execution, the Paris council drew up a statement of the revenues owed by the king of France to his late sister-in-law.[55] The largest amount was in unsatisfied assignations (*parties*) of 23,030 *écus* 48s 4d on the *chambre des comptes* of Paris but there were also significant sums in unpaid pensions as well as some outstanding loans to the king and the duke of Nevers. The total sum was 164,595 *écus* 27s 1d or the equivalent of just over eight year's worth of revenues of her original portion of 60,000 *livres*. In her last wishes, Mary asked for her council to be allowed to enjoy the revenues of her estates for a year after her death in order to be able to compensate for these debts; she also requested permanent pensions for her servants.[56] In fact, the duchy of Poitou was promptly sold on royal orders and there is no sign that any pensions were organized for Mary's remaining servants.[57]

The history of Mary's interests in France after her capture is, in some respects, predictable. It accords with all that we have known for over a century — since the publications of Chéruel and Teulet — about the ambiguously paternal French royal concern for Mary during her English captivity. France's politics abroad during the civil wars has to be interpreted in the light of her domestic divisions; coherence was not one of its most evident features. Although many at the French court believed that the best way to unite the realm was to engage its hearts and minds in foreign conquest, as the earlier Valois had done, the later Valois were generally persuaded that this was more likely to weaken the monarchy than strengthen it. Limited commitments, the containment of sources of conflict and the maintenance of traditional allegiances, were their minimalist objectives — when they were free to pursue them. The major Valois concerns were, of course, dominated by the Spanish presence in northern Europe and particularly by events in Flanders. Mary's captivity presented a number of perplexing conundrums to France's rulers. How could Mary be protected without that becoming more than a limited commitment? How could it be harmonized with the need for an English alliance against the Spanish in Flanders? How could the internal divisions in Scotland be healed so that its monarchy could be strong and yet not become more deeply embroiled, sustaining a French party which would increase, rather than diminish, the divisions in the Scottish polity? How, in short, could the auld alliance be sustained without abandoning Mary?

Mary was, of course, to be protected, her life assured and her confinement rendered as tolerable as possible. This much the Valois owed a close relative and could be secured through diplomatic channels. Doubtless they had some marginal effect on Elizabeth's councillors and the conditions of Mary's captivity. What more might have been considered? Stronger measures such as a commercial blockade (proposed by the Spanish ambassador in England to the French in 1569) were never seriously entertained; such a blockade would merely have further disrupted the commerce in north-west European waters and given needless legitimacy to the already worrying activities of the Protestant privateers operating from La Rochelle.[58] What countenance was given to assisting discontented Catholic elements in England on her behalf? Tempting though this possibility may have looked, especially with the English and Scottish Catholic exiles in France, it was always rejected. The Valois had good cause to know the dangers of 'setting light to other men's barns', and there was always the risk of such actions benefiting Spain rather than France. In any case, the contacts which the exiles had at the French court were fragile and intermittent. English noble. *emigrés* were, with few exceptions, not sufficiently well endowed to support themselves for long at that expensive establishment while seminary activists had a more pressing ministry to perform than dancing attendance in a court whose political direction they suspected and whose moral atmosphere they disapproved of. Some Scottish nobles attached to Mary's service had an entry via her ambassador Beaton, but he was in a somewhat ambiguous position there, forever playing a delicate quadrille between Guise, Valois and papal interests, whilst trying to promote Mary's interests in whatever way seemed appropriate.[59] The French court had more pressing problems of its own to be over-concerned with the introverted world of refugees from the British Isles.

So it is not surprising that Catherine de Médicis, acting on behalf of her son Charles IX who was still in tutelage, showed neither support nor sympathy for the northern rebels in 1569. Her response to the Ridolfi plot's discovery in the spring of 1571 was to indicate in every possible way that the French monarchy knew nothing of it and to plead for Mary's life despite her folly.[60] The following year, Charles IX, now in the plenitude of power, put his seal to the Treaty of Blois with Elizabeth which omitted all references to Mary and allowed for the mutual extradition of politically inconvenient exiles. Mary was outraged at this abandonment.[61] French royal diplomacy would help to keep her alive, but it would not secure her release.

If Mary had lingering hopes that Henri III might abrogate the Treaty of Blois, they were dispelled when it was confirmed in London on 26 March 1575; detailed questions about Mary's access to her estate officials were raised in the course of the delegation but the ambassadors prided themselves on the 'modération' which they had shown in accordance with the king's instructions.[62] On several occasions thereafter, particularly when the diplomatic corridors were buzzing with rumours of forthcoming invasion plots to rescue Mary, or with the Anjou match, Henri III reminded his ambassador, Michel Castelnau de Mauvissière, to stick rigidly to his brief and not to excite 'suspicion' in the English queen over Mary.[63] In May 1584, he told him to limit his contacts with the Scottish queen to the affairs of her dowry alone.[64] Such prudent passivity on the part of the French crown was already counted on by Walsingham during Mary's second trial and the events leading to the execution.

Had events in Scotland moved in a different direction, France's concerns for Mary might have been more positive. Had Elizabeth broken to any significant degree the engagement agreed between the two crowns and intervened militarily north of the Scottish border, the French monarchy might have defended her more ardently. In fact, with the exception of the events surrounding the Northern Rising of 1569, there were no substantial border incursions from England, although rumours of military action, such as those of March 1581, produced predictably fierce reactions from the French ambassador in London.[65] Equally, had the Marian and French faction in Scottish politics shown more staying power, particularly after the fall of Morton in 1580, Henri III would have had more cards in his hand. As it was, French influence was limited both by the difficulty of establishing a permanent accredited embassy in Scotland (and thus implicitly accepting James VI as king of Scotland in place of his mother) and perhaps by a failure to bribe prominent individuals within the easily pensionable Scottish polity. The French king's languid reaction to the news in 1582 of the Ruthven raid reflected his scepticism that the Scots could ever be fashioned into a solid pro-French alliance again: 'les Escossais sont coutumiers de faire souvent entreprises les ungs contre les autres, et de veoir des divisions entre eulx.'[66] Shortly after this date, France's rulers ceased to hope for anything more than a slow building of bridgeheads to the new Scottish ascendancy. From the despatch of baron d'Esneval as permanently accredited ambassador to the Scottish court in October 1585, Mary had become little more than a burdensome irrelevance to French foreign policy.

This did not prevent the trial and execution of Queen Mary being a substantial humiliation to Henri III in both personal and political terms. With the dynastic misfortunes of the Valois, Henri had precious few kin to protect; in 1587, he sacrificed his only royal sister-in-law at the precise moment when he was fighting a war against his only royal brother-in-law. French royal diplomacy had worked to keep the Scottish queen alive and it failed. At the eleventh hour, Pomponne de Bellièvre, Henri's most subtle and experienced negotiator, was instructed to offer Elizabeth a ransom for the queen's life of 20–30,000 *écus*, to be funded from the dowry along with personal pledges from the duke of Guise that he would play no part in any conspiracy against the English queen.[67] The offers were rejected completely. Elizabeth's letter to the French king as Bellièvre packed his bags to return to France on 18 January 1587 is a remarkable document, departing from all the normal courtesies between crowned heads of Europe; vituperative, bossy, oblivious to the wider issues which the trial raised, she accused the French king of protecting a murderess and seeking to destabilize her kingdom and threaten her as an enemy. The letter ended with an offensive reference to France's internal problems: 'Pourtant, étudiez, je vous prie, plutôt à conserver notre amitié que pour la diminuer. Vos États, mon bon frère, ne permettent trop d'ennemis, et ne donnez, au nom de Dieu, la bride à chevaux effarouchés, de peur qu'ils n'ébranlent votre selle.'[68] Had Elizabeth intended consciously to undermine the French king's authority in early 1587, there was little that she could have undertaken more immediately effective than having Mary's head chopped off.

Henri III's benevolent inactivity towards Mary must also be seen in the context of his personal and obsessive fear of Henri, duke of Guise although we should beware of taking too seriously the somewhat hysterical attitudes towards the Guise clan which tended to predominate in English diplomatic circles.[69] Guise made little secret of his interest in the possibilities of a Catholic rebellion in England, supported by an invasion. He had a direct stake in upsetting the status quo in England. His press in Rheims kept alive the case for Mary's claim to the English throne.[70] If Mary Stewart, following the normal course of succession or even after a rebellion in her favour should replace Elizabeth, who could tell what the effects on France's polity might be? Yet Guise's positive support for schemes for invasion was circumscribed. It cannot be traced back before April 1578 and it had evaporated by January 1585, principally because England was always subordinated to France in his priorities. He took up the cause of *l'Impresa* in 1578, following the collapse of the first Catholic League in the wake of the edict of Beaulieu in 1576. He dropped it with the declaration of the Catholic League in France in March 1585; except for projects of small-scale raids presented to him by Charles Arundel, there is no evidence that he took any further interest in the matter.[71]

Since the details of these invasion schemes is already so well known, they need no further rehearsal here. For our purposes, it is important to note merely that the duke of Guise moved into a somewhat closer proximity to English *emigré* Catholic circles. His contacts with English gentry remained inevitably limited — he had neither the resources nor the need to act as patron and employer of gentry from outside France. Among seminary activists, though, the position was different. The favour of the Guises had permitted Allen to establish the English seminary at Rheims. In the same way, the school at Eu was established in the original buildings of the Jesuit college founded by the duke of Guise and to which he gave an annual pension.[72] A proportion of Scottish clerics in seminaries in Paris and elsewhere, as well as in French universities, were prepared to volunteer for missionary endeavour back in Scotland and would naturally have looked to the Guise family for protection.[73] Guise patronage came to dominate the geography of the Catholic migration from the British Isles to France, whether it was through the southern Netherlands to northern France via the duchy of Guise, lying on the border between Amiens and Cambrai, or whether it involved the sea route to the ports of Picardy and through Champagne, both provinces in Guise control, towards Lorraine. Of the places of any significance for *emigré* settlement in France, only Rouen and Paris remained outside Guisard influence in 1587.

But while the duke of Guise was no longer seriously interested in invading England after 1585, either to rescue Mary Stewart or to establish Catholicism there, his pose as the champion of Catholicism in France meant that he needed the prestige which association with these objectives would give him. So it came about that an abstracted image of Mary, carefully contrived for the purpose — imprisoned, wronged, maltreated, innocent, the Catholic martyr at the hands of Elizabeth — was of greater practical use to the duke of Guise than the real Mary, now a pathetic prisoner in Tutbury.

The public perception of Mary had already developed a life of its own in France, just as it had in England. Gradually, the English *emigrés* in France moulded an image which had a creative and significant impact on French consciousness. Both the bibliographical and thematic treatments of this subject have been exhaustively undertaken.[74] The close contacts between John Leslie and Adam Blackwood, her chief 'image-builders' in France, Mary's council and the Guise clan are easily demonstrated.[75] Through them, Mary had more power to influence French politics beyond the grave than she ever had during her lifetime.

The reaction to Mary's execution was almost exclusively a Parisian phenomenon; provincial cities — even those with English *emigré* minorities

— were muted in comparison with the French capital where it was but one part of a battle for the hearts and minds of its citizens between the French king and the Catholic League. The radical *Sixteen*, the clandestine Catholic Paris confraternity, had been established in 1585 to preserve the traditional religion and it appears to have had some success in recruiting individuals from among the respectable members of the city's corporations as well as among its legal, publishing and clerical fraternities.[76] It had been obliged to keep to its secrecy for fear of royal reprisal and suspicion and had lacked an obvious issue on which to rally popular support.[77] Mary's execution provided the *Sixteen* with an occasion to orchestrate overt Catholic solidarity in the capital, separate from, and, by implication, critical of the French king. The duke of Guise was naturally willing to lend his support to an issue which could legitimately be presented as affecting his family, faith and the future of royalty too. Henri III was not openly criticized in the immediate reactions but the execution laid the basis for a more open criticism of royal attitudes towards the heretic queen Elizabeth in the following year.[78] Mary's death became an epiphany in the raising of Catholic consciousness in Paris, one step on the road to the French king's exclusion from his capital fourteen months later.

A great collector of ephemera such as Estoile could hardly fail to be excited by the 'pasquils, placards, tombeaux et discours sur cette mort' which the event inspired.[79] Some were, of course, officially inspired. But the English ambassador had failed even to gain entry at the French court to present the orthodox view of the council in England that the execution had been undertaken 'withoute her Majesties intent and menyinge' and English versions of Mary's death, emphasizing that she had been tried for crimes against the state and casting doubt on whether she had died a good Catholic, were received with little credence in Paris.[80] This was partly because the French ambassador in London, Châteauneuf de l'Aubespine, had smuggled out a sketchy and evidently hearsay report of the execution a day or so after 27 February 1587; it arrived in Paris around 6 March, a week after the initial news of the execution, and was hastily published more or less as it had come.[81] This was then supplemented by a version which appears to have originated at the court of Henri III and which was probably distributed to the resident ambassadors there. This built on the fragmentary details in the Châteauneuf account to present a more solid and well-founded, Catholic description of Mary's execution.[82]

These circulated in Paris during the Lenten penitential season before the English version arrived. The English ambassador had already been threatened with house arrest.[83] He was reduced to reporting impotently the rising popular wrath around him. Four days after the news had arrived he wrote; 'Truly I fynde all men here in a furye and all that love not her Ma[jes]tie in a great hope to buyld some great harme to her ma[jes]tie uponn ytt.' Three days later he reiterated that 'there is fyre enough kyndled ...'[84] Walsingham was so alarmed that he replied: 'And yet you shall do well to forebeare hereafter to wryte any more of the sharpe humour that this accident hath bred there because yt increaseth the more her Ma[jest]ie's offence against her Counssell.'[85] He resorted to censuring Stafford's letters and told the ambassador to counter English critics with the view that no sound French patriot could possible want a Guise on the English throne; and that, if Henri III did, then he was not long for this world.[86] Even after Easter, Stafford was still impressed,[87]

seeing the eagerness of mynds here aggravated, continued, maintained and increased as they be in this matter of the Quene of Scottes; which in truthe I dare not write them to you by a great many parts soe eager as I doe find them, for I cannot saie that I have yet founde anie one, nor spoken withe anie, nor heard of anie, what relligion, state, passion, affection or age soever theie were of, but doe utterly in publicke and in private speake against ytt and in hard terms, especially against the manner of ytt ...

We may approach this extraordinary explosion of sentiment through the sonnets, epitaphs, odes and invectives against Elizabeth, proposed inscriptions for Mary's tomb and a variety of epigrams on the execution, published in Paris at the time.[88] Although mostly anonymous, a number are assignable to known French literary figures — including Malherbe, Gilles Durant, Robert Garnier and perhaps Charles, later Cardinal, Du Perron.[89] Among the exiles, Adam Blackwood seems to have been the principal force and we now know he was responsible for the Latin poem extolling Mary's martyrdom and abusing Elizabeth, which was posted at the cathedral door of Notre-Dame on 13 March, the day of the official requiem mass.[90] Other examples appear to have been written by Blackwood's son-in-law, George Crichton.

The themes behind these compositions are of a piece; as l'Estoile succinctly put it, they 'criaient et disaient tout haut qu'elle était morte martyre pour la foi catholique, apostolique et romaine, et que la reine anglaise ne l'avait fait mourir pour autre choses que pour la religion ...'.[91] Elizabeth was Jezebel, guilty of all the female vices. As the verses dedicated to the English Jezebel began:[92]

Bâtarde incestueuse et paillarde publique,
Perfide, déloyale et fille de ta soeur,

Que ton père et le sien découvrant son erreur,
Père et mari cruel, fit mourir impudique...

She was a she-wolf in a country which prided itself on having none.[93] Mary was a martyr, already a saint protecting France from its enemies.[94] Her death was a conscious sacrificial act on behalf of all English Catholics; it was also a warning to all sovereigns of the dangers to their thrones. In one version of her last words, she calls on the crowned heads of Europe to witness the wrongs done to her by heretics and, with remarkable powers of mental arithmetic on the foot of the scaffold, demonstrates that the name 'Calvin' is the equivalent to the mystic number of the Beast.[95] She demanded that the French king avenge her death and most of the poems urge Henri III to take punitive action against the English murderess.[96]

'Time will lay these blazes' remarked the English agent Waad to Burghley. This was the hope of the English and also of the French king himself. Henri III hoped, at least in the short term, to deflect the impact of the execution from damaging his own reputation. He personally involved himself in the requiem preparations and prevailed upon the 'politique' prelate, Renaud de Beaune, archbishop of Bourges, to preach the sermon there.[97] Other measures, including the seizure of English ships in French ports undertaken just before the news of the execution broke, helped him to pose as the champion of the queen's honour and rights.[98] But the indefinite suspension of French diplomacy towards England was inconceivable in the overall circumstances of 1587 and, in late May, normal diplomatic channels were reopened, both in London and in Paris.[99]

One consequence of the restoration of diplomatic relations was the possibility of demanding that French royal authorities stem the tide of Jezebel literature. A complaint was almost immediately lodged against one pamphlet, apparently entitled the 'Advertissement des advertissements' and copies of it were seized and destroyed, the printer and bookseller imprisoned. Once more, popular emotions were aroused against this easy compliance with the wishes of the English Jezebel by 'politiques'. Engravings, taken perhaps from the Rome edition of Robert Persons's *De Persecutione Anglicanae* of 1582 or the *Briefve Description* of Richard Verstegen, prepared in Paris around 1583, of the sufferings of the English Catholics, were placed on a board in the cemetery of St Séverin church by order of Jean Prévost, its curé, a member of the *Sixteen*.[100] Clerics were on hand with pointers to explain the posters and they were seen, according to Stafford, by up to 5,000 people, before the display was removed, on royal orders, on 9 July.[101] The fact that Mary's chancellor, du Ruisseau, was a churchwarden at St Séverin leads one to suspect the direct involvement of her Parisian council in keeping her memory green among the Parisian notability.[102]

Mary's personal servants returned from England to Paris in the late autumn of 1587. With them, they brought more information about the conditions of her imprisonment and more reliable testimony about her final moments.[103] Such first-hand and often moving detail could be woven afresh into the story of Mary's death and this is why the enduring statements of the Marian image in France appear after October 1587. Blackwood's *Martyre de la Royne d'Escosse* drew on these experiences to formulate an impassioned account of Mary's indignities at the hands of the English from the moment she left France to her burial at Peterborough; it appeared anonymously towards the end of 1587 and was subsequently reprinted five times before the end of 1589.[104] The French king retaliated weakly by organizing the publication of one of Bellièvre's harangues to Elizabeth I and also the sermon of Renaud de Beaune (with the complimentary references to the Guise family excised).[105] But, as he gradually lost control of political events in his capital on the eve of the Day of Barricades, so Marian literature played a significant contributory part in his loss of moral command there. Mary thus became an image for revolution in France; it was an altogether surprising apotheosis for an absentee dowager queen.

Notes

[1] Labanoff, vii, 485.

[2] H. L. Lightman, 'Sons and Mothers: Queens and Minor Kings in French constitutional Law' (Bryn Mawr College Ph. D., 1981) explores the legal and constitutional position of French queens and queen mothers.

[3] AN, X^{1a} 8624, fos 189–190 (*Lettres patentes d'évocation* to Mary, following the general terms of a royal ordinance of Apr. 1561, confirmed 23 June 1561); also 8625, fo. 35v (Confirmation of the privileges of royal officers conferred on her domestic officers residing in France, 27 Nov. 1563); also 8627, fo. 431 (Confirmation of privileges of *committimus* to her domestic servants, 29 May 1568).

[4] *CSP Scot.*, ii, 967–8.

[5] Fraser, *Mary*, 90–3. PRO, SP 52/8, fo. 32 (Randolph to Cecil, St Andrews, 18 Mar. 1563) for her reactions to the news of the assassination of François, duke of Guise — 'maynie of the fayre faces are greatlie impayred. The Queene herself mervilous sadde, her ladies sheddinge of teares lyke showers of rayne'. Ibid., fo. 55 (1 Apr. 1563) for the reception of a copy of the duke's will that was 'well washed with many a salte tear'.

[6] Labanoff, iv, 270 (6 May 1575) asking Louis, cardinal de Guise 'd'avoir soing et tenir la mayn à mes affaires'.

[7] AN, Y3129 (*Registres des insinuations*) fo. 323 (12 Oct. 1581); grant of a pension to George Douglas, referring also to a *rente* constituted in favour of William Douglas by the cardinal of Lorraine on Mary's behalf on 21 Feb. 1574.

[8] Deduced from comments in Labanoff, iv, 164, 203, 234, 254, etc. The 'poco liberalita' of the cardinal of Lorraine and his desire 'spraregniare la douariere delle Regina in Francia' in Apr. 1566 is noted in *Papal Negs.*, 493. I am grateful to the editor for this reference.

[9] Labanoff, iv, 444 (Sheffield, 29 Apr. 1574).

[10] After Mary's death, according to Michel, *Ecossais,* ii, 82, her French seals were surrendered to the duke of Guise who then (reluctantly) finally handed them over to the French chancellor. He cites Estoile's *Mémoires-Journaulx* but I have been unable to locate the reference.

[11] Fraser, *Mary,* 92.

[12] For the court of France under Henri III see J. Boucher, *Sociétés et mentalités autour de Henri III* (1981).

[13] Keith, *History,* i, 353–9. F. Mignet, *History of Mary, Queen of Scots* (1851), 27, mistook this for 600,000 *livres* and the error is repeated in, among others, Fraser *Mary,* 87.

[14] Teulet, *Relations,* ii, 153.

[15] BN, MS Fr. 3335, fo. 95 (Estat sommaire et abrégé de l'évallua(ti)on de soixante mil livres tournois de rente pour le douaire ...). See Table 1, above.

[16] BN, MS Dupuy 722, fol. 143 (Remonstrance sur le supplement de l'assigna-(ti)on du douaire ..., 25 July 1561).

[17] BN, MS Fr. 3335, fol. 80 (9 Aug. 1561). Further remonstrances of the parlement fo. 81v (5 Sept. 1561) with king's acceptance of them (12 Sept. 1561) fo. 82.

[18] ibid., fo. 96

[19] Labanoff, iv, 239; the item also figured among the outstanding debts in France owed to Mary; Teulet, *Relations,* iv, 205–6.

[20] Labanoff, iv, 216. Her last will disposed of a putative 4,900 *écus* to Gilbert Curle, Claude Nau and the sieur de Beauregard on the hope that the case would be finally decided in her favour (ibid., vii, 485).

[21] ibid., i, 148 (10 Aug. 1562).

[22] References to the assignation on Poitiers receipts occur later in ibid., v, 239. See also ibid., ii, 1, 68. The 25 per cent fall in value of the Scots £ against the French *livre* 1561–7 compensated (Gilbert, 'Usual money of Scotland', 145–6); see also Lynch, ch. 1 above.

[23] Labanoff, ii, 129 (26 June 1568).

[24] ibid., iii, 177 (8 Feb. 1570/1) refers to the urgent need for 'reparations of ruynes and other disorders happened during the last troubles' in Poitou.

[25] Teulet, *Relations,* ii, 268–81; 252 salaried or pensioned servants with a budget of 33,320 *livres.*

[26] L. Paris, *Négociations, lettres et pièces diverses relatives au règne de François II*

(1841), 744−50; 286 salaried or pensioned servants with a budget of 58,551 *livres*.

[27] R. Raymond, 'Notes, extraites de comptes de Jeanne d'Albret et de ses enfants, 1552−1608', *Revue d'Aquitaine et du Languedoc*, xi (1867), 119−25 (account for the year 1565).

[28] Teulet, *Relations*, ii, 269.

[29] He was appointed chancellor of the university of Poitiers, abbot of the Benedictine abbey of l'Absie in Poitou (formerly held by David Paniter, bishop of Ross, McRoberts, *Scottish Reformation*, 314) and also treasurer of St Hilaire-le-Grand in Poitiers. Later he was to be made prior of the priory of St Pierre at Pontoise, also within Mary's gift (D. Sammarthanus, *Gallia Christiana* (1873), ii, cols 1383−4). Labanoff, iii, 203 (Mary to James Beaton, 4 Mar. 1571) mentions the cardinal of Lorraine's offer to him of the casual revenues from her lands in Champagne; ibid., iv, 234 (Mary to Charles, cardinal of Lorraine, 8 Nov. 1574) requests a benefice for James Beaton; fo. 242 grants him 4,000 *livres*, etc.

[30] *CSP Ven.*, viii, 517.

[31] Labanoff, iv, 120.

[32] *Dictionnaire de biographie française*, v, cols 1048−9.

[33] H. Baguenault de la Puchesse (ed.), *Lettres de Catherine de Médicis* (Paris, 1899), x, 524.

[34] H. Michaud, *La grande chancellerie et les écritures royales au XVIᵉ siècle* (1967), 169, 172 for the family.

[35] D. Kelley, *François Hotman* (1973), 335; E. Barnavi, *Le parti de Dieu* (1980), 39; G. de Pimodan, *Le mère des Guises; Antoinette de Bourbon* (1925), 403−4 indicates that he was dealing with the succession of the cardinal of Guise in 1578.

[36] N. M. Sutherland, *The French Secretaries in the Age of Catherine de Medici* (1962), 99−101.

[37] A. Lang, 'The household of Mary, queen of Scots in 1573', *SHR,* ii (1905), 345−55. I am indebted to the editor for this reference.

[38] Labanoff, iv, 203; ibid., 120 (29 Mar. 1574) and 162 (8 May 1574) mention his long years in Mary's service and that she had promised him the post.

[39] ibid., v, 41; iv, 267; *CSPF*, xv, 270.

[40] Labanoff, iv, 216, 249, accuse him of becoming compromised in his service to the king's finances − see also ibid., iv, 254.

[41] ibid., 307; see also *CSP Scot.*, ii, 923−4.

[42] Fraser, *Mary*, 513.

[43] *DNB entry*; E. Murdin, *Burghley Papers* (1759), ii, 435−539 (letters from Jan. 1584 to Mar. 1586). See Holmes, ch. 9 below, for Morgan and Paget.

[44] Labanoff, v. iv, 313 (Mary to James Beaton, 21 May 1576). Mary explains that Dolu's reluctance to dispense funds to the exiles as 'tant pour le peu de fonds qu'il dit avoir entre les mains, que pour la conséquence laquelle il m'a remonstré que ceste ouverture pourroit tenir, et qu'elle ne serviroit, estant sceue, que d'appeller d'Escosse tous ceulx qui m'ont faict service, et inviter les aultres à m'importuner de pareilles requestes, au lieu que, si je voullois retenir

une bonne somme de deniers pour les occasions qui me peuvent souvenir, comme celle de la mort de cette Royne, je ne manquerois d'hommes qui servoient plus prestz de me faire service que ceulx qui, m'estant tousjours sur les bras, diminueroient mes moyens, et me mecteroient en nécessité pour subvenir à la leur'.

[45] Fraser, *Mary*, 514.

[46] Teulet, *Relations*, iii, 92−3.

[47] M. P. Holt, *The Duke of Anjou and the Politique Struggle during the Wars of Religion* (1986), 67.

[48] Labanoff, iv, 337 (Mary to Louis de Gonzague, duke of Nevers, 30 July 1576). She described the duchy as 'la plus belle pièce de mondit douaire' in 1581 (ibid., v, 239).

[49] Teulet, *Relations*, iii, 10 (*ordonnance*, Henri III, 31 Oct. 1576); BN, MS Dupuy 832, fo. 4 (Commission de Henri III à Guillaume Bailly, président de la chambre des comptes de Paris ... to evaluate the revenues of Vermandois, 27 Jan. 1577). In 1587, Mary's council claimed the loss of a year's revenue during this period (Teulet, *Relations*, iv, 205).

[50] BN, MS Dupuy 148, fo, 381; initial registered opposition to the apanage grant in favour of Anjou by the *parlement* of Paris, 23 May, 1576. Ibid., fo. 310; legal acts of opposition registered in the joint names of Elisabeth de France and Marie Stuart (n.d., 1576).

[51] Teulet, *Relations*, iii, 62.

[52] *CSP Scot.*, ii, 932; Labanoff, v, 275 (Mary to Henri III, 3 Dec. 1581), asking for the king's intervention in the legal case on her behalf. The Vitry estates were challenged by a grant of half their value to the sieur de St Belin on the recommendation of Catherine de Médicis; see Mary's complaints in Labanoff, vi, 267.

[53] *CSP Scot.*, ii, 935 (?1582); Teulet, *Relations*, iii, 271 (Articles of Scottish ambassador sent to Henri III, 26 Apr. 1584).

[54] Fraser, *Mary*, 512−13.

[55] Teulet, *Relations*, iv, 205−6.

[56] Labanoff, vii, 485.

[57] *CSP Ven.*, viii, 525.

[58] P. A. Chéruel, *Marie Stuart et Catherine de Médicis* (1858), 58. For the activities of the privateers, see B. Dietz, 'Privateering in North-West European Waters' (London Univ. Ph.D., 1959).

[59] e.g. Teulet, *Relations*, iii, 199 (*c* Apr. 1583) − Beaton acting as the agent for access to the French court of Maxwell and Lennox.

[60] Chéruel, *Marie Stuart*, 58−61. See Holmes, ch. 9 below, for the Northern Rising and the Ridolfi plot.

[61] ibid., 62; cf. Labanoff, iii, 182, 204, 207.

[62] 'Mémoires remis au roi par La Châtre ...' (Apr. 1575) reprinted in Chéruel, *Marie Stuart*, 178−88 with accompanying correspondence.

[63] Teulet, *Relations*, iii, 50 (Henri III to Castelnau de Mauvissière, 8 July 1579); ibid, iii, 62−3 (12 Jan. 1580) − an additional revealing sentence in the letter is reprinted in M. François (ed.), *Lettres d'Henri III* (Paris, 1984), iv, 325−6 to the

effect that the ambassador was to contact Mary about the affairs of her duchy secretly because, otherwise, Elizabeth I 'en feroit sinistre interpretation ainsi qu'elle a de coustume quand elle me veoit avoir souvenance d'elle et de ses affaires'. See also the similar instructions given to Châteauneuf de l'Aubespine, 16 Feb. 1586 (Teulet, *Relations*, iv, 88−9).

[64] ibid., iii, 278.

[65] ibid., iii, 101.

[66] ibid., iii, 135.

[67] R. Kierstead, *Pomponne de Bellièvre* (1968), 49−50; Chéruel, *Marie Stuart*, chs xiii−xiv; Teulet, *Relations*, iv, 115−53. The French king's final offer is contained in BN, MS Fr. 5933, fo. 417.

[68] Chéruel, *Marie Stuart*, 167−8.

[69] A valuable corrective is outlined in M. R. Thorp, 'Catholic conspiracy in early Elizabethan foreign policy', *Sixteenth Century J.*, xv (1984), 431−48.

[70] See the works of John Leslie, appearing from the presses at Rheims, identified in J. D. Scott, *A Bibliography of Works relating to Mary Queen of Scots* (1901), nos. 116, 123, 125, etc. Also *Bibliotheca Bibliographica Aureliana* (1973), fasc. 121 (Rheims) nos. 48, 95, 96, etc.

[71] A. Lynn Martin, *Henry III and the Jesuit Politicians* (1973), 65 and refs. The last positive sign of Guise's interest in any form of invasion appears in Jan. 1585, *CSP Scot.*, ii, 960.

[72] J. Bossy, 'Elizabeth Catholicism; the Link with France' (Cambridge Univ. Ph. D., 1960), 55−8; I am grateful to Professor Bossy for permission to read and summarize his conclusions which I have followed closely in this section. Cardinal Guise spoke of the Rheims seminary as his 'clientela' (*Douai Diaries*, 139). For the college at Eu, see F. Fabre, 'The English College at Eu, 1582−92', *Catholic Historical Rev.*, xxxvii (1951), 257−80.

[73] Forbes Leith, *Narratives*, 196, presents a petition from exiled Scottish clerics in France of the early 1580s.

[74] J. E. Phillips, *Images of a Queen* (1964), esp. 88−110.

[75] See, in addition to Phillips, *Images*, D. M. Lockie, 'The political career of the bishop of Ross, 1568−80', *Univ. Birm. Hist. J.*, iv (1953), 98−137; C. H. Hay, 'George Buchanan and Adam Blackwood', *BHR*, viii (1946), 166−71.

[76] Outside Paris, there were muted responses in Rheims and Rouen, most notably on 22 May in Rheims when William Gifford, professor at the seminary, preached a sermon before the League princes including laudatory references to Mary as 'ornament of the family of Lorraine and Phoenix of the North' (the sermon is printed in *Warrender Papers*, ii, 18−28). The history of the Catholic League in Paris has recently been the subject of renewed intensive research, the results of which can be seen in D. Pallier, *Récherches sur l'imprimerie à Paris pendant la Ligue* (1976); E. Barnavi, *Le parti de Dieu* (1980); R. Descimon, *Qui étatient les seize?* (1985).

[77] Pallier, *Récherches*, 58−64.

[78] See the analysis in S. E. A. Haynie, 'The Image of Henri III in contemporary French Pamphlets' (Michigan Univ. Ph. D., 1971), chs iii, iv, which seeks to demonstrate that the degree of personal criticism of the French king was not as great as sometimes supposed before 1588.

[79] P. de l'Estoile, *Journal du règne de Henri III* (ed. L. R. Lefèvre, 1943), 488.

[80] PRO, SP 78/17, fo. 58 (22 Feb. 1587/4 Mar. NS); Phillips, *Images*, 155−61.

[81] ibid., 147; Teulet, *Relations*, iv, 169−78. As Teulet noted (170), his information about the execution seems to have come from a gentleman in his household, Claude de la Châtre, whose manuscript account of the exectuion survives in BN, MS 500, Colbert 35. La Châtre was active on Guise's behalf in Paris in 1587, and his account of that year, published in 1587, lays considerable emphasis on Mary's execution and Guise's desire to avenge Mary's death (*Discours . . . contenant les plus memorables faits . . . en l'année 1587* (Paris, 1588)). The published version had the title *Discours de la mort de . . . Marie Stuard Royne d'Ecosse*; see Scott, *Bibliography*, 160, and Pallier, *Recherches*, 229.

[82] Phillips, *Images*, 150−1. It was printed in W. R. Humphries, 'The execution of Mary, queen of Scots', *Aberdeen Univ. Rev.*, xxx (1943), 20−5. This version was notable for its account of Mary's reception of the eucharist from a disguised priest in her cell and its corruption of the Châteauneuf version of Elizabeth receiving the news of the execution whilst out riding to Elizabeth's taking to horse to ride to London and proclaim the news to the joyful London citizenry.

[83] PRO, SP 78/17, fo. 40 (31 Jan. 1586/7, Waad to Cecil). This was in reprisal for the house arrest of the French ambassador in London.

[84] ibid., fo. 58 (Stafford to Secretaries of State, 22 Feb. 1586 (7)/4 Mar. NS); fo. 62 (ibid., 25 Feb. 1586 (7)/7 Mar. NS).

[85] ibid., fo. 75 (9 Mar. 1587/19 Mar. NS).

[86] *CSPF, 1586−88*, 266, 276; also 246, 255; Bellièvre's reaction to English justifications for English actions, including the covert support offered to Henri of Navarre was the crisp 'vous voulez faire les valets du diable . . .' (PRO, SP 78/17, fo. 92).

[87] ibid., fo. 99 (Stafford to Walsingham, 24 Mar. 1587/3 Apr. NS).

[88] Phillips, *Images*, 162−9. I have not been able to consult the *De Jezabelis Angliae Parricidio Varii Generis Poemata Latina et Gallica*, a collection to be found in the Folger library; but most are to be found in Estoile and the various editions of Blackwood's *Martyre de la Royne d'Écosse* and I have also consulted BN, MS Dupuy 644, fos 459−62 which contains four Latin poems in her memory as well as the long French verse elegy 'Sur le trespas de la royne d'Escosse', by Gilles Durant, an *avocat* at the *parlement* of Paris. BN, MS Fr. 15888, fos 492−500 has a long Latin verse elegy in hexameters entitled *Querela de morte Maria Regina Scotiae adversus Isabellam Angliae Reginam* which does not appear to have been seen by Phillips.

[89] Jacques Davy, Cardinal Du Perron was the author assigned by l'Estoile to the vitriolic 'Vers funèbres' for Mary which contain the lines about Elizabeth I: 'Ce vieil monstre, conçu d'inceste et d'adultère Qui sa dent acharnée au meurtre va souillant, Et le sacré respect des sceptres dépouillant Vomit contre les cieux son fiel et sa colère.' When reprinted in 1608, the English ambassador registered a vigorous protest with the French king (Estoile, *Journal pour le règne de Henri IV*, ed. A. Martin (1958), 359).

[90] Phillips, *Images*, 164.

[91] Estoile, *Journal*, 487.

[92] ibid., 515.

[93] ibid., 516.

[94] Phillips, *Images*, 165−7.

[95] ibid., 168.

[96] ibid., 168−9.

[97] Teulet, *Relations*, iv, 178−80; Phillips, *Images*, 152.

[98] Orders from the king to the lieutenant general in Guienne to seize all English ships and forbid the payment of all English debts were given on 7 Feb. 1587 (*Archives du palais de Monacco,* Series J 58, fo. 144).

[99] *CSPF.*, xxi, pt. i, 267, 301, 309−10.

[100] PRO, SP 78/18, fo. 191 (Stafford to Walsingham, 22 June 1587/2 July NS). For Richard Verstegen's *Briefve description des diverses cruautez que les Catholiques endurent en Angleterre pur la foy* see A. G. Petti, 'Richard Verstegen and Catholic martyrologies', *Recusant History*, v (1959), 72−7. No copies of the *Advertissement* appear to have survived.

[101] It proved a difficult matter − with the court briefly absent from Paris − to remove the posters; the commissioner sent from the *parlement* was so intimidated by the crowd that he was unable to proceed. It required the authority of the master of Ordnance from the Arsenal and the first president of the *parlement* to enforce the law, and even the president was menaced that 'he would have his throat cut for it'.

[102] Bossy, 'Elizabethan Catholicism', 95, citing AN, LL 924, 21, 53.

[103] Phillips, *Images*, ch. vii.

[104] ibid., 174−9.

[105] Pallier, *Recherches*, 245−6; Scott, *Bibliography*, 167; Teulet, *Relations*, iv, 115.

9

Mary Stewart in England

P. J. HOLMES

Mary Stewart arrived at Workington on 16 May 1568 and remained in England until her execution on 8 February 1587. Close to nineteen years were spent in England, nearly half her lifetime. The importance of these years lies, historians tell us, above all in the connection between Mary and the various attempts that were made to dethrone Queen Elizabeth I. Mary's presence in England stirred up dissident elements, especially Roman Catholics, and she was at the heart of a series of rebellions and conspiracies.[1] There are certain defects in this analysis. It is not possible to deny, of course, that Mary was involved in treason and plot, but it may be worth asking how dangerous to Elizabeth these conspiracies were, and how central Mary's role in them was. The main objection to the accepted interpretation of Mary's exile is that to concentrate on the plotting is to misunderstand the considerable value to Elizabeth of Mary's presence in custody in England. It solved quite neatly for Elizabeth two interrelated issues: the Scottish question and the succession problem. It was worth enduring a little danger for that. As an anonymous correspondent of the earl of Leicester put it in 1574: 'Providence seems to have sent the Scottish Queen to England for no other end than to have her power and wicked will restrained from all opportunity of doing any harm to the Church and people of England.' This was a view also expressed (probably early in 1570) before the queen in Council by Sir Ralph Sadler: 'As for the Queen of Scots, she is in your own hands, Your Majesty may so use her as she shall not be able to hurt you; and to that end surely God hath delivered her into your hands, trusting that Your Majesty will not neglect the benefit by God offered unto you in this delivery of such an enemy into your hands.'[2]

Elizabeth did not choose to have Mary Stewart in England: like so much else in Elizabeth's reign it was a matter of luck, or Providence as

Protestants might put it — luck based on Mary's extraordinary stupidity. Mary is often described as 'fleeing' to England. It was not flight; she came of her own accord, as she herself admitted, and against the counsel of her chief advisers. Mary had escaped from Lochleven Castle fourteen days before she arrived in England. The first blunder had been committed when Mary's supporters allowed themselves to be brought to battle before they had all assembled in full strength, and consequently they were defeated at Langside. The Queen did then flee, but when she reached Terregles Castle near the Western Borders she was in safety, for a time at least. She could have remained in Scotland, although no doubt a certain degree of rapid movement would have been required. Her support in the country was strong and the see-saw of politics seemed to be tipping against her half-brother and enemy, the earl of Moray.[3] Alternatively, she could have sailed for France, following the same route she had taken as a child when she first left Scotland. Her brother-in-law, Charles IX of France, would have found it difficult to give her immediate military aid, but he certainly would not have incarcerated, then killed her. Mary's foolish decision to come to England was based on a misunderstanding of Elizabeth's personality and of English policy. She assumed from Elizabeth's letters and the exchange of tokens that the queen of England was her friend. There was something in this, but not much. Elizabeth had used her diplomatic muscle to protect Mary after her imprisonment in Scotland, even perhaps saving her life, and she had maintained since 1562 reasonably cordial relations with the Scottish court. She had also congratulated Mary on her escape from Lochleven. But it took a rather narrow view of Anglo-Scottish relations for Mary to assume that it was safe to come to England. Elizabeth may have written Mary sweet letters, but she had refused to recognize her as heir to the throne of England; she had supported the Chaseabout raiders, then received them in England when they had failed; she had been sharply critical of Mary's conduct after Darnley's death, and had done nothing to prevent her deposition.[4] What makes Mary's decision the more extraordinary is that she came to England not just seeking temporary refuge or as a staging-post before going to the Continent. She came to ask Elizabeth to restore her by armed force to the throne of Scotland.[5] The only reasonable explanation for the queen of Scots' behaviour in May 1568 is that given by Sir James Melville of Halhill, who describes her as acting out of fear.[6] It is possible that she suffered some sort of breakdown, similar to that which overtook her after her second husband's murder. Whatever the case, it was the greatest mistake of her life and one which she would have ample cause to regret, every day for the next nineteen years. All efforts to see Mary as a great stateswoman must founder eventually on consideration of the folly she committed in 1568. Nor is her conduct once she was in England inconsistent with the view that she was politically inept, although after she left Scotland and gave herself into the care of her cousin, she only had pawns to play with, and not many of them.

Mary's policy while in England followed five principal lines.[7] First, she negotiated with Elizabeth for her release from custody. Generally, this was to be part of an agreement with the Scots for her return to the throne of Scotland. These negotiations involved the various Scottish regents and then James VI himself, while Mary also sought to involve the French, using them to bring pressure to bear on the English government to agree to her terms. This line of policy seemed to come close to success on one or two occasions before 1572, but was then broken off for a decade until its revival in 1583. During this decade, the main aim of Mary's policy was merely to secure better conditions for herself in prison, which was for most of the time at Sheffield: more servants, more riding and above all more visits to the baths at Buxton, a thing she considered essential to her health, which was never good. The third concern of Mary while in captivity in England was with her estates in France, her property as queen dowager, a subject for frequent letters and a number of visits by French officials.[8] Fourthly, Mary used her diplomatic talents and her money to influence Scottish events, by corresponding with her supporters north of the Border and by working through French intermediaries on their behalf. Finally, Mary did plot, with English subjects and with foreigners in secret conspiracy, largely to escape, but also to subvert the state of England. What a study of Mary's correspondence and papers reveals is the preponderance of her Scottish interests, and then her close contacts with France; there is not much concern with English affairs, except in so far as they may effect her release. Her famous claim to the English throne is never forgotten, but it is by no means her chief interest. Mary's plotting was, therefore, only a part of her political activity in England. Again, it is difficult not to be harsh in our assessment of Mary's political acumen when this plotting is considered. Mary was probably right, at first anyway, if she thought that she did not risk her life by such involvement. No doubt she had justice on her side too; her imprisonment was clearly illegal. But if the plots were revealed before they were successful, they did absolutely nothing to further what should have been her principal concern, her release from captivity. Indeed, if there was anything which would harden Elizabeth's heart against setting Mary free it was the sort of conspiracy in which she engaged.

If plotting was harmful to Mary's cause, was it dangerous to Elizabeth? Did the presence of Mary in England stir up the Catholics to a dangerous level of political activity? It might be argued, on the contrary, that Mary's captivity in England made life for Catholic insurgents not more, but less easy. Rebels had now to organize not merely an uprising or the assassination of Elizabeth, but had also to release Mary from captivity, and if possible arrange a foreign invasion at the same time. This was a trick which no one even came close to pulling off. As Mary recognized herself, in all enterprises directed against England by foreign powers, 'the greatest difficulty which hath been always objected unto me' was how to effect her release from captivity. In a way, the imprisonment of Mary in England served as a hostage to Catholic good behaviour. Even John Leslie, Mary's ambassador at the English court, saw the danger, saying in 1570, 'that in case any stir were made for her, they should have delivered her dead but not living'.[9] Mary's ambassador in France, James Beaton, archbishop of Glasgow was also aware that Mary's life was at risk as a result of plotting. In a letter of 1580 he said that the Guise would not help Mary with armed force, 'pour l'opinion qu'ils ont que nostre entreprise est mener la Roine à la boucherie'.[10] Mary's gaolers understood the position and Sir Amyas Paulet made it quite clear that in the event of an attempt to release Mary he would kill her.[11] After the Bond of Association had been drawn up, Mary wrote to Elizabeth: 'pour vous dire librement, madame, je ne puis pancer que ceulx qui attempteront à vostre vie, n'en fissent autant à la mienne'.[12] The wily William Maitland of Lethington had seen, as early as 1570, that another, more sinister danger faced Mary if she plotted: 'I fear deadly the craft of her enemies, who will not stick to make offers to convey her away, and then, being privy to it, trap her in a snare, and so to execute against her person their wicked intention.'[13]

What contacts did Mary have with English Catholics? Clearly the conspiracies show some link, but it would be wrong to exaggerate the connection. After perhaps a little initial laxity, access to Mary was extremely difficult and it is not right to think of northern Catholics flocking to pay her court. Mary's collected correspondence, which runs to seven substantial volumes, contains only a handful of letters addressed to English Catholic leaders like William Allen, Robert Persons and Sir Francis Englefield.[14] Persons, the greatest of the Elizabethan Catholics, did, it is true, engage in a political enterprise on Mary's behalf in the early 1580s, but its purpose was largely Scottish and after about 1584 he played only a small part in her affairs.[15] One reason for this was that Mary's chief English agents in France, Charles Paget and Thomas Morgan, were by this time on very bad terms with Persons and Allen.

Persons had reason to doubt the political wisdom of Paget and Morgan and even their real loyalty to Mary in the light of their contacts with Walsingham. Hence for the last years of her life, Mary was linked most closely to English Catholics who were regarded with grave suspicion by the men whose brains, influence and contacts in Rome and Madrid placed them as the natural leaders of Elizabethan Catholicism.[16]

There is no doubting that Mary was true to the Catholic faith in her fashion, but it is possible that there were those in England who might have hoped for a little more outward piety. As long as she was in England she attended Anglican services and sermons, and is even reported to have shown her liking for them.[17] She was treated to a course of lectures given by the bishop of Coventry.[18] By no means all her attendants were Catholic — none, of course, was English. She sent abroad from time to time for *agnus dei* and other devotional objects, and in the 1580s she had occasional secret visits from a French Jesuit disguised as a physician.[19] She made a declaration in 1568 in the hall of Bolton Castle that despite her attendance at heretic services she was a true Catholic, but she later claimed that she had done so for foreign consumption, and it was a statement made when few people were present.[20] She wrote abroad in the same vein, but more frequently complained of her physical treatment in captivity than of the spiritual torture she suffered. In her later years there are passages in her letters which suggest a sense of identification with the English Catholics suffering for their faith, and clearly their plight moved her to pity, though arguably not to recusancy.[21] At the very end of her life, she sought to prepare her reputation as a martyr and this theme is found in some of her last pronouncements.[22] In her public capacity in Scotland, Mary had generally been more politique than papalist, and in the course of negotiations with Elizabeth for her release, she was prepared to allow the continued free exercise of Protestantism there.[23]

How far English Catholics ever really took Mary to their hearts is not clear, especially after the publication of what had happened in Scotland in 1567. It may be that some Catholics were prepared to agree with the assessment of Pius V when the admitted that of Elizabeth and Mary he did not know who was worse.[24] Before Mary arrived in England Catholic books had already been composed in favour of her claim to the succession. Her pretensions were given wider currency during the years of her imprisonment in the writings of her agent, John Leslie, and eventually in pamphlets published by Robert Persons and William Allen.[25] Whatever they may have thought of her religious observances, or of her marital conduct, most Catholics probably accepted that she was heir to the throne of England. Even such a political quietist as Sir Thomas Tresham supported Mary's rights in his private writings, indeed her claim to the throne in 1558.[26] A correspondent of William Cecil described meeting a group of gentlemen somewhere in the provinces in 1575; they protested their loyalty to Elizabeth but said that they were banded together to take action in the event of her death when Mary's cause would require support.[27] Such an attitude was probably quite typical among the Elizabethan Catholics.

But plots there were. What part did Mary play in them? She was accused by Elizabeth of being 'the principal author' of the Rising of the Northern Earls, and on another occasion of being 'the principal hidden cause of these troubles'.[28] It is agreed that the rebellion grew in some way out of a conspiracy among courtiers to arrange the marriage of Mary and the duke of Norfolk. Mary clearly played a part in this affair, although how fully her interests were engaged is unclear. She herself admitted that Norfolk was not a brilliant match, partly because his Protestantism alienated Spanish and French support, and even disturbed the English Catholics like the earl of Northumberland, who at first disapproved of the marriage.[29] At about this time Mary considered other suitors, including Don John of Austria, Philip II and the duke of Anjou and reconsidered the Archduke Charles of Austria and Don Carlos.[30] Nevertheless, Mary did enter into romantic correspondence with Norfolk on and off between 1569 and 1571, and there was further contact through John Leslie. Clearly Mary's presence in England sparked off this court conspiracy, which was emphatically not a Catholic affair, although Mary seems to have made little of the running herself. Meanwhile, real plotting had been going on in the North in 1569 and there is no doubt that Mary was involved. She had come into England the previous year at Workington, which was in the earl of Northumberland's liberty of Cockermouth, and he immediately claimed her as his guest, with at first the influential support of the Council in the North.[31] Some very astute work by Lowther, deputy to the governor of Carlisle prevented this, though not without a public slanging-match with the earl. Northumberland had had contact with Mary before she came to England and so had a certain Christopher Lascalles, who attempted to visit her when she first arrived at Carlisle. He is described as a 'lewd and arrogant papist' and was a friend of the earl.[32] While she was at Carlisle and Castle Bolton, Northumberland lent the queen some furniture, and the countess and other gentlewomen sent her neighbourly presents of 'wild meat' and so forth.[33] Northumberland and Westmorland were both present at the concluding sessions of the enquiry called by Elizabeth in the winter of 1568—9 to look into relations between Mary and her subjects.[34] Mary seems to have won sympathy in the North: Sir Francis Knollys said that if Mary escaped from Bolton the country people would laugh in their sleeves rather than help catch her.[35] In 1569 when Mary was brought down from Bolton to Tutbury in Staffordshire she may have stayed the night at Ripon with Richard Norton, a veteran of the Pilgrimage of Grace and soon to be the geriatric Che Guevara of the Rising.[36] There seems to have been a romantic connection between Christopher, one of 'Old' Norton's many sons, and Mary Seton, the Scottish queen's lady-in-waiting, and this may have been a cover for something more serious.[37] Mary Stewart was certainly aware of the plans hatched in 1569 by the rebels; letters and messages passed between her and Northumberland and also Thomas Markenfeld, another leading figure in the Rising. The chief intermediaries were her attendants, Lord Livingston and his son, John; the latter was reported to be in Yorkshire on the eve of the outbreak of the rebellion.[38] Northumberland also met John Leslie, Mary's agent, on a number of occasions and through him made contact with the Spanish ambassador.[39]

This evidence is insufficient, however, to justify Elizabeth's accusation that Mary was the chief instigator of the Northern Rising. As Anthony Fletcher shows, the rebellion had its political, social, religious and regional causes which had nothing to do with Mary.[40] The work of Wallace MacCaffrey also suggests that both an internal political crisis and international pressures were coming to a head in 1569, and that Mary's presence in England was just one ingredient in this unpleasant recipe.[41] Indeed, there is good evidence that Mary sent word at the last minute to the rebels, urging them not to proceed with their rebellion, as did John Leslie.[42] It is sometimes said that the Northern rebels aimed to release Mary from captivity, although Fletcher rightly casts some doubt on this assertion.[43] Elizabeth feared they might try to do so, ordering that Mary's guard be increased and that she be moved south to Coventry, a walled city inhabited by commendably godly citizens.[44] However, the evidence of the interrogations taken of the rebels after the Rising suggests that they had decided before they rebelled that it was impossible to seize her, even from Tutbury. Northumberland related how in the months before the rebellion Leonard Dacre and Francis Norton conferred with Markenfeld about the possibility of rescuing the queen, and that Dacre and Norton actually went to Shropshire to spy out the land but returned within two days, reporting that it was impossible.[45] There is a story that Northumberland himself went with his wife to stay at Wentworth, near Sheffield, presumably in the summer of 1569, intending to send the countess disguised as a midwife to Tutbury to attend one of Mary's ladies who was pregnant, and thus secure a Toad-of-Toad-Hall escape, but that they gave up the attempt when they learned of the high level of care exercised in the protection of Mary.[46] In October 1569, just before the Rising, Thomas Bishop went to Shropshire on behalf of the conspirators 'to get ... true word how and in what manner she is kept and who guardeth her'. He sent back his son with a pessimistic report, describing how the queen was held 'with great guard and great watch of the country'.[47]

The Rising of the Northern earls was an event not only in English, but also in Scottish history. There is evidence that the earls received Scottish help during the rebellion, and Leonard Dacre, who rose right on the Border, certainly did. He advertised for Scottish troops in Jedburgh and his army was as much Scots as English.[48] It is probably too much to argue from this that Mary's supporters, who were strong in the Marches, acted in concert with the English rebels, although it is a tempting hypothesis. A remarkable recrudescence of support for Mary in Scotland occurred at the same time as the rebellion in England. There were traditional ties of friendship and family across the Border; Dacre in particular was very well connected in Scotland.[49] Many of the English rebels were well received by the Marians after the failure of their rising and stayed in Scotland in some cases for nearly a year, attending an important assembly of the queen's party held at Linlithgow in the summer of 1570.[50] In retaliation, Elizabeth sent north the largest army she ever sent to Scotland, which co-operated with the forces of the regent, attacking Marian strongholds on the Borders and then as far up as Glasgow.[51] It was proudly reported home that they had 'burnt and spoiled as much ground within Scotland as any army of England did in one year these hundred years'.[52] Two Scottish strongholds on the Border, Hume and Fast Castles, were held by the English until 1573.[53] After the rebels left Scotland for the Netherlands, Mary helped maintain them there with her charity; there are references in her correspondence to this until as late as 1586.[54] The one who failed to get away was Northumberland himself, and when it was reported that the regent had returned him to the English, Mary 'wept so till I was all swollen three days after', which was large-scale weeping even by Mary's standards.[55]

Part of the blame for the Ridolfi plot which followed the Northern Rebellion lies with Elizabeth, who failed to let enough noble blood in 1569, although she was particularly harsh with the commons. Norfolk, an ideal match for Mary in terms of political misjudgement, considered his life was charmed and having escaped the block once continued to plot. Ridolfi no doubt deserves our condemnation, but he too had been arrested at the time of the Rising and then released to conspire another day. His interest in the plot which bears his name may have been as much financial as political — he was a banker after all. There were large sums involved and Ridolfi had already handled some payments from the pope and Alva remitted to English conspirators, and had also made advances on his own credit, which he sought to recover by developing another plot and raising further cash on the Continent.[56] Mary was certainly badly served by John Leslie, who had a childish taste for irresponsible plotting on her behalf, but there is no doubt that she was herself deeply involved in this conspiracy to encourage a Spanish invasion. Mary's main interest was as usual with the Scottish situation; the memorandum drawn up on her behalf by Ridolfi speaks of an invasion of Scotland, while Norfolk's corresponding document deals with an attack on England.[57] As Ridolfi's plot was developing, one wing of the Marian party in Scotland, with Mary's approval, was itself urging Alva to send military support to Scotland. Mary's close associate, the Catholic loyalist, Lord Seton, was the chief negotiator sent to the Netherlands to press for this aid to be given.[58] So Ridolfi represented only one line of communication between Mary and her supporters on the one hand and the Spanish on the other. It has been suggested that Ridolfi was a double agent, having been forced into government service after his brief imprisonment in 1569,[59] but there seems to be little evidence to support this and it is difficult to see how, if he were being blackmailed into being an *agent provocateur*, he could be held loyal to this course once he had gone abroad in 1571 with his messages for the Catholic powers. It also shows his genuine enthusiasm for Mary's cause that in 1584 he emerged from his retirement in Florence in order in attempt again to interest Pope Gregory XIII in an enterprise to secure her release.[60] Nevertheless, there were *provocateurs* at work in these years and the government rounded up the plotters quite easily — apart from the banker himself — before the conspiracy came to anything.[61] Cecil had his spies before Walsingham took over as the security expert. In view of Alva's failure to respond very favourably to Ridolfi's plans, it is clear that the plot never enjoyed much chance of success and hence that there was no great danger to Elizabeth. What should have been more worrying to the government than the spectre of international Catholicism massing its forces against the Protestant isle was the way in which the years 1568–71 revealed dangerous fissures in the fabric of the Anglican establishment itself; for example, Lord Cobham's failure to reveal to Cecil the Ridolfi despatches which he intercepted as warden of the Cinq Ports but deliberately concealed to protect Norfolk.[62]

In comparison with the events just described, the later plots were trivial. This is not to say that Mary was not involved in them, but after 1569 no rebellion occurred, Elizabeth's life was not in any real danger,

and the conspiracies of small men in small numbers replaced the major
upheavals of the earlier years. It is tempting to see a gradually escalating
problem of security for Elizabeth, linked to the arrival of missionary
priests in England in the late 1570s and early 1580s, the development of
recusancy, the breakdown of relations with Spain and the slide into
mayhem on the Continent. This is emphatically not the case, although
the Elizabethan government tried to make it look like that. Mary
plotted still, but after 1571 her activities were much restricted – at least
at first – by the harsher terms of imprisonment imposed on her.
Others also plotted on her behalf. In 1577 the English government paid
a great deal of interest in reports they received of a plan to marry Mary
to Don John of Austria. Mary herself seems not to have been consulted
by the advocates of this scheme, and her letters of the time contain
what seem to be genuine expressions of surprise at the idea of the
match.[63] What we know as the Throgmorton plot, which came to light
in 1583 and led to the expulsion of the Spanish ambassador, the execution
of Francis Throgmorton and the flight of a number of Catholic gentlemen, was indeed a serious affair, though nipped successfully in the bud
by Walsingham.[64] Whether the bud would have flowered is not clear.
Throgmorton was no more than a courier whose confessions revealed
some part of a long-woven strand of Mary's policy which concerned
interesting her Guise relatives and the Spaniards in an invasion of
Scotland, in order to rescue the young James VI from Protestant influence
and to lead on to, or to coincide with, an invasion of England. Again,
Mary's overriding concern with Scottish rather than English affairs is
demonstrated here, and the pernicious influence of the house of Guise,
which had been acting intermittently in conspiracy on her behalf against
England for some time.[65] How far Scottish, or French circumstances
would have allowed this plan to come is unclear, but the involvement
of Spain is significant, since it marks an important stage in the development of a Spanish interest in England, which culminated in the Armada.
None the less, it is clear that even if Mary had not been in England,
relations between Elizabeth and Philip II would have worsened and that
the affairs of the Netherlands were the main factor in this deterioration.

    The Parry plot of 1584 is a fitting introduction to the final unravelling
of the story. Parry was a lunatic and a government agent and his
connection with Mary was most tenuous, although he had been in
touch with one of the men on her council in Paris, Thomas Morgan.[66]
If he was a danger to Elizabeth, which he almost certainly was not,
then it was the fault of the royal councillors who had encouraged his
plotting. In the same way, the Babington plot can hardly have been a
serious threat to the Queen since it was a conspiracy devised in part – if

not in whole — by her own secretary, who knew about it from start to finish.[67] Mary certainly did become involved, although she hoped to interest the plotters in Scottish affairs as well as English, and her support for the assassination of Elizabeth is not proven, though it seems likely. Two letters to Babington were enough to bring Mary to the block; letters sent through a 'secret' postal system which Walsingham himself had organized. The tone of other letters by Mary at this time, however, suggests a total dedication to the overthrow of the English state — a feeling which may be comprehensible after such a long imprisonment.[68]

The Elizabethan spy system and the close interest in security shown by Cecil and Walsingham helped prevent the plots of Mary seriously threatening the throne. We tend to exaggerate these days the difficulties of communication in the Tudor age, and in a society where the people who mattered were all largely known to one another and where privacy did not exist it was difficult to keep secrets long. The rack also helped. The government knew about the Northern Rising before it happened, indeed they caused it by arresting Norfolk, although possibly preventing a rising in East Anglia as a result. The other plots were also discovered quite easily; when Alva described Ridolfi as a 'gran parlaquina' he probably meant not so much that he talked rubbish as that he talked indiscriminately.[69] But there was a flaw in English security, and this lay in the freedom allowed to Mary to engage in political activity. The reasons for this laxity are to be found in the curiously uncertain nature of Mary's position in England, at least before 1571. She was not strictly speaking a prisoner, but a guest of the queen and hence she was allowed to send and receive messages and visitors. It is true that access to her was limited and a check kept on her movements, but she was generally permitted over thirty male servants and a handful of women, and she lived in some style. Her entourage ran up debts of £286 sterling in the period of less than two months they spent at Carlisle.[70] Elizabeth was careful to make Mary's position in England as honourable as possible. At the height of the concern over the Northern Rising, Elizabeth wrote to Mary's gaolers rebuking them for lodging her in an inn at Coventry, recommending instead the house which she herself had stayed in, 'The Friars', when she had visited the city.[71] After the discovery of the Ridolfi plot there was a much tougher regime, but it gradually relaxed, and by the early 1580s Mary was corresponding almost as freely as she had been when she first arrived in England. This was due in part to French pressure; it was necessary for a queen of France, and perhaps more important a member of the house of Lorraine to be treated with dignity. Mary was also in her own right a woman of means. She was after all 'duchesse de Touraine, comtesse de Poictou, Chaumont en Bassigny, Vermandoys et Senlis, dame d'Espernay, St Menelhoud et Victry'.[72] Her French dowry had originally been worth 60,000 *livres*, though by the end of her life it was sadly diminished to as little as 20,000.[73] She had been talked into a number of unfavourable exchanges, and had renounced the duchy of Touraine in order to endow the duke of Anjou in 1576 and thus reconcile him to his brother, Henri III. Her estates had suffered during the wars of religion, and both the quality and honesty of her officials deteriorated after 1574.[74] Nevertheless, this money gave her the means to relieve Scottish and English exiles, to send help to her supporters in Scotland, to finance her clandestine correspondence and to run a substantial household in England. The parsimony of Elizabeth allowed this unsatisfactory situation to continue, although Mary was permitted after a while to receive only 2,000 crowns a year in England.[75]

Some criticism can also be made of the earl of Shrewsbury as a gaoler. He was willing, but not very able. He had by his own estimate a household of 240 at Wingfield, apart from Mary's establishment, and it was inevitable that she would be able to corrupt some of them.[76] Elizabeth felt he was the only man sufficiently loyal and distinguished among her nobles to lodge a queen, but there was danger in keeping the queen of Scots permanently in the north, where Catholic sympathy was strongest, and not at a great distance, even at Sheffield, from the Border. Elizabeth, however, resolutely refused to allow her to be taken further south until 1585 and even then would not consider the Tower of London.[77] Shrewsbury and especially his wife, Bess of Hardwicke, were on terms of some familiarity with Mary, and there is a suggestion that the countess engaged in mild plotting with the queen, to warn her when news should arrive of Elizabeth's death and allow her to escape. Mary's trust in Shrewsbury was absolute, but perhaps this was as Elizabeth wanted it.[78] On several occasions a change of prison and of warder was discussed and it came close to being put into effect in 1578 after the scare over Don John.[79] Shrewsbury would have been glad to be relieved of the burden; he described himself as a 'prisoner', being so long kept from court and council.[80] In the end, however, Mary stayed with Shrewsbury, partly because the only alternative which was seriously considered, the earl of Huntingdon, was anathema to her. Complete security was possible, despite Mary's great knowledge of secret writing and other techniques of subterfuge. This was shown when she was transferred to the charge of Sir Amyas Paulet in 1585. Had this change been made as early as 1571 – or even before – Elizabeth would have had little to complain of. The paradox is that in order to draw Mary into a plot, it was necessary deliberately to relax Paulet's regime, indeed to open up lines of communication between Mary and her fellow conspirators which were actually supervised by the authorities themselves.

Elizabeth's treatment of the captive Mary was inextricably intertwined with her policy towards Scotland: from the two strands were woven the right circumstances for the eventual union of the two kingdoms in 1603. It is true that the foundations had been laid earlier, by the marriage of Margaret Tudor and James IV, by the policy of Henri VIII and Protector Somerset, and by the famous Cecilian *démarche* of 1559–60. But developments in Scotland during the personal rule of Mary Stewart had shown that the gradual coming together of two ancient enemies might not continue,[81] and that Scotland might yet play an independent role again. The 'flight' to England of Mary in 1568 prevented this development continuing, and the detention of Mary led to the gradual acceptance by the majority of the Scottish ruling class of the need for an accord with Elizabeth. The twisted path of negotiations after 1568 led, at the expense of Mary's liberty, to the Treaty of Berwick signed in 1586 and so, after the execution of Mary, to the accession of James VI of Scotland to the throne of England.

Mary, queen of Scots had given the English a considerable surprise when she first arrived in England, but gradually a policy emerged which was masterly, if lacking in any morality except that of 'reason of state'. Cecil made all the running in this first phase; afterwards it was Walsingham, who became secretary in 1574. Elizabeth was also deeply involved, especially at times of crisis. Elizabeth's influence in English affairs is often analysed from a sentimental point of view. We learn, for example, that her handling of the affairs of Mary was governed by her heart. If this is the case, Elizabeth must have had a very cold heart. The first thing to accomplish after Mary's arrival was her imprisonment. This may be said to have been achieved with Sir Francis Knollys's arrival in Carlisle on 29 May 1568, not quite a fortnight after Mary's coming to the city. On that day, Knollys reported to Cecil that Mary was already asking to be released, and he expressed the fear that she might escape by tying together towels and letting herself out of a window.[82] On 30 May, in a letter to France, Mary said she was 'arrestée' in England, though honourably treated. Three days later Knollys described himself as a 'gaoler'.[83] Imprisonment was made more effective by 14 July, when despite her tears and protests ('je ne veulx bousger') she was taken to Castle Bolton, the house with the highest walls in England and a further fifty miles from the frontier.[84] There were reports at this time that the English intended to keep Mary a perpetual prisoner, and Mary herself had also heard rumours 'que je seray seurement guardée jamays de retourner en Escosse'.[85] Nothing in the record seems to justify this, but as a possible line of policy it must have been considered. The plan which emerged in the minds of Cecil and Elizabeth was to hold an enquiry into the affairs of Scotland. The Regent Moray was willing to submit to this, but Mary reluctant, asking instead to see Elizabeth in person or be set free.[86] In the end, Mary agreed to the tribunal, having been told that whatever the outcome, she would be restored to Scotland and that no accusations would be made regarding her conduct as queen or wife.[87] This promise (which was not kept) was quite contrary to what was told to Moray's party; they were assured that if Mary could be found guilty of crimes she would not be restored.[88] It is difficult to know what was going on at this stage; Elizabeth and Cecil were playing for time and developing their ideas, assessing the danger of various courses of action and testing the conflicting opinions of privy councillors. The purpose of the tribunal might be seen simply as being to justify Mary's deposition in the eyes of the world and hence her imprisonment. This is probably too simple: the intention in the summer of 1568 was rather to sound the Scots out, to see if their dangerous disputes might be settled. Even the restoration of Mary could not be ruled out, but it would have to be arranged on terms favourable to England. What could not be allowed to happen was foreign intervention in Scotland, which might result from the release or escape of Mary. The enquiry, or diet as Cecil called it, finally met in the autumn and winter of 1568−9, first at York, from where it was adjourned to Westminster and Hampton Court. The commissioners for all three parties (Mary, Elizabeth and Moray) were confused over their roles. The result was a sort of stalemate, though hardly one very favourable to Mary since she stayed in prison and the famous Casket Letters were revealed to the English council. The regent, on the other hand, returned to Scotland with a loan of £5,000 sterling and the opportunity to consolidate his position still further.[89] What the diet must have revealed to the English was that no real compromise was possible. The regent would not have Mary back on terms she would accept, so there was now no choice but to keep her in prison. It was clear to Mary that she had been tricked by 'the chief of my rebels and the ancient and natural enemies of my realm'. She was understandably bitter: 'Thus all the equity of my cause, the connaissance of the which I trusted in the said Queen of England, has been renounced, and miserably sold for the ruin of my realm.'[90]

The beginnings of a clear English policy emerged after the ending of the diet, one which had been forming in the minds of the more audacious or more Protestant of Elizabeth's councillors for some time. Moray's party, the adherents of the infant James VI, became the English party. Money was given them, even military aid. At the centre of this connection between Moray and Elizabeth was the detention of Mary in England. In prison, Mary was unable to influence Scottish affairs much and her party, led by the duke of Châtelherault, who was incompetent and himself held in England for a while, dwindled away. Moray's loyalty to Elizabeth was secured, since his position depended on Mary's captivity. But the wider international scene was threatening, and Elizabeth was unhappy about the perpetual detention of Mary, which reflected badly on English hospitality. So negotiations with the Scottish queen did not cease entirely. In discussions with John Leslie which began in the spring of 1569 a form of agreement was drafted satisfactory to Elizabeth and Mary, but after long delays Moray rejected it.[91] In October he sent an embassy to London to explain the impossibility of restoring Mary, and even of some sort of joint position with her son, which suggested instead that she be kept permanently in England or sent back to prison in Scotland.[92] The idea of returning Mary to her Scottish captors now began to be considered seriously by Cecil and it remained a theme in English policy for the next six years.[93] Such thoughts were doubtless strengthened by the outbreak of the Northern Rising, which inevitably interrupted negotiations with Mary and led to a distinct hardening of Elizabeth's attitudes towards her cousin. Everything was done in the aftermath of the rebellion to help the king's men, leaderless since the murder of Moray in January 1570. A council meeting of 29 April came to the conclusion that it was not now possible to restore Mary and that the earl of Morton (now assuming Moray's place, if not yet the actual office of regent) should be supported to the hilt.[94]

Elizabeth, however, was not yet ready openly to adopt such a radical course. It may be that the Marian revival in Scotland worried her — clearly there was some danger of backing the wrong horse, but the most significant factor was the desire to remain on good terms with France, a policy which the deterioration in relations with Spain encouraged. The French were unhappy about the English forces sent into Scotland after the Northern Rising, a clear breach of the Treaty of Edinburgh of 1560, and national, or at least dynastic, honour was bound up with the treatment of Mary. So the English forces under the earl of Sussex were called back, and another year (May 1570–June 1571) was spent negotiating a tripartite agreement by which Mary was to be restored, to rule jointly with her son, who himself was to be sent to England for his education, while the English held Dumbarton and Hume Castle as pledges.[95] Behind the scenes, however, English support for the king's men continued, as the election of the earl of Lennox as regent in July 1570 indicates; he had lived in England for twenty years, had returned to Scotland with an English passport, and as the father of Darnley was not likely to be very favourable to the queen of Scots.[96]

The treaty for Mary's restoration was bogged down in diplomatic complications, largely the work of the king's party, until the uncovering of the Ridolfi plot in the spring of 1571 allowed Elizabeth herself to add to the delay.[97] At the beginning of October, when the case against the Ridolfi plotters had been thoroughly prepared, and after the murder of the 'English regent', as Lennox was known, had shown that compromise in Scotland was dangerous, the English finally dropped the pretence that the negotiations with Mary were continuing. Elizabeth wrote to the new regent, the earl of Mar, plainly announcing that she no longer intended to treat further with Mary to the prejudice of the king's estate.[98] This letter marked a real turning-point in relations between Elizabeth and Mary, and it ended three and a half years of negotiation and equivocation. Similar letters were sent to the Marians, and the siege of Edinburgh Castle, their last stronghold, began.[99] Throughout these protracted diplomatic discussions, the French had been at the centre of Elizabeth's thoughts, and they continued even now to exert a restraining influence. The French hoped still to do something to help the Marians in Scotland and save them from complete defeat. But for Catherine de Médicis's 'very dear and beloved daughter-in-law', Mary, the best the French crown could hope for now was that Elizabeth would spare her life.[100] By 1572 Catherine was prepared to make a treaty with Elizabeth which omitted all reference to Mary, thus abandoning her to the English. This represented a major triumph for Elizabeth's diplomacy, but was largely the fruit of Mary's own plotting with Ridolfi. French attitudes were clearly expressed in the interview between Catherine and Walsingham held on 31 March, 1572:

CATHERINE: [Mary] is allied to the king and to me, and brought up here, and we for our part could do no less but entreat for her what we could obtain at the Queen my sister's hands. She seeketh an other way to ruinate herself, to deserve no pity nor favour, and sorry we must be for her. And if she be so dangerous (as it appeareth) we can not nor dare not require liberty for her, which is so perilous to the Queen my sister's state. Yet if it shall please her for our sake to give her life, and for the rest to provide for her own safety, as reason is, she shall do a deed of pity, and in this matter we will trouble the Queen your mistress no further ...

WALSINGHAM: Yea, but while we two shall be at strife, if you would set up again the Scottish Queen, whom by reason the Queen our mistress cannot abide, if in the mean while a third shall come in, and set foot in Scotland, would it not trouble you and us also?

CATHERINE: Yes, and we would be as loth to see that as you.

WALSINGHAM: Well, madam, then take heed of the puthawk, for he is ready.

CATHERINE: I know who you mean, and he is ready in deed, and loves to be meddling in every place. But I doubt not but the Queen your mistress and we shall agree.[101]

The Ridolfi plot was as offensive to Catherine de Médicis as it was to Elizabeth, since Mary's attempt to involve Spain (the 'puthawk') in the affairs of Scotland, threatened to break the auld alliance as well as to break faith with England.

Abandoned by her French family and under fierce attack from the English parliament, Mary Stewart nearly lost her life in 1572, as she herself realized.[102] Elizabeth sent a high-powered team of councillors to charge her with crimes against the state, and a trial seemed certain.[103] What saved her was Elizabeth's caution and procrastination rather than her squeamishness. As the days ticked away, it became less and less likely that Mary would be tried. What may have clinched matters was the St Bartholomew's Day Massacre in France. At first this seemed to strengthen the hand of the Catholics and the house of Guise and hence made the public execution of Mary in England dangerous. It is significant that one of the first actions taken by the English government after news of the Massacre reached England was to send Henry Killigrew on an embassy to Scotland; his secret instructions were to negotiate the return of Mary, to trial there and possible execution. This 'great matter', as it was coyly referred to in the despatches, now took the place of plans for Mary's death in England.[104] The Scots, however, were not keen and the death of another regent in October interrupted discussions. Burghley hoped that Elizabeth would now find the strength to execute Mary, but she preferred to wait and continue to negotiate in Scotland.[105] If no conclusion to the question of what to do with Mary was reached, the civil war in Scotland was at least brought to an end. The outbreak of fighting in France early in 1573 had allowed Elizabeth finally to give military support to the king's party in its struggle to capture Edinburgh Castle. Something in the region of a thousand men and a siege battery were sent north, and after a few days bombardment in which 3,000 great shot were bestowed on the castle walls, it fell on 29 May 1573.[106] The earl of Morton, at last regent in name, appointed as he himself admitted at Queen Elizabeth's behest, was now master of the entire realm. There was never again to be a significant Marian party in Scotland.

For the rest of the decade, Mary's captivity was not relieved by any talk of her release or restoration. The English continued to consider the possibility of returning her to captivity in Scotland. This is a topic referred to in ambassador Killigrew's correspondence until the summer of 1574, but by then it was quite plain that the Scots did not want her.[107] The following year the queen accepted that it might prove dangerous to return Mary, although in a paper composed by Burghley after the Don John 'plot' had been revealed in 1577, this option was still considered. Burghley, however, still wanted her executed in England.[108]

The English settlement of Scotland made in the years 1568–73 was to last for the rest of the century, but it was not to be an easy path, nor one to which contemporaries could see a clear end. In the late 1570s Scottish affairs again became confused and potentially dangerous for the English. Two factors were mainly responsible for the growth of such fears and both seemed to afford some comfort to Mary.[109] First, the young king was growing to maturity, which threatened the position of Morton and hence the stability he had created. It was feared by the English and hoped by Mary that James VI might feel some sympathy for the plight of his mother and might seek in the long term to pursue a more independent Scottish policy than his regents had. The second problem for the English was represented by the arrival in Scotland in 1579 of Esmé Stewart, sieur d'Aubigné, later duke of Lennox, who quickly wormed his way into the confidence of the king. The English suspected him of being a favourer of Mary, although in fact she was rather suspicious of him too;[110] at any rate, he was French and pro-Catholic, a reminder of Scottish tendencies which the English thought they had overcome.

The result of this growing independence in the young James VI was that the English reopened discussion with Mary for the last time. After some preliminary talks in 1581, negotiations began in February 1583 and continued until October 1584.[111] Their purpose was to devise a treaty for her release from captivity, and then, at least in Mary's eyes, to arrange an 'association' of herself with James VI in the joint government of Scotland. The English seem to have entered into these talks with some genuine hopes of their success, and they were continued despite the discovery of the Throgmorton plot late in 1583, which would have given them a very good excuse for dropping the matter. What led to the failure of the negotiations on this occasion was the growing realization in England that James VI was not sincere in his concern for his mother, or at least not so concerned as to be willing to give up any real power in order to secure her release. Again, the fact that Mary was in prison in England gave English diplomats a considerable advantage when dealing with James, since in effect they had the key to his continued hold over Scotland, and also to his succession to the throne of England. As James showed a growing appreciation of the realities of the situation, an agreement with him alone was devised, and by the Treaty of Berwick of 1586 the stability in Anglo–Scottish affairs which had first been achieved in 1573 at the end of the civil war was recovered. The consequence for Mary was that there was clearly nothing to be gained by the English in releasing her, indeed nothing much to be gained by keeping her alive.

The Treaty of Berwick marked the end of any hopes that Mary might still have entertained of her restoration to Scotland. Scotland was now linked to England by ties which even the execution of Mary in 1587 could not weaken. There were certainly twists and turns between 1587 and 1603, but it is reasonable to say that the treaty and then the death of Mary assured the accession on Elizabeth's death of James to the throne of England. In the 1560s the question of the succession had been one of the great political problems which England faced: parliamentary opposition, conciliar factions and a battle of books had resulted from the uncertainty surrounding the future of the Tudor dynasty. Mortimer Levine, the historian of this great issue, argues that this problem, disappeared in 1568 with the death of Catherine Grey.[112] Certainly the coincidence of date seems to be clear: after 1568, the great debates in the House of Commons cease and controversy abates. But Levine's thesis ignores the fact that Catherine Grey had children, let alone other relatives. If the members of the Protestant establishment could accept Catherine as the heir to the throne, which in itself involved a considerable disregard for the rules of primogeniture, they could surely suspend disbelief further and accept her children as legitimate. Perhaps the really significant event of 1568 which led to an end of debate on the succession was the arrival in England of Mary Stewart, Catherine Grey's rival as heir. As long as she remained in safe custody, the future seemed less unclear to English councillors. If Elizabeth should die, at least Mary's imprisonment would allow a breathing space in which to decide on a successor. The succession debate of the early years of Elizabeth's reign had had little to do with the promotion of the claims of Catherine Grey, it had almost entirely been concerned with the exclusion of Mary Stewart. What better way to ensure that she might be cut out of the succession than to keep her in prison in England? There was after 1568 little need for further debate.

The hallmark of Elizabeth's policy towards Mary had been fabianism.

She knew that to return Mary or release her was to play a card of great value, and Elizabeth never found anything that was worth bidding for with this trump. Hence, the imprisonment was prolonged and its benefits gradually reaped. The same had been true of Mary's life: it had been preserved by the good sense of a queen who knew that this too was an ace which could not be used twice. Elizabeth's attitude to Mary can be interpreted in a romantic fashion, but there was more *realpolitik* than sentiment in it. In 1572 Elizabeth was willing to give Mary up perhaps to be killed in Scotland, but not to kill her herself. It would upset France, and certainly in the long run might harm relations with Scotland. Mary was worth far more alive than dead. In any case, the patriotic feeling she aroused among the English strengthened Elizabeth's hand at home, particularly perhaps in parliament. Mary helped to bind queen, Commons and Lords together in a common sense of siege.[113]

By 1587 the case was very much altered. The Scots were now firmly tied to England and the adult James VI had everything to gain from the death of his mother. The French were about to be consumed again in civil strife, and in any case over the years they had made it quite clear that Mary was not a major concern of theirs. Above all, the Spanish were now preparing for open war on England. Already by 1586 as Nau, Mary's secretary noted, the most active English Catholic politicians had turned away from Mary Stewart and were prepared to recognize a Spanish princess as the potential Catholic ruler of England.[114] Mary may have acted in the past as a shield against Spanish attack, but no longer. None the less, Elizabeth was understandably reluctant to commit herself finally to the public execution of Mary. Elizabeth at first tried to persuade Sir Amyas Paulet to murder the queen of Scots, but when he refused, the farce was played that Davison had deceitfully procured the death warrant against Elizabeth's wishes.[115] It is possible that Elizabeth intended to wait until 9 or 10 February, the anniversary of Darnley's death, but that enthusiastic officials wanted to complete the job early to avoid any last-minute changes of the royal mind. Elizabeth was right to be cautious; she had to receive very high-level representations from the French, even if only to reject them, Walsingham throwing up a smoke-screen by discovering another entirely fabricated plot involving the French embassy. Scottish reaction was surprisingly hostile, and even so experienced a statesman as Hunsdon feared war, although he was able to assure the Scots that Elizabeth had not been responsible for Mary's death.[116] James VI had the sense to see that much depended now on his conduct towards England; if he sympathized with the mother he had never known, he may also have reflected on his father's memory too. Great nations are not united without a little blood and iron, and in the end the final assurance of the Union of England and Scotland which developed from the imprisonment of an unfortunate woman, lay in her death on a sordid stage in Fotheringhay Castle.

Notes

[1] A. G. R. Smith, *The Emergence of a Nation State* (1984), 151; R. Ashton, *Reformation and Revolution* (1984), 68–70, 112ff., 144–7; C. Russell, *The Crisis of Parliaments* (1971), 159–61, 240–2; G. R. Elton, *England under the Tudors* (1969), 292–309, 367–70.

[2] *CSP Scot.*, v, 71; A. Clifford (ed.), *State Papers of Sir Ralph Sadler* (1809), ii, 566.

[3] *CSP Scot.*, ii, 466–8; Labanoff, vi, 472; Donaldson, *Mary*, ch. 5; *Donaldson, Queen's Men*, ch. 6.

[4] R. B. Wernham, *Before the Armada* (1966), 270–3.

[5] *CSP Scot.*, ii, 416–17.

[6] Melville, *Memoirs*, 202.

[7] What follows is based on Labanoff, ii–vii, and on *CSP Scot.*, ii–vi.

[8] See Greengrass, ch. 8 above, for the jointure.

[9] Labanoff, vi, 409; *CSP Scot.*, iii, 160; cf. ibid., ii, 623–5.

[10] Labanoff, vii, 153.

[11] ibid., vi, 176

[12] ibid., vi, 139

[13] *CSP Scot.*, iii, 312.

[14] Labanoff, vi, 323–4, 404–12 (to Englefield); vi, 333–7 (to Persons); iv, 374–7 (to Allen); A. Teulet, *Supplément au recueil du Prince Labanoff* (1859), 324–30 (to Allen). Cf. T. F. Knox (ed.), *The Letters and memorials of William Cardinal Allen* (1882), 29–30, 229–30, 243–4, 264–5, 247–8; L. Hicks (ed.), *Letters and Memorials of Fr Robert Persons* (Catholic Record Society, 1942), 246–52.

[15] Hicks, *Letters of Persons*, Introduction, xlv–lxix.

[16] L. Hicks, *An Elizabethan Problem* (1964), esp. 132–5.

[17] *CSP Scot.*, ii, 466; Labanoff, ii, 240; iv, 95–6; vii, 16–18; *HMC Salisbury*, i, 400.

[18] *CSP Scot.*, iii, 63; Labanoff, iv, 97.

[19] J. H. Pollen, 'Mary Stuart's Jesuit chaplain', *The Month*, cxvii (1911), 11–24, 136–49.

[20] *CSP Scot.*, ii, 510, 515; Labanoff, ii, 182–7, 237–41; Teulet, *Supplément*, 294–7.

[21] Labanoff, iv, 295; vi, 151–8, 159–64, 296. This is a difficult matter to pronounce on in a paragraph and I am conscious of perhaps being unjust here to Mary; for suggestions of a recusant outlook, see Labanoff, iv, 95–9, but see also iv, 278–81 for her requests for dispensation.

[22] Labanoff, vi, 438–40, 447–56.

[23] ibid., ii, 208; cf. ibid., v, 216; *CSP Scot.*, ii, 465; iii, 164.

[24] A. O. Meyer, *England and the Catholic Church under Queen Elizabeth*, trans. J. R. McKee (1916), 74.

[25] P. J. Holmes, *Resistance and Compromise: The Political Thought of the Elizabethan Catholics* (1982), 23–6, 133–4, 137.

[26] ibid., 178–9; BL, Add. MS 39829, fos 119–24.

[27] *HMC Salisbury*, ii, 74.

[28] ibid., i, 445, cf. 560; *CSP Scot.*, iii, 236–7.

[29] Labanoff, iii, 180–7; C. Sharp, *Memorials of the Rebellion of the Earls of Northumberland and Westmorland* (1975), 189–92.

[30] Labanoff, ii, 280, iii, 180–7; *CSP Scot.*, ii, 623–4, 651–2. See Adams, ch. 6 above, for the earlier marriage negotiations.

[31] *CSP Scot.*, ii, 410–11, 412–13.

[32] ibid., ii, 458; Sharp, *Memorials,* 193–4.

[33] *CSP Scot.*, iii, 237; Sharp, *Memorials,* 191.

[34] Donaldson, *First Trial,* 191.

[35] *CSP Scot.*, ii, 541.

[36] ibid., ii, 605.

[37] Fraser, *Mary,* 510.

[38] Sharp, *Memorials,* 189ff.; *CSP Scot.*, ii, 672, 685; *HMC Salisbury*, i, 468–71, 561; ii, 17.

[39] Sharp, *Memorials,* 189ff.; *HMC Salisbury*, ii, 16–17.

[40] A. Fletcher, *Tudor Rebellions* (1968), 91–106.

[41] W. T. MacCaffrey, *The Shaping of the Elizabethan Regime* (1968), part v.

[42] *HMC Salisbury*, i, 468; ii, 17, 25–6.

[43] Fletcher, *Tudor Rebellions,* 96.

[44] *CSP Scot.*, ii, 675, 676, 677–8; iii, 8, 9.

[45] Sharpe, *Memorials,* 192ff.; *HMC Salisbury*, ii, 25–6.

[46] *CSP Scot.*, iii, 646.

[47] *HMC Salisbury*, i, 470.

[48] ibid., i, 459–60; Sharp, *Memorials,* 68–9, 125–6, 219, 220; *CSP Scot.*, iii, 69, 78, 85–6, 108.

[49] ibid., iv, 637; *HMC Salisbury,* i, 419–20.

[50] ibid., i, 459; *CSP Scot.*, iii, 29, 30, 31–2, 47–53, 87–8, 131–3, 178–80, 216, 219, 262, 274, 309, 310–11, 323, 330, 340.

[51] ibid., iii, 95–6, 97, 109–10, 115–16, 169, 171–3, 178, 183–5, 196–9, 205–6, 326–8.

[52] ibid., iii, 217.

[53] ibid., iv, 623, 624–6.

[54] Labanoff, vi, 359, 367.

[55] ibid., iii, 48.

[56] *CSP Scot.*, iii, 607, 637–9, 647–8, 570–1; iv, 196, 274–5; *HMC Salisbury*, i, 562–3, 570.

[57] Labanoff, iii, 221–50.

[58] *CSP Scot.*, iii, 303–4, 305–6, 307, 323, 324–5, 330, 334, 336, 344, 348, 392–3, 456–8, 570, 592–3; iv, 68, 110–11, 139, 165, 197.

[59] F. Edwards, *The Dangerous Queen* (1964), 166−7, 303−4.

[60] Labanoff, vii, 169−72.

[61] C. Read, *Lord Burghley and Queen Elizabeth* (1965), 17ff.

[62] *CSP Scot.*, iv, 9−10.

[63] C. Read, *Mr. Secretary Walsingham* (1925), ii, 355−9; Labanoff, iv, 344−50, 363ff., 368ff., 377ff., 382ff.; v, 2−11; *HMC Salisbury*, ii, 158−9.

[64] Read, *Walsingham,* ii, 381ff.

[65] See Greengrass, ch. 8 above, for Guise activity.

[66] ibid., ii, 400ff. See also Greengrass, ch. 8 above, for Morgan.

[67] J. H. Pollen (ed.), *Mary, Queen of Scots and the Babington Plot* (SHS, 1928), Introduction.

[68] Labanoff, vi, 312ff., 404ff.

[69] Fraser, *Mary,* 502.

[70] *CSP Scot.*, ii, 633.

[71] ibid., iii, 13.

[72] Labanoff, vi, 82.

[73] ibid., iv, 137−55; v, 238ff., 275−7; vi, 276.

[74] ibid., iv, 337−8; v, 238ff; vi, 336; *CSP Scot.*, v, 457. See Greengrass, ch. 8 above, for the administration of the dowry.

[75] *CSP Scot.*, v, 364, 529; *HMC Salisbury*, ii, 443−6.

[76] *CSP Scot.*, ii, 671.

[77] ibid., v, 71.

[78] Labanoff, iv, 127; v, 139ff., 433ff.; vi, 45−9.

[79] *CSP Scot.*, v, 271−3, 274.

[80] ibid., iv, 580.

[81] See White, ch. 3 above, for anti-English feeling after 1560; also Lynch, ch. 1 above.

[82] *CSP Scot.*, ii, 296−7, 416−17.

[83] Labanoff, ii, 87, 108; *CSP Scot.*, ii, 421.

[84] Labanoff, ii, 123; *CSP Scot.*, ii, 420, 449.

[85] Labanoff, ii, 102.

[86] ibid., ii, 96ff.; *CSP Scot.*, ii, 431−5, 438−40, 448, 459, 462−3, 465.

[87] ibid., ii, 432−5, 465; Labanoff, ii, 139ff., 147−50, 184−5.

[88] *HMC Salisbury*, i, 365−6, cf. 375−6.

[89] *CSP Scot.*, ii, 603, 626. The diet is fully discussed in Donaldson, *First Trial*; the documents are transcribed in *CSP Scot*, ii, 510ff.

[90] *HMC Salisbury*, i, 385−6, cf. 391−2.

[91] *CSP Scot.*, ii, 641, 642−6, 647; *HMC Salisbury*, i, 411−12.

[92] ibid., i, 420−1; *CSP Scot.*, ii, 682−3.

[93] ibid., ii, 683−4, 688.

[94] ibid., iii, 136−9, 162; Clifford, *Sadler State Papers*, ii, 562−9.

[95] *CSP Scot.*, iii, 162−4, cf. 176−7, 452−3; *HMC Salisbury*, i, 411−12; Labanoff, iii, 88−105.

[96] *CSP Scot.*, iii, 212, 709.

[97] ibid., iii, 600−1.

[98] ibid., iv, 1−2, 690.

[99] ibid., iv, 3—4, 64, 106—9; J. R. Dasent (ed.), *Acts of the Privy Council* (1894), viii, 50; Labanoff, iii, 399.

[100] *CSP Scot.*, iv, 112; cf. 111—12. See also Greengrass, ch. 8 above, for French policy.

[101] *CSP Scot.*, iv, 208—11.

[102] Labanoff, iii, 367, 376, 383, 391ff.

[103] ibid., iv, 47ff.; *CSP Scot.*, iv, 323, 324—7, 330—2.

[104] ibid., iv, 384—6, 428, 432, 434—5, 471, 485; Read, *Lord Burghley*, 87ff.

[105] *CSP Scot.*, iv, 429, 431—2.

[106] ibid., iv, 534—5, 547—50, 564, 572—3, 579—80.

[107] ibid., iv, 676; v, 28, 32, 33, 39.

[108] ibid., v, 112—13, 267; cf. 152—4, 265—6.

[109] Read, *Walsingham*, ii, ch. ix.

[110] *CSP Scot.*, v, 456—8, 504, 505, 514—16, 595, 606, 608—10, 620—2, 633, 637.

[111] Read, *Walsingham*; Labanoff, v, 220—5, 260—72, 347, 441—6, 453, 463, 473; vi, 2—3, 6ff., 35—42.

[112] M. Levine, *The Early Elizabethan Succession Question* (1966), 202—6.

[113] J. E. Neale, *Elizabeth I and her Parliaments*, i, (1953), 247—90, ii, (1965), 103—144; interpreted in the light of G. R. Elton, 'Parliament in the sixteenth century: functions and fortunes', *Historical J.* (1979), 255—78.

[114] Labanoff, vii, 202.

[115] Read, *Burghley*, 366—7.

[116] *Calendar of Letters and Papers relating to the Border*, ed. J. Bain (1894), i, 242, 245, 246, 252, 265, 297—9, 305; F. H. Mares (ed.), *The Memoirs of Robert Carey* (1972), 7—8.

Bibliography

The bibliography is confined to a list of the works cited by the contributors to this volume, otherwise it might be many times its present length. All works were published in London, unless otherwise stated.

Aberdeen. *Extracts from the Council Register of the Burgh of Aberdeen*, 2 vols (Spalding Club, 1844–8).

Accounts of the Lord High Treasurer of Scotland, ed. T. Dickson and Sir J. Balfour Paul (Edin., 1877–).

Acta Curiae Admirallatus Scotiae 1557–1561 (Stair Soc., 1937).

Acts and Proceedings of the General Assemblies of the Kirk of Scotland (1560–1618), ed. T. Thomson (Bannatyne Club, 1839–45).

Acts of the Lords of Council in Public Affairs, 1501–1554, ed. R. K. Hannay (Edin., 1932).

Acts of the Parliaments of Scotland, ed. T. Thomson and C. Innes (Edin., 1814–75).

Acts of the Privy Council of England, ed. J. R. Dasent (1890–1907).

Adams, S., 'The Lauderdale papers, 1561–1570: the Maitland of Lethington state papers and the Leicester correspondence', *SHR*, lxvii (1988).

Adamson, P., *De papistarum, superstiosis ineptiis* (Edin., 1564).

Adamson, P., *Serenessimi ac Noblissimi Scotiae Angliae Hybernie Principis Henrici Stuardi . . . et Mariae Reginae* (Paris, 1566).

Anderson, P. D., *Robert Stewart, Earl of Orkney, Lord of Shetland* (Edin., 1982). 4 vols (1777).

Anderson, P. D., *Robert Stewart, Earl of Orkney, Lord of Shetland* (Edin., 1982).

Anglo, S., *Spectacle, Pageantry and Early Tudor Policy* (1969).

Apted, M. R., and Hannabus, S., *Painters in Scotland* (SRS, 1978).

Armstrong-Davison, M. H., *The Casket Letters* (1965).

Ascoli, G., *La Grande Bretaigne devant l'opinion française* (Paris, 1927).

Ashton, R., *Reformation and Revolution* (1984).

Axton, M., 'Lord Robert Dudley and the Inner Temple revels', *Historical J.*, xiii (1970).

Bannatyne Manuscript, ed. W. Tod Ritchie (STS, 1934).

Barnavi, E., *Le parti de Dieu* (Brussels, 1980).

Barry, J. C. (ed.), *William Hay's Lectures on Marriage* (Stair Soc., 1967).

Barwick, G. F., *A Book bound for Mary, Queen of Scots* (1901).

Barwick, G. F., 'A sidelight on the mystery of Mary Stuart', *SHR*, xxi (1924).

Bath, Marquess of, *Calendar of the Manuscripts at Longleat*, ii (Dublin, 1907).

Batho, G., 'A prisoner's pursuits: the captivity of Mary, Queen of Scots', *The Historian*, xii (1986).

Beaugue, J. de, *Histoire de la guerre d'Écosse: pendant les campagnes 1548 et 1549* (Maitland Club, 1830).

Bercher, W., *The Nobility of Women* (Roxburghe Club, 1904).

Bibliotheca Bibliographica Aureliana (Baden Baden, 1973).

Bigalli, D., *Immagini de principe* (Milan, 1985).

Bizzari, P., *Varia Opuscula* (Venice, 1565).

Bontems, C., et al. *Le prince dans la France des XVIᵉ et XVIIᵉ siècles* (Paris, 1965).

Bossy, J., 'Elizabeth Catholicism: the link with France', (Cambridge Univ. Ph.D., 1960).

Boucher, J., *Societés et mentalités autour de Henri III* (Lille, 1981).

Bouille, René de, *Histoire des ducs de Guise* (Paris, 1850).

Boutier, J., Dewerpe, A., and Nordman, D. (eds), *Un tour de France royal: le voyage de Charles IX, 1564–1566* (Paris, 1984).

Bradner, L. (ed.), *The Poems of Queen Elizabeth* (Providence, USA, 1964).

Brosse, J. de la, *Histoire d'un capitaine bourbonnais au XVIᵉ siècle: Jacques de la Brosse, 1485(?)–1562: ses missions en Écosse* (Paris, 1929).

Brown, J. M. (ed.), *Scottish Society in the Fifteenth Century* (1977).

Brown, K., 'Much ado about nothing?', *History Today* (Feb. 1987).

Brown, P. H., *History of Scotland*, 3 vols (Cambridge, 1905–11).

Brown, P. H., *Scotland in the Time of Queen Mary* (1904).

Buchanan. *The History of Scotland, by George Buchanan*, ed. J. Aikman, 4 vols (Glasgow, 1827–9).

Burghley Papers, ed. E. Murdin, 2 vols (1749–57).

Burns, C., 'Papal gifts to Scottish monarchs: the golden rose and blessed sword', *IR*, xx (1959).

Bushnell, G. H., 'Diane de Poitiers and her books', *The Library*, ser. 4, vii (1926–7).

Calderwood, D., *History of the Kirk of Scotland*, ed. T. Thomson and D. Laing, 8 vols (Wodrow Soc., 1842–9).

Calendar of Letters and Papers relating to the Borders, ed. J. Bain (Edin., 1894–6).

Calendar of Shrewsbury Papers (Derbyshire Arch. Soc., 1966).

Calendar of State Papers relating to Scotland and Mary, Queen of Scots, 1547–1603, ed. J. Bain et al. (Edin., 1898–1969).

Calendar of State Papers, Domestic, Elizabeth, Addenda 1580–1625 (1872).

Calendar of State Papers, Foreign, of the reign of Elizabeth, ed. J. Stevenson et al. (1863–1950).

Calendar of State Papers, Rome, ed. J. M. Rigg (1916–26).

Calendar of State Papers, Spanish, Elizabeth, ed. M. A. S. Hume (1892–9).

Calendar of State Papers, Venetian, ed. R. Brown and C. G. Bentinck (1864–98).

Camden, W., *Annales*, trans. R. Norton (1625).

Canongate. *The Buik of the Kirk of the Canagait, 1564–1567*, ed. A. B. Calderwood (SRS, 1961).

Cantinelli, R., and Dacier, E. (eds), *Les trésors des bibliothèques de France* (Paris, 1926).

Catalogue of the Tercentenary Exhibition of Mary, Queen of Scots (Peterborough, 1887).

Cauchie, M., 'Les psaumes de Janequin', *Mélanges de musicologie offerts à M. Lionel de La Laurencie* (Paris, 1933).

Chambre (or Chalmers), D., *Histoire abbregée de tous les rois de France, Angleterre et Escosse* (Paris, 1579).

Chéruel, P. A., *Marie Stuart et Catherine de Médicis* (Paris, 1858).

Cloulas, I., *Henri II* (Paris, 1985).

Coleccion de documentos ineditos para la historia de España, ed. M. F. Navarette and others (Madrid, 1842–95).

Collection de manuscripts, livres estampes et objets d'art relatifs à Marie Stuart, reine de France et d'Ecosse, ed. G. T. Bliss (Paris, 1931).

Collection of State Papers left by William Cecil, Lord Burghley, ed. S. Haynes and W. Murdin, 2 vols (1740–59).

Constant, J.-M., *Les Guises* (Paris, 1985).

Correspondence du Cardinal de Granvelle, ed. E. Poullet and C. Poit (Brussels, 1878–96).

Correspondencia de Felipe II con sus embajadores en la corte de Ingleterra (Codoin, lxxxix, 1887).

Cowan, I. B. *The Enigma of Mary Stuart* (1971).

Cowan, I. B. *The Scottish Reformation* (1982).

Cowan, I. B., Mackay, P. H. R., and Macquarrie, A. (eds), *The Knights of St John of Jerusalem in Scotland* (SHS, 1983).

Cowan, I. B., and Shaw, D. (eds), *The Renaissance and Reformation in Scotland: Essays in honour of Gordon Donaldson* (Edin., 1983).

Cowan, S., *The Last Days of Mary Stuart*, 2 vols. (1907).

Craig, T., *Henrici ... et Mariae ... epithalamium* (Edin., 1565).

Cust, L., *Notes on the Authentic Portraits of Mary, Queen of Scots* (1903).

Davenport, C., *Cameo Book-Stamps* (1911).

Davidson, J., *Inverurie and the Earldom of Garioch* (Aberdeen, 1878).

Dawson, J. E. A., 'Mary, queen of Scots, Lord Darnley and Anglo-Scottish relations in 1565', *International History Rev.*, viii (1986).

Decrue de Stoutz, F., *Anne, duc de Montmorency, connétable et pair de France sous les rois Henri II, François II et Charles IX* (Paris, 1889).

Descimon, R., *Qui etaient les seize?* (Paris, 1985).

Dickson, R., and Edmond, J. P., *Annals of Scottish Printing* (Cambridge, 1890).

Dictionnaire de biographie française.

Didbin, T. F., *A Bibliographical Tour in the Northern Counties of England and in Scotland* (1833).

Dietz, B., 'Privateering in North-West European Waters' (London Univ. Ph.D., 1959).

Digges, D., *The Compleat Ambassador* (1655).

Dilworth, M., 'A book of hours of Mary of Guise', *IR*, xix (1968).

Dilworth, M., 'The commendator system in Scotland', *IR*, xxxvii (1986).

Dimier, L., 'About Mary Queen of Scots' portraits', *SHR*, iv (1907).

Discours du grand et magnifique triomphe faict du mariage de François et Marie Stuart, ed. W. Bentham (Roxburghe Club, 1818).

Diurnal of Remarkable Occurents that have passed within the country of Scotland, since the death of King James the Fourth, till the year 1575, ed. T. Thomson (Bannatyne and Maitland Clubs, 1833).

Donaldson, G., (ed.), *Accounts of the Collectors of Thirds of Benefices 1561–1572* (SHS, 1949).

Donaldson, G., *All the Queen's Men: Power and Politics in Mary Stewart's Scotland* (1983).

Donaldson, G., 'The bishops and priors of Whithorn', *Trans Dumf. and Galloway Nat. Hist. and Antiq. Soc.*, xxvii (1948–9).

Donaldson, G., *The First Trial of Mary, Queen of Scots* (1969).

Donaldson, G., *Mary, Queen of Scots* (1974).

Donaldson, G., *Scotland: James V to James VII* (Edin., 1965).

Doughty, D. W., 'The library of James Stewart, earl of Moray, 1531–1570', *IR*, xxi (1970).

Drummond, H., *The Queen's Man* (1975).

Dufour, A., 'Le mythe de Génève au temps de Calvin', *Revue suisse d'histoire*, ix (1959).

Dunbar, J. G., 'The palace of Holyroodhouse', *Archaeological J.*, cxx (1964).

Durkan, J., 'George Buchanan: some French connections', *The Bibliotheck*, iv, (1964).

Durkan, J., 'George Hay's *Oration at the purging of King's College, Aberdeen, in 1569', Northern Scotland*, vi (1985).

Durkan, J., 'Henry Scrimgeour, Renaissance bookman', *Edin. Bibl. Soc. Trans.*, v (1978).

Durkan, J., 'James, third earl of Arran: the hidden years', *SHR*, lxv (1986).

Durkan, J., 'Native influences on George Buchanan', in *Acta Conventus Neo-Latini Sanctandreani*, ed. I. D. Macfarlane (1982).

Durkan, J., 'The royal lectureships under Mary of Lorraine', *SHR*, lxii (1983).

Durkan, J., 'William Murdoch and the early Jesuit mission in Scotland', *IR*, xxxv (1984).

Durkan, J., and Ross, A. (eds), *Early Scottish Libraries* (Glasgow, 1961).

Earl of Stirling's Register of Royal Letters, ed. Sir W. Alexander (Edin., 1885).

Edinburgh. *Extracts from the Records of the Burgh of Edinburgh, 1403–1603*, ed. J. D. Marwick and M. Wood (Scot. Burgh Rec. Soc., 1869–1927).

Edwards, F., *The Dangerous Queen* (1964).

Ellis, H. (ed.), *Original Letters illustrative of English History*, 11 vols (1824–46).

Elton, G. R., *England under the Tudors* (1969).

Elton, G. R., 'Parliament in the sixteenth century: functions and fortunes' *Historical J.*, xxii (1979).

Elton, G. R., *Policy and Police: The Enforcement of the Reformation in the Age of Thomas Cromwell* (Cambridge, 1972).

Etheridge, D. T., 'Political Prophecy in Tudor England' (Univ. of Wales, Swansea, Ph.D., 1979).

Exchequer Rolls of Scotland, ed. J. Stewart et al. (Edin., 1878–1908).

Fabre, F., 'The English College at Eu, 1582–92', *Catholic Historical Rev.*, xxxvii (1951).

Facsimiles of the National Manuscripts of Scotland, 3 vols (1867–71).

Ferguson, D., *Tracts* (Bannatyne Club, 1860).

Ferguson, W., *Scotland's Relations with England: A Survey to 1707* (Edin., 1977).

Finnie, E., 'The house of Hamilton: patronage, politics and the church in the Reformation period', *IR*, xxxvi (1985).

Fleming D. H., *Mary, Queen of Scots* (1897).

Fletcher, A., *Tudor Rebellions* (1968).

Forbes Leith, W., *Narratives of Scottish Catholics under Mary Stuart and James VI* (Edin., 1885).

Forbes Leith, W., *The Scots Men-at-Arms and Life Guards in France, 1418–1830*, 2 vols (Edin., 1882).

Foreign Correspondence with Marie de Lorraine, Queen of Scotland, from the originals in the Balcarres Papers, ed. M. Wood, 2 vols (SHS, 1923–5).

Forneron, H., *Les ducs de Guise et leur époque: étude historique sur le seizième siècle* (Paris, 1877).

Fraser, A., *Mary, Queen of Scots* (1969).

Fraser, G. M., *Historical Aberdeen* (Aberdeen, 1905).

Fraser, W., *The Lennox* (Edin., 1874).

Fraser, W., *Memorials of the Earls of Haddington* (Edin., 1889).

Fraser, W., *Memorials of the Montgomeries, Earls of Eglinton* (Edin., 1859).

Fraser, W., *The Red Book of Menteith* (Edin., 1880).

Fraser, W. (ed.), *The Sutherland Book*, 3 vols (Edin., 1892).

Frescoln, K. P., 'A letter from Thomas Randolph to the earl of Leicester', *Huntington Library Q.*, xxxvii (1973).

Frescoln, K. P., 'Thomas Randolph: an Elizabethan in Scotland' (West Virgina Univ. Ph.D., 1971).

Froude, J. A., *The Reign of Elizabeth* (Everyman edn, n.d.).

Furgol, E., 'The progresses of Mary, queen of Scots, 1542–48 and 1561–68', *Procs. Soc. Antiqs. Scot.*, cxvii (1987).

Gilbert, J., 'The usual money of Scotland and exchange rates against foreign coin', in *Coinage in Medieval Scotland*, ed. D. M. Metcalf (British Arch. Reports, xlv, 1977).

Gore-Browne, R. F., *Lord Bothwell* (1937).

Greengrass, M., *France in the Age of Henri IV: The Struggle for Stability* (1984).

Guiffrey, J., *Artistes parisiens du XVIᵉ et XVIIᵉ siècles* (Paris, 1915).

Guillemin, J. J., *Le cardinal de Lorraine, son influence politique et religeuse au XVIᵉ siècle* (Paris, 1847).

Halliwell, R. E., 'Prince humaniste ou prince chévaleresque: a French Renaissance debate', *Kentucky Romance Q.*, xxi (1974).

Hamer, D., 'The marriage of Mary, Queen of Scots to the dauphin: a Scottish printed fragment', *Bibl. Soc. Trans.* (1932).

Hamilton Papers. Letters and Papers illustrating the political relations of England and Scotland in the XVIth century, ed. J. Bain, 2 vols (Edin., 1890–2).

Hay, C. H., 'George Buchanan and Adam Blackwood', *BHR*, viii (1946).

Haynie, S. E. A., 'The Image of Henry III in contemporary French Pamphlets' (Michigan Univ. Ph.D., 1971).

Henderson, T. F., *Mary, Queen of Scots*, 2 vols (1905).

Herries, Lord, *Historical Memoirs of the Reign of Mary, Queen of Scots* (Abbotsford Club, 1836).

Hewitt, G. R., *Scotland under Morton* (Edin., 1982).

Hicks, L., *An Elizabethan Problem* (1964).

Hicks, L. (ed.), *Letters and Memorials of Fr Robert Persons* (Catholic Record Soc., xxxix, 1942).

Hobson, G. D., *Les reliures à la fanfare* (1935).

Hobson, G. D., 'Parisian binding, 1500–1525', *The Library*, 4th ser., xi (1931).

Hoffman, V., 'Le Louvre de Henri II: un palais impérial', *Bulletin de la Société de l'Histoire de l'Art français 1982* (Paris, 1984).

Holmes, P. J., *Resistance and Compromise: The Political Thought of the Elizabethan Catholics* (Cambridge, 1982).

Holt, H. F., 'Observations upon a "shilling" of Francis the Dauphin and Mary Stuart', *PSAS*, vii (1870).

Holt, H. F., 'On the great seal of Francis II of France and Mary, queen of Scots, as king and queen of France, Scotland, England and Ireland', *J. of British Arch. Assoc.*, xxiv (1868).

Holt, M. P., *The Duke of Anjou and the Politique Struggle during the Wars of Religion* (Cambridge, 1986).

Hosack, J., *Mary, Queen of Scots and her Accusers*, 2 vols (Edin., 1870–4).

Hume, M. A. S., *The Love Affairs of Mary, Queen of Scots: A Political History* (1903).

Humphries, W. R., 'The execution of Mary, queen of Scots', *Aberdeen Univ. Rev.*, xxx (1943).

Jack, R., *The Italian Influence on Scottish Literature* (Edin., 1972).

Jacquart, J., *François I* (Paris, 1981).

Jaech, S. L. J., 'The "prophisies of Rymour, Beid and Marlying"': Henry VIII and a sixteen-century political prophecy', *Sixteenth Century J.*, xvi (1985).

James, M. E., 'English politics and the concept of honour', *Past and Present* suppl., iii (1978).

James, M. E., 'Obedience and dissent in Henrician England: the Lincolnshire Rebellion, 1536', *Past and Present*, xlvi (1970).

Jebb, S., *De Vita et Rebus Gestis Mariae Scotorum Regina*, 2 vols (1725).

Keith, R., *The History of the Affairs of the Church and State in Scotland down to 1567*, 3 vols (Spottiswoode Soc., 1844–50).

Kelley, D., *François Hotman* (Princeton, 1973).

Ker, N. R., *Medieval Manuscripts in British Libraries* (Oxford, 1977).

Kierstead, R., *Pomponne de Bellièvre* (Providence, 1968).

Knecht, R. J., *Francis I* (Cambridge, 1982).

Knox. *John Knox's History of the Reformation in Scotland*, ed. W. C. Dickinson, 2 vols (Edin., 1949).

Knox. *The Works of John Knox*, ed. D. Laing, 6 vols (Edin., 1846–64).

Knox, T. F. (ed.), *The Letters and Memorials of William Cardinal Allen* (1882).

L'Estoile, P. de, *Journal du règne de Henri III*, ed. L. R. Lefèvre (Paris, 1943).

L'Estoile, P. de, *Journal pour la règne de Henri IV*, ed. A. Martin (Paris, 1958).

L'Hospital, M. de, *Oeuvres completes* (Paris, 1825).

La Ferrière-Percy, H. de la, 'L'entrevue de Bayonne', *Revue des questions historiques* (1883).

Labanoff, Prince, *Lettres et mémoires de Marie, reine d'Ecosse*, 7 vols (Paris, 1844).

Lang, A., *History of Scotland*, 4 vols (Edin., 1900−7).

Lang, A., 'The household of Mary, queen of Scots in 1573', *SHR*, ii, (1905).

Lang. A., *The Mystery of Mary Stuart* (1901).

Lang, A., 'New light on Mary, Queen of Scots', *Blackwood's Magazine*, clxxxii (1907).

Lang, A., *Portraits and Jewels of Mary, Queen of Scots* (1906).

Lavaud, J., *Un poète de cour au temps des derniers Valois: Philippe Desportes* (Paris, 1936).

Lavisse, E., *Histoire de la France*, 9 vols (Paris, 1901−11).

Lee, M., *James Stewart, Earl of Moray* (New York, 1953).

Leslie, J., *The History of Scotland from the Death of King James I in the Year 1436 to the Year 1561* (Bannatyne Club, 1830).

Leslie. *Diary of John Leslie, Bishop of Ross*, ed. D. Laing (Bannatyne Misc., iii, 1855).

Lesure, F. and Thibault, G., *Bibliographie des éditions d'Adrian le Roy et Robert Ballard* (Paris, 1955).

Lesure, F., *Musique et musiciens français de XVIᵉ siècle* (Geneva, 1976).

Letters of James IV, ed. R. K. Hannay (SHS, 1953).

Letters and Memorials of Fr. Robert Persons, ed. L. Hicks (Catholic Record Soc., 1942).

Lettres de Catherine de Médicis, ed. H. de la Ferrière-Percy and B. de Puchesse, 11 vols (1880−1909).

Lettres d'Henri III, ed. M. François, 3 vols (Paris, 1984).

Lettres inédites de Henri II, Diane de Poitiers, Marie Stuart, François, roi dauphin adressées au connétable Anne de Montmorency (Paris, 1818).

Levine, M., *The Early Elizabethan Succession Question* (Stanford, Calif. 1966).

Levine, M., *Tudor Dynastic Problems 1460−1571* (1973).

Liber Officialis S. Andree (Abbotsford Club, 1845).

Libraries of Mary, Queen of Scots and James VI (Maitland Club Misc., 1834).

Lightman, H. L., 'Sons and Mothers: Queens and Minor Kings in French Constitutional Law' (Bryn Maur College Ph.D., 1981).

Lockie, D. M., 'The political career of the bishop of Ross, 1568−80', *Univ. of Birmingham Hist. J.*, iv (1953).

Lynch, M. *Edinburgh and the Reformation* (Edin., 1981).

Lynch, M. 'Scottish Calvinism 1559−1638', in M. Prestwich (ed.), *International Calvinism, 1541−1715* (Oxford, 1985).

Lynch, M. (ed.), *The Early Modern Town in Scotland* (1987).

MacCaffrey, W. T., *The Shaping of the Elizabethan Regime* (New Jersey, 1968).

MacDonald, A. A., 'The Bannatyne Manuscript: a Marian anthology', *IR*, xxxvii (1986).

MacDonald, R. H. (ed.), *The Library of Drummond of Hawthornden* (Edin., 1971).

Macfarlane, I. D., *Buchanan* (1981).

McGowan, M. B., 'Form and themes in Henri II's entry into Rouen', *Renaissance Drama*, i (1968).

McGrath, J., 'The Administration of the Burgh of Glasgow, 1574–1586', (Glasgow Univ. Ph.D., 1987).

Mackenzie, P. Stewart, *Queen Mary's Book* (1907).

McKerlie, E. M. H., *Mary of Guise-Lorraine, Queen of Scotland* (1931).

McNeill, P., and Nicholson, R. (eds), *An Historical Atlas of Scotland, c.400–c.1600* (St Andrews, 1975).

McNeill, W. A., 'Documents illustrative of the Scots College, Paris', *IR*, xv (1964).

MacQueen, J. (ed.), *Ballattis of Luve* (Edin., 1970).

McRoberts, D. (ed.), *Essays on the Scottish Reformation, 1513–1625* (Glasgow, 1962).

McRoberts, D., *The Fetternear Banner* (Glasgow, 1956).

Maitland Quarto Manuscript, ed. W. A. Craigie (STS, 1920).

Mares, F. H. (ed.), *The Memoirs of Robert Carey* (Oxford, 1972).

Marshall, R. K., *Mary of Guise* (1977).

Martin, A. L., *Henry III and the Jesuit Politicians* (Geneva, 1973).

Melville, Sir James of Halhill, *Memoirs of his Own Life, 1549–93*, ed. T. Thomson (Bannatyne and Maitland Clubs, 1827).

Memoires-Journaux de Pierre de l'Estoile (Paris, 1876).

Meyer, A. O., *England and the Catholic Church under Queen Elizabeth*, trans. J. R. McKee (1916).

Michaud, H., *La grande chancellerie et les écritures royales au XVIe siècle* (Paris, 1967).

Michel, F.-X., *Les Français en Ecosse. Les Écossais en France*, 2 vols (1862).

Mignet, F. A., *The History of Mary, Queen of Scots*, trans. A. R. Scoble (1851).

Miscellaneous Papers principally illustrative of Events in the Reigns of Queen Mary and King James VI, ed. W. J. Duncan (Maitland Club, 1834).

Miscellany of the Spalding Club (Spalding Club, 1841–52).

Mitchell, W. S., *A History of Scottish Bookbinding* (Edin., 1955).

Montaiglon, A. de, *Latin Themes of Mary Stuart* (Warton Club, 1855).

Mumby, F. A., *Elizabeth and Mary Stuart* (Boston, 1914).

Murray, J. A. H. (ed.), *The Romance and Prophecies of Thomas of Erceldoune* (Early English Text Soc., 1875).

Nau, C., *Memorials of Mary Stewart*, ed. J. Stevenson (Edin., 1883).

Neale, J. E., *Elizabeth I and her Parliaments*, 2 vols (1953–7).

Neale, J. E., *Queen Elizabeth* (1952).

Nixon, H. M., 'Binding forgeries', *Sixth International Congress of Bibliophiles 1969* (Vienna, 1971).

Nixon, H. M., *Sixteenth-century Gold-tooled Bindings in the Pierpont Morgan Library* (New York, 1971).

Nugent, D., *Ecumenism in the Age of the Reformation: The Colloquy of Poissy* (Cambridge, Mass., 1974).

Omond, G. W. T., *The Arniston Memoirs* (Edin., 1887).

Pallier, D., *Recherches sur l'imprimerie à Paris pendant la ligue* (Geneva, 1976).

Papiers d'état du Cardinal Granvelle, ed. C. Weiss, 9 vols (Paris, 1841–52).

Paris, L. (ed.), *Négociations, lettres et pièces diverses relatives au règne de François II* (Paris, 1841).

Parker, G., *Spain and the Netherlands: Ten Studies* (1979).

Pasquier, E., *René Benoist, le pape des Halles, 1521–1608* (Paris, 1913).

Paterson, J., *History of the County of Ayr* (Edin., 1852).

Pemberton, C. (ed.), *Queen Elizabeth's Englishings of Boethius, Plutarch, Horace* (Early English Text Soc., 1899).

Pepys MSS preserved at Magdalene College, Cambridge (HMC, 18th Report, 1911).

Perlin, E., *Description des royaulmes d'Angleterre et d'Escosse* (Paris, 1558).

Petti, A. G., 'Richard Verstegen and Catholic martyrologies', *Recusant History*, v (1959).

Philippson, M., *Histoire du règne de Marie Stuart* (Paris, 1891).

Phillips, J. E., *Images of a Queen: Mary Stuart in 16th Century Literature* (California, 1964).

Pimodan, G. de, *La mère des Guises: Antoinette de Bourbon* (Paris, 1925).

Pitcairn, R. (ed.), *Criminal Trials in Scotland from 1488 to 1624*, 3 vols (Edin., 1833).

Poetical Works of Gavin Douglas (STS, 1874).

Pogson, R. H., 'Reginald Pole and the priorities of government in Mary Tudor's church', *Historical J.*, xviii (1975).

Pollen, J. H. (ed.), *A Letter from Mary, Queen of Scots to the Duke of Guise* (SHS, 1904).

Pollen, J. H. (ed.), *Mary, Queen of Scots and the Babington Plot* (SHS, 1922).

Pollen, J. H., 'Mary Stuart's Jesuit chaplain', *The Month*, cxvii (1911).

Pollen, J. H. (ed.), *Papal Negotiations with Mary, Queen of Scots* (SHS, 1901).

Powis, J., *Aristocracy* (Oxford, 1984).

Protocol Books of Dominus Thomas Johnsoun 1528–78 (SRS, 1920).

Purvey, P. F., *Coins and Tokens of Scotland* (1972).

Quynn, D. M., 'The early career of John Gordon, dean of Salisbury', *BHR*, vii (1945).

Raymond, R., 'Notes, extraites de comptes de Jeanne d'Albret et de ses enfants,' *Revue d'Aquitaine et du Languedoc*, xi (1867).

Read, C., *Lord Burghley and Queen Elizabeth* (1965).

Read, C., *Mr. Secretary Cecil and Queen Elizabeth* (New York, 1955).

Read, C., *Mr. Secretary Walsingham*, 3 vols (Oxford, 1925).

Records of Aboyne, 1203–1681 (New Spalding Club, 1894).

Redondo, A., *Antonio de Guevara et L'Espagne de son temps* (Geneva, 1976).

Register of the Privy Council of Scotland, 1545–1625, ed. J. H. Burton et al. (Edin., 1877–98).

Registrum Honoris de Morton, 2 vols (Bannatyne Club, 1853).

Registrum Magni Sigilli Regum Scotorum, ed. J. M. Thomson et al. (Edin., 1882–1914).

Registrum Secreti Sigilli Regum Scotorum, ed. M. Livingstone et al. (Edin., 1908–).

Relations politiques des Pays-Bas et de l'Angleterre sous le règne de Philippe II, ed. Baron Kervyn de Lettenhove (Brussels, 1882–1900).

Robertson, J. (ed.), *Inventaires de la royne d'Escosse, douairière de France* (Bannatyne Club, 1863).

Romier, L., *Les origines politiques des guerres de religion* (Paris, 1913–14).

Rose, D. M., 'Mary, queen of Scots and her brother', *SHR*, ii (1905).

Ross, A., 'More about the archbishop of Athens', *IR*, xiv (1963).

Royal Commission on Ancient and Historical Monuments. *Inventory of the City of Edinburgh* (Edin., 1951).

Ruble, A. de, *La première jeunesse de Marie Stuart* (Paris, 1891).

Ruble, A. de, *La traité de Cateau-Cambrésis* (Paris, 1889).

Russell, C., *The Crisis of Parliaments* (Oxford, 1971).

Russell, E., *Maitland of Lethington* (1912).

Salisbury, Marquess of, *Calendar of Manuscripts at Hatfield House* (HMC, 1883–5).

Sammarthanus, D., *Gallia Christiana* (Paris, 1873).

Sanderson, M. H. B., 'Catholic recusancy in Scotland in the sixteenth century', *IR*, xxi (1970).

Scots Peerage, ed. Sir J. Balfour Paul, 9 vols (Edin., 1904–14).

Scott, J. D., *A Bibliography of Works relating to Mary Queen of Scots* (Edin., 1901).

Scottish Correspondence of Mary of Lorraine, 1542–1560, ed. A. I. Cameron (SHS, 1927).

Sedgwick, H., *The House of Guise* (1938).

Sharman, J., *The Library of Mary, Queen of Scots* (1889).

Sharp, C., *Memorials of the Rebellion of the Earls of Northumberland and Westmorland* (repr. edn, 1975).

Skelton, J., *Maitland of Lethington and the Scotland of Mary, Queen of Scots* (Edin., 1894).

Small, J., 'Queen Mary at Jedburgh in 1566', *Procs. Soc. Antiqs. Scot.*, iii (1881).

Smith, A. G. R., *The Emergence of a Nation State* (1984).

Smith, D. Baird, 'Archibald Craufurd, lord of Session', *Juridical Rev.*, xlv (1933).

Smith, M., *Joachim du Bellay's Veiled Victim* (Geneva, 1974).

Smith, M. C., 'Ronsard and Queen Elizabeth I', *BHR*, xxix (1967).

State Papers and Letters of Sir Ralph Sadler, ed. A. Clifford (Edin., 1809).

Stevenson, J. (ed.), *Selections from Unpublished Manuscripts ... illustrating the Regin of Mary, Queen of Scotland, 1543–68* (Maitland Club, 1837).

Stewart, H. C., 'Two letters and poems of Mary Stewart', *The Stewarts*, viii (1947–50).

Stoddart, J. T., *The Girlhood of Mary, Queen of Scots* (1908).

Strickland, A., *Lives of the Queens of Scotland*, 8 vols (Edin., 1850–9).

Strong, R., *Art and Power* (1984).

Strong, R., *Splendour at Court* (1973).

Sutherland, N. M., *The French Secretaries in the Age of Catherine de Medici (1962)*.

Swain, M., *The Needlework of Mary, Queen of Scots* (1973).

Teulet, A. (ed.), *Lettres inédites de Marie Stuart* (Paris, 1859).

Teulet, A. (ed.), *Papiers d'état, pièces et documents inédits ou peu connus relatifs à l'histoire de l'Ecosse au XVIe siècle*, 3 vols (Bannatyne Club, 1852–60).

Teulet A. (ed.), *Relations politiques de la France et de l'Espagne avec l'Ecosse au XVIe siècle*, 5 vols (Paris, 1862).

Thorp, M. R., 'Catholic conspiracy in early Elizabethan foreign policy', *Sixteenth Century J.*, xv (1984).

Turbow, G., 'Mary, queen of Scots, patroness of the arts of France', *Scotia*, iii (1979).

Tytler, P. F., *History of Scotland*, new edn, 4 vols (Edin., 1882).

Wainwright, J. B., 'Selected letters and papers of Nicholas Sander', *Miscellanea* (Catholic Record Soc., 1926).

Warner, G. F., 'The library of James VI' (SHS *Misc.*, 1893).

Warrender Papers, ed. A. I. Cameron, 2 vols (SHS, 1931–2).

Weber, B. C., *The Youth of Mary Stuart, Queen of Scots* (Philadelphia, 1941).

Wedderburn, R., *The Complaynt of Scotland*, ed. A. M. Stewart (STS, 1979).

Wernham, R. B., *Before the Armada* (1966).

White, A., 'Religion, Politics and Society in Aberdeen, 1543–1593' (Edinburgh Univ. Ph.D., 1985).

Williamson, A. H., *Scottish National Consciousness in the Age of James VI* (Edin., 1979).

Wood, M., 'The domestic affairs of the burgh', *Bk. of the Old Edinburgh Club*, xv (1928).

Works of James VI (1616).

Wormald, J., *Court, Kirk and Community: Scotland 1470–1625* (1981).

Wright, T., *Queen Elizabeth and her Times* (1838).

Zeller, G., *Histoire des relations internationales* (Paris, 1953).

Index

231